OUR WAR: IRELAND AND THE GREAT WAR

AN IRISH HERO!
1 IRISHMAN DEFEATS 10 GERMANS.

'An Irish hero!', 1915.
Reproduced by permission of the
Board, Trinity College Dublin.

FOR VALOUR

SERGEANT
MICHAEL O'LEARY, V.C.
· IRISH GUARDS ·
HAVE YOU NO WISH TO EMULATE THE SPLENDID BRAVERY OF YOUR FELLOW COUNTRYMAN
JOIN AN IRISH REGIMENT TO·DAY

OUR WAR

IRELAND AND THE GREAT WAR

THE 2008 THOMAS DAVIS LECTURE SERIES

Edited by John Horne

RTÉ

RIA

Our war: Ireland and the Great War

First published 2008

by Royal Irish Academy
19 Dawson Street
Dublin 2

www.ria.ie

The editor and publisher are grateful to the following for granting
permission to reproduce the documents, photographs and illustrations
in this book: Belfast City Hall, National Archives of Ireland, National
Library of Ireland, National Museum of Ireland, Royal Irish Academy
Library, RTÉ Stills Library, Somme Heritage Centre, Trinity College
Dublin Library and UCD Archives, School of History and Archives.

Every effort has been made to trace the copyright holders of these
items and to ensure the accuracy of their captions.

ISBN 978-1-904890-50-8

British Library Cataloguing in Publication Data. A CIP catalogue
record for this book is available from the British Library.

Printed in Spain by Centro Grafica Ganboa

10 9 8 7 6 5 4 3 2 1

CONTENTS

WILLYOUMAKE A FOURTH ?

'Will you make a fourth?' A poster issued by the Department of Recruiting for Ireland (DRI), *c.* 1916. The DRI replaced the ineffective Central Council for the Organisation of Recruiting in Ireland (CCORI) in October 1915. Reproduced by permission of the Board, Trinity College Dublin.

Right: TCD, Papyrus 53–55. Proclamation taken from the walls of the GPO. Pasted underneath it were many different recruitment posters, including 'Will you make a fourth?' which has been made visible here for demonstrative purposes. Reproduced by permission of the Board, Trinity College Dublin.

POBLACH ___ A H EIREANN.

THE PROVISIONAL GOVERNMENT
OF THE
IRISH REPUBLIC
TO THE PEOPLE OF IRELAND.

IRISHMEN AND IRISHWOMEN : In the name of God and of the dead generations from which she receives her old tradition of nationhood, Ireland, through us, summons her children to her flag and strikes for her freedom.

Having organised and trained her manhood through her secret revolutionary organisation, the Irish Republican Brotherhood, and through her open military organisations, the Irish Volunteers and the Irish Citizen Army, having patiently perfected her discipline, having resolutely waited for the right moment to reveal itself, she now seizes that moment, and, supported by her exiled children in America and by gallant allies in Europe, but relying in the first on her own strength, she strikes in full confidence of victory.

We declare the right of the people of Ireland to the ownership of Ireland, and to the unfettered control of Irish destinies, to be sovereign and indefeasible. The long usurpation of that right by a foreign people and government has not extinguished the right, nor can it ever be extinguished except by the destruction of the Irish people. In every generation the Irish people have asserted their right to national freedom and sovereignty ; six times during the past three hundred years they have asserted it in arms. Standing on that fundamental right and again asserting it in arms in the face of the world, we hereby proclaim the Irish Republic as a Sovereign Independent State, and we pledge our lives and the lives of our comrades-in-arms to the cause of its freedom, of its welfare, and of its exaltation among the nations.

The Irish Republic is entitled to, and hereby claims, the allegiance of every Irishman and Irishwoman. The Republic guarantees religious and civil liberty, equal rights and equal opportunities to all its citizens, and declares its resolve to pursue the happiness and prosperity of the whole nation and of all its parts, cherishing all the children of the nation equally, and oblivious of the differences carefully fostered by an alien government, which have divided a minority from the majority in the past.

Until our arms have brought the opportune moment for the establishment of a permanent National Government, representative of the whole people of Ireland and elected by the suffrages of all her men and women, the Provisional Government, hereby constituted, will administer the civil and military affairs of the Republic in trust for the people.

We place the cause of the Irish Republic under the protection of the Most High God, Whose blessing we invoke upon our arms, and we pray that no one who serves that cause will dishonour it by cowardice, inhumanity, or rapine. In this supreme hour the Irish nation must, by its valour and discipline and by the readiness of its children to sacrifice themselves for the common good, prove itself worthy of the august destiny to which it is called.

Signed on Behalf of the Provisional Government,

THOMAS J. CLARKE,

SEAN Mac DIARMADA, THOMAS MacDONAGH,

P. H. PEARSE, EAMONN CEANNT,

JAMES CONNOLLY. JOSEPH PLUNKETT.

The term **"MISSING"** does not necessarily mean that the soldier is killed or wounded. He may be an unwounded prisoner or temporarily separated from his regiment. Any further information received will be at once sent on to you.

G. 3250   100,000 9/14 H W V

Books of this nature are in every sense a collective venture, and in the present case a number of people must be thanked. This book originated in two events held in Trinity College Dublin, in June 2007. The first was an exhibition organised in the Library on 'Ireland and the First World War' by Charles Benson, Keeper of Early Printed Brooks. It was a revelation of the richness of print culture in Ireland related to this event. The second was the Loretta Glucksman Symposium organised by the Dean of Arts and Humanities, Terence Brown. It presented an afternoon of readings and talks by writers, poets and historians on 'The unthinkable: Europe, Ireland and the Great War', to a large and appreciative audience.

The success of both events was a further indication of a resurgence of interest in the Great War in Ireland. This is related to the peace process in Northern Ireland which has unlocked more complex visions of the past in both parts of the island. It is due also to the increased visibility of the Great War following the end of the Cold War as the seminal event in the cycle of violence and ideological extremism that marked the twentieth century. The fact that Ireland was deeply involved in the war is of fundamental importance to an understanding of its own place in European and international history.

This made it all the more appropriate to observe the ninetieth anniversary of the end of the Great War in 2008 with a public discussion of its place in Irish history and its legacy for Ireland today. Lorelei Harris, Editor of Features, Arts and Drama in RTÉ Radio 1, seized the opportunity with enthusiasm by commissioning the 2008 Thomas Davis Lecture series, with its distinguished history of bringing important topics to a wider public, on the subject of 'Our war: Ireland and the Great War'. I am grateful to the nine colleagues who contributed lectures. Peter Mooney, producer of the radio series, showed his strong personal commitment to the project not only by recording all ten of us but also by lending his private collection of the letters of his grandfather, who fought in the war, for use in the book. Finally, thanks must go to Malachy Moran, Manager, Audio Services and Archives RTÉ Radio, for his enthusiasm and drive in getting the project off the ground.

The Thomas Davis lectures are published here as a joint enterprise by RTÉ and the Royal Irish Academy (RIA). Pauric Dempsey, Head of Communications and Public Relations at the RIA, proposed that the book should be enriched with a multitude of documents and objects related to the war, all but a handful of them unfamiliar, and all reproduced in colour. In this way, the RIA and RTÉ have taken the project to a new level, enhancing the ideas and arguments of the lectures for what will hopefully be a wide readership. Lucy Hogan, the Production Editor of the Publications Department of the Academy, showed the highest editorial skill allied to a deep sense of what the book could be—and seemingly infinite patience—in bringing the volume into being. Without the vision and commitment of Pauric, Ruth Hegarty, Managing Editor at RIA and Lucy, the book would have been much the poorer. In this they were supported by Fidelma Slattery's design and Helen Litton's indexing skills.

To call this an illustrated book is a misnomer. For the documents and illustrations reproduced in it are much more than pictures supporting the ten chapters. They stand alone as an argument about the impact of the Great War in Ireland by the traces that it left not only in the print culture of the country, as the Trinity Library exhibition had shown, and in what one might call the manuscript culture (diaries, letters, drafts of speeches) but also in the material culture. Collections such as those at the National Irish War Memorial at Islandbridge and the National Museum at Collins Barracks, Dublin, the Royal Ulster Rifles Museum in Belfast and the Somme Heritage Centre at Newtownards, Co. Down, reveal the material involvement of Ireland and Irish people in the twentieth century's initiation into the horrors of industrialised warfare. Whether from print, manuscript or material culture, the items shown in this volume are merely an indication of the riches that await the researcher and the interested public.

Establishing an inventory of the manuscripts, print documents and objects in holdings across Ireland from which the illustrations might be drawn was a daunting preliminary task. It would have been impossible in the time available without the work of Eneclann, the campus company of Trinity College Dublin, which specialises in historical and genealogical research and records management. Fiona Fitzsimons and her team made lists of materials from archives and museums across the country. Their work was invaluable for this book and provides the basis for a print or electronic publication of Irish sources on the Great War.

Assembling the documents called on the goodwill of many individuals and institutions. My nine colleagues all made useful suggestions and Caitriona Clear, David Fitzpatrick, Jane Leonard and Philip Orr kindly lent materials in their own possession. Keith Jeffery was unstinting not only in providing material but also in drawing on his extensive knowledge to suggest where other items might be found. Charles Benson allowed us to draw on the riches of Trinity College Library and, with great generosity, to make use of his own notes and captions for the 2007 exhibition, which thus lives on in this volume. Invaluable counsel and documents were supplied from the National Archives of Ireland by Catriona Crowe, Aideen Ireland and Eamonn Mullally. Lar Joye and Finbarr Connolly unhesitatingly placed the resources of the splendid new military history display at the National Museum, and its reserves, at the disposal of the book and provided photographs of the objects and documents requested. Gerard Lyne, with Harriet Wheelock, supplied vital manuscripts from the National Library of Ireland while Mary Broderick, the Ephemera Librarian, supplied cartoons, posters and hand bills with great enthusiasm. Jaki Knox and Terence Nelson, at the Royal Ulster Rifles Museum in Belfast, and Noel Kane, at the Somme Heritage Centre, were generosity itself in allowing us to make full use of their collections. Seamus Helferty made available important documents from the University College Dublin Archives. Other institutions to be thanked are the Imperial War Museum, London, and the Library of the Royal Irish Academy.

The Great War also left its trace in art, architecture and monuments either in Ireland or realised elsewhere by Irish people. One of the great Irish artists of the period, William Orpen was an official British war artist, and drew and painted some of the most moving and powerful images of the Western Front. The presiding genius of the British cemeteries and war memorials on the Western Front, Edwin Lutyens, achieved one of his finest creations in Dublin, with the National Irish War Memorial at Islandbridge. Although in lesser numbers than elsewhere (for reasons explained in this volume), war memorials of one kind and another were erected across the country, though we still have no inventory of them. One does not have to travel to Macedonia or the Somme to find the connections between Ireland and the Great War. They are, if only we look for them, all around us.

John Horne
Dublin, August 2008

Members of the 7th Batallion, Royal Dublin Fusiliers, taken at Collins Barracks, *c.* 1915.
© English Collection

Lance Corporal, R.I.R., by William Conor, 1918. William Conor (1881–1968) was a popular artist who painted scenes of everyday life in Belfast. He went with the 36th (Ulster) Division to France and recorded both officers and soldiers (see also p. 94)

A sign for the Berlin Road, which has been renamed 'Tipperary Road', *c.* 1918. © 2007 Getty Images.

THE CALL TO ARMS

NLI, Ephemera Collection, WAR/1914-18/7: 'The call to arms', 1916. Irish recruiting poster. A piper rallies the troops as an Irish wolfhound looks on. Courtesy of the National Library of Ireland.

DAVID ALLEN & SONS
40. Gt. Brunswick St.
DUBLIN.
(Copyright Res.)

IRISHMEN
DONT YOU HEAR IT?

CHAPTER 1

Our war, our history

JOHN HORNE

THE
ROYAL MUNSTER FUSILIERS

are earning eternal fame fighting for YOU

Will the fine lads of KERRY, CORK, LIMERICK & CLARE do nothing to help their kinsmen?

COME ALONG AND ASSIST IN DESTROYING THE
German Menace

(1048). Wt. 2614. 12,000. 8/'16.   CAHILL & CO., Ltd., DUBLIN.

Few countries were more decisively affected by the Great War than Ireland. Not only did Irishmen from all backgrounds fight and die in greater numbers than in any other conflict in the country's past, but Ireland's modern political shape to a great extent derives from it. Yet ninety years after it ended, perceptions of this central episode in our history remain strangely blurred. In countries that paid a terrible price but were 'victors', such as Britain, France and Australia, the war has always been a strong presence. In Germany, its effect is masked by the greater catastrophe of its sequel in 1939–45. In Russia, the Bolsheviks erased it from official memory, while in Poland and the Czech Republic, since the end of Soviet domination, the public has struggled to recover its inter-war history when their independence was won as a result of the Great War. Ireland, however, has been a study in contested memory. For the terrible sacrifice in the war underwrote the *refusal* of Irish independence by unionist Northern Ireland, whereas the Easter Rising and the path to independence were founded on *rejection* by nationalists of the British war effort.

In the last decade, much has been done to end this dichotomy. When Queen Elizabeth II and President Mary McAleese dedicated the Irish Peace Tower in Flanders on 11 November 1998, all the Irish soldiers of the Great War were at last commemorated on the

Left: 'The Royal Munster Fusiliers are earning eternal fame fighting for you', 1914–18. Reproduced by permission of the Board, Trinity College Dublin.

Western Front. In 2006 the participation of Irish soldiers in the Battle of the Somme was honoured for the first time by a state ceremony in the Republic, complementing the official celebration of the ninetieth anniversary of the Easter Rising. Ireland's role in the Great War is increasingly acknowledged in the Republic while awareness of the part played by Catholics and nationalists has grown in Northern Ireland, where as recently as 1987 the IRA blew up the Enniskillen war memorial on Remembrance Sunday, killing eleven people.

But what does the new 'memory' consist of? Are we doing anything more than recognising for the sake of current political correctness that soldiers from the whole island participated in the war? The soldiers' war is certainly important, and we still have much to discover about the ordinary men who fought in it.[1] But how did the soldiers' experiences relate to the larger meaning of the conflict? In what way was the Great War 'our war'? Few books have addressed these questions in substance.[2] Our island's conflicting memories of the war still blur the retrospective view and prevent us from taking the war's full measure. History is not the same as memory, so changing the lens means recovering Irish experiences of the war. But all memory has a history so it also requires study of how different Irish memories of the war evolved. These are the issues addressed by the Thomas Davis lectures and by this book.

Recently, a revolution has taken place in the understanding of the Great War more generally, and this new understanding affects how we re-evaluate its impact on Ireland. The transformation has been driven by social and cultural history, which have helped to disentangle memory from history, to explore contemporary experiences of the war and to study the ways in which those experiences were remembered or forgotten in the different societies involved.[3] Three major features of the Great War have emerged. The first is the intensity with which societies engaged in it. The second is the mass death caused in combat. The third is remembrance—how people came to understand an event whose trauma none had anticipated.

Some historians have argued that the cultural and political engagement in the war by the European nations, or by peoples who in Ireland and much of eastern Europe hoped to achieve nationhood, amounted to a modern crusade.[4] Of course, hard political issues were involved—the fate of empires, the formation of new nations, colonial rivalries and the potential domination of Europe by Imperial Germany. But everywhere the enemy was pictured as a threat to the very existence of the national communities concerned, and it was this antagonism that created the sense of a crusade. We think of Sigmund Freud as the father of psychoanalysis. But partly owing to the war, he became an astute observer of collective psychology and in a remarkable essay written in 1915 he conveyed this ability of European civilisation to mobilise intense antagonisms.

> Then the war [...] cuts all the common bonds between the contending peoples and threatens to leave a legacy of embitterment that will make any renewal of those bonds impossible for a long time to come [...] It has brought to light an almost incredible phenomenon: the civilized nations know and understand one another so little that one can turn against the other with hate and loathing. [5]

This mobilisation of society for war—we might even refer to it as self-mobilisation—was extremely powerful.[6] Afterwards, when it became hard to reconstruct the war-time mood, it was explained away by propaganda and censorship. Indeed, the idea of propaganda as manipulation dates precisely from the 1920s, when it became a tool to explain how rational people had accepted the folly of war.[7] In Ireland, there has been a republican version of the myth that sees nationalist support for a 'British imperialist' war in just these terms. Even in the scholarly literature, a case has been made for understanding the war in Ireland as propaganda.[8] Both censorship and propaganda were certainly part of the mobilisation process, but they have to be understood in terms of governments and important segments of public opinion that were intensely committed to their visions of the war. The concept of 'war cultures' has been coined to better capture this sense of something more substantial and self-determined, which requires understanding through its own values and internal dynamics.[9]

Military service was central to the cultures of war-time. Universal conscription was the norm in continental Europe, resulting in the armies of millions that fought the war. It met with remarkably little resistance and the opposition that did occur emerged late in the war and, even then, mainly in Russia and Austria–Hungary. The United Kingdom achieved the feat of raising a Continental-style army of 2.5 million by calling for volunteers before being forced to introduce conscription in 1916 in order to find the same number again. Ireland, as part of the UK, played an important role in this voluntary war effort, contributing some 210,000 recruits. However, in 1918 it proved impossible to introduce conscription here.[10] But everywhere, whether voluntary or compulsory, military service raised issues of national identity and political rights. It was the crux of acceptance—or refusal—of the war.

The second key feature of the war to be underlined by recent scholarship is combat-related death on an unprecedented scale. Modern technology, notably high-explosive artillery and machine-guns, not only made the Great War the most lethal conflict to date, but also gave an overwhelming preponderance to the combatants' ability to defend themselves. The result was the trench warfare in which the great powers were mired for four years without being able to convert the military losses into a decisive victory. Even in 1918 when the use of tanks and aircraft foreshadowed future conflicts, Germany and Austria–Hungary were defeated mainly by exhaustion. Hence the particular experience of combat in 1914–18. This was not just of high losses, but of high losses for unclear gains. Freud, who was also a family man with two sons and a son-in-law at the front, noted in the essay already cited that whereas modern society had grown unused to death, now: 'Death will no longer be denied; we are forced to believe in it. People really die; and no longer one by one, but many, often tens of thousands, in a single day'.[11]

Irish soldiers who served as professionals in the British Army were killed from the outset in the intense fighting as the British Expeditionary Force (BEF) helped stem the German invasion of France. On 1 September 1914, for example, a Catholic Lieutenant–Colonel in the Irish Guards (and son of a former Lord Chief Justice of Ireland), George Morris, died commanding a rearguard as the BEF retreated to the Marne. He is commemorated by a stained glass window in the parish church of Spiddal, Co. Galway, While historians disagree on the precise figure, by the time the war was over, some 27,000 to 35,000 Irish soldiers were dead.[12]

These two dimensions of the war, mass engagement in the conflict and mass death in battle, shaped how the experience of the conflict played out in the different societies concerned. It proved hard to sustain the self-mobilisation of society in the face of military stalemate and soaring casualties. Moreover, destruction on an industrial scale required an equivalent production of the materials of war, and the belligerent countries had to improvise an industrial effort that generated its own social and political tensions, not to mention an agricultural effort to keep soldiers and civilians adequately fed. The political strain of managing the war effort became intense. Yet, the scale of losses incurred and the high stakes involved sustained hostility toward the enemy despite some voices calling for an early peace. The last two years of the war were marked by the need for endurance at both a personal and a collective level. Where social cohesion, national identity or the legitimacy of the state were weakest—for example, in Russia and Austria–Hungary—endurance turned into refusal, producing revolution along class or national lines. Elsewhere, dogged endurance sustained the populations as the war reached its military climax. Ireland experienced both.

The relationship between mass mobilisation and mass death shaped the third feature of the war underlined in recent historical writing—remembrance. Death lay at the heart of remembrance. Almost everywhere there was a profusion of monuments and rituals of collective mourning. The tradition before 1914 was to subsume the war dead in the figure of their great commander or military unit.[13] The scale of death in 1914–18 made such a hierarchy of commemoration impossible. It democratised those in death who had not always experienced such equality in life. Almost spontaneously, the commemorations in London and Paris in July 1919 took place in the presence of the dead—in the form of the cenotaph or symbolic empty tomb—erected in Whitehall and at the Arc de Triomphe.[14] The two minute silence and the grave of the unknown soldier completed a commemorative ritual that has since become the norm. This form of remembrance also took place in Ireland.[15]

However, the function of such rituals was to preserve a relationship between death and the purposes for which the war had been fought. The equation turned on the notion of 'sacrifice'—that is, of meaningful death. As such it proved highly unstable given the actual outcome of the war. In defeated Germany, for example, monuments flourished for the men who had died for the *Heimat*, that untranslatable term for a local homeland. But no successful national monument was built nor could any national ritual be agreed upon because there was no consensus on the meaning of defeat.[16] In Britain and France, by contrast, Armistice Day continued to express a sense of necessary sacrifice, though it was often tinged by a belief that future war must be avoided for the sacrifice to be fully justified.[17] War memorials and national rituals were a transaction between the purpose of the war and mass death, in an effort to give meaning to its memory.[18] In Ireland, they proved one of the principal ways in which memory of the conflict divided.

Looking at the war in terms of mass engagement, mass death and remembrance seems to provide a good framework for re-evaluating the conflict's place in Irish history. Let us explore each of them a little further. In terms of nationalist engagement, there was particular sympathy for the fate of the two small nations, Belgium and Serbia, which were invaded by Germany and its Austrian ally. For unionists, the idea that the British Empire embodied civilisation and fear that the defeat of France by Germany would menace British security were sufficient to depict a national community under threat.[19] For much of nationalist opinion, the violation of Belgian neutrality, the atrocities that the German Army committed against Belgian civilians (including the deliberate destruction of the Catholic university library at Louvain) and the mass exodus of refugees, some of whom materialised in Irish towns, made the issue of Prussian 'militarism' very real.[20] The nationalist intellectual and former Home Rule MP, Tom Kettle, was unusual in that he was actually in Belgium illegally buying arms for the Irish National Volunteers[21] when the invasion occurred, and was able to see its effects at close quarters. But his belief that 'this last crusade' was about defending the same democratic values and self-determination that Home Rule was to bring to Ireland matched the Liberal view of the war in Britain or that of republican France. The same case was put by Redmond when he urged the National Volunteers (who had by this point spilt from the more militant Irish Volunteers) to serve in the British Army: it was the war as a democratic crusade, along with the belief that Belgium had suffered due to its Catholicism.[22]

In other countries the war brought a suspension of politics in 1914, and for a brief moment, as the country pulled back from the brink of civil war, it seemed as if this was so in Ireland too. But the war in fact reactivated politics as nationalists and unionists pursued their opposed goals by participating in the war effort. This was entirely compatible with the belief that the war embodied the values for which they stood. Although there were some dissidents (including the militant minority group, the Irish Volunteers), in both cases politics were underpinned by a 'self-mobilisation' that perhaps entitles one to talk of unionist and nationalist 'war cultures'.

Churchmen played a key role as Presbyterian or Church of Ireland clergy invoked British traditions of religious liberty while the Catholic clergy denounced the German oppression of Catholic Belgium and most (but not all) the bishops endorsed the nationalist crusade.[23] Women mounted a formidable charitable effort in support of soldiers and prisoners of war or nursed with the forces. In both communities, unionist and nationalist, the war was a palpable presence—from silk embroidered postcards of the Allied flags to disparaging portraits of the enemy. An officer of the Royal Inniskilling Fusiliers training in Donegal carved a fretwork clock that portrayed an Irish soldier bayoneting a German officer, with his distinctive spiked helmet, who inadvertently stabs a German soldier below him as he falls. He gave the clock to a local family before departing for the front in 1915, the violence of war imagined, then put aside for the real thing.

By 1916 'self-mobilisation' for the war was on the wane. Not only had the conflict lasted beyond all expectations but its human cost had become clear, at least at a local level. Even before the British Army sustained 420,000 dead, missing, wounded and captured at the Battle of the Somme from July to November 1916, men from Dublin, Cork and elsewhere in Ireland had suffered in the Gallipoli campaign the previous year.[24] But in most combatant states, military casualties were highest in the first half of the war, and by 1917 the conflict had turned into a grim endurance test. What mattered was whether the required resources could be found to sustain the effort to the bitter end, and if so on what terms.

In this regard, the economic dimension was perhaps the least important as far as Ireland was concerned. Grinding poverty remained a scourge of the unskilled working class and the 'congested districts' of the rural west, but farm incomes rose as Britain fought the German submarine menace by expanding home food production. Farmers, large and small, were well satisfied with high prices. In Russia and Italy, land-hunger among the poorest peasants became a critical issue for war-time society. It was a major factor in the revolution that broke out in March 1917 in Russia, while in Italy land reform was demanded by peasant soldiers as the national effort was re-launched following the defeat at Caporetto in October 1917.[25] In Ireland, by contrast, land agitation and reform by British governments had largely resolved this issue, so that recruiters in 1915 could only appeal to farmers to defend what they had already secured (see pp. 20–1).[26]

Potentially more important was the industrial mobilisation. Across Europe and the United States, the vast output of munitions created a war-time working class centred on coal mines, steel foundries and munitions plants. Whether for reform or revolution, organised labour became a force to be reckoned with, while governments feared that strikes might turn into class opposition to the war—as indeed happened in Russia, Italy, Austria and Germany.[27] The tight labour-market conferred an unusual degree of influence on Irish trade unions, still struggling in Dublin to recover from the 1913 lockout, and this helped workers defend themselves against war-time inflation. But Ireland remained on the margins of the munitions effort, except in the industrial north-east where skilled workers were overwhelmingly loyalist. Irish labour posed little threat to the UK's war economy (unlike Scotland, where Red Clydeside was a hotbed of disaffection), and the Irish state in which it might have entrenched its bargaining-power did not yet exist.

The real Irish contribution to the war remained military. Not only did recruitment make this highly tangible, it also supplied the symbolic currency of nationhood during the war. The assumed right of a state to call on its subjects or citizens to defend it in time of need, let alone to conscript them, had become deeply political with the advent of mass armies in the nineteenth century.[28] Military service and war-time 'sacrifice' were a prime means of creating national communities, which meant they could also be used to demand reciprocal rights and reforms. Both unionist and nationalist leaders traded on this understanding of military service. While the 36th (Ulster) Division recruited from the Ulster Volunteer Force (UVF) and the 16th (Irish) Division contained nationalist activists and several Home Rule MPs, it would be foolish to imagine that most men joined up for political motives. But the pattern of enlistment was very different from that of peacetime volunteering by Irishmen for the small, professional British Army, a tradition that was in decline. Men joined up for many reasons, but they came (in varying degrees) from all backgrounds and enlisted in the context of a social self-mobilisation that made volunteering seem not an irrational but a decent and 'manly' thing to do.[29]

Because the war reactivated Irish politics, different kinds of volunteer expressed the competing versions of nationality that came to a head in the conflict.[30] The result, however, was to define and dramatise four varieties of statehood in Ireland: unionist, Ulster unionist, nationalist and republican. The war marked the definitive failure of unionism on the island as a whole, and thus of that historic attempt to include Ireland in a British nation that had bedevilled Anglo–Irish relations since 1800. Yet if that option had long been doomed, it still represented the status quo, and its swan-song came with the self-mobilisation of Protestant families and institutions outside the north-east for the war effort and the readiness with which their sons volunteered for the army. The war service of Trinity College Dublin, a largely though not exclusively Protestant institution by the early twentieth century, is a good example. The casualty rate of its alumni was comparable with Oxford and Cambridge, as the Hall of Honour and adjacent Library still testify.[31] Among those commemorated is Robert Bernard, whose father was the Provost of Trinity after the war and Church of Ireland Archbishop of Dublin during it, and who died with the Royal Dublin Fusiliers at Gallipoli.

The strength and density of Protestantism in the north-east, which had found expression in the 100,000 armed militia volunteers of the pre-war period, allowed a different option. Its volunteers, and especially those in the 36th Division, fed a war-time culture of fortress unionism that anticipated partition and was reinforced in the second half of the war by the supposed 'treason' of the Easter Rising and Sinn Féin. In 1917 a painting by James P. Beadle recorded the exploits of the men of the 36th Division on the first day of the Somme when, some wearing Orange sashes and shouting loyalist slogans, they stormed five lines of German trenches. The fact that it should be donated to the people of Belfast by the UVF during the war testifies to the potent symbolism of the northern unionist volunteer. The painting still hangs in Belfast City Hall and has appeared on countless Orange Order sashes.

Home Rule nationalists, by contrast, invoked the model of the loyal dominion, such as Australia or Canada, achieving national status within the empire.[32] The double-edged symbolism of the nationalist volunteer, we have seen, represented the cause of democratic national self-determination both internationally and at home. While the best remembered words of Tom Kettle come from his moving poem to his daughter, in which he defined the war as 'not for flag, nor King nor Emperor/But for a dream, born in a herdsman's shed/And for the Secret Scripture of the poor', they are less typical than his frequently expressed belief that Britain owed Ireland 'colonial Home Rule' because of the 'seal of the blood given in the last two years'—a phrase used in a letter published after he died in September 1916, fighting with the 16th Division at the Somme.[33]

Blood sacrifice of a different sort was the key to the Republic proclaimed by the insurrectionary Volunteers of Easter 1916. This had everything to do with the war. For the minority that rejected Redmond's crusade systematically inverted what we might consider the war culture of Irish nationalism. The British Empire, not Germany, was the enemy, and for Pádraig Pearse and James Connolly the empire meant not the 'white' dominions but British oppression in Egypt and India as well as Ireland. 'We do not love the [British] Empire', Connolly wrote in 1915; 'we hate it with an unqualified hatred.'[34] The nation had to mobilise, but for a war *against* Britain, which turned insurrection and collaboration with Germany into acts of patriotism. Above all, the notion of 'sacrifice' that lay at the heart of the war cultures became a weapon against nationalist recruitment for the war. There is no better illustration of this than a copy of the Proclamation torn down from the walls of the GPO by a British officer after the insurrection.[35] What came away with it were the recruiting posters over which it had been pasted. Dublin's walls were a contested space for opposed forms of volunteering and competing views of the nation (see pp. *vi–vii*).

The relative strengths of these identities changed across the war, and there have been important historical debates on the reasons, from the resilience or weakness of the Home Rule Party on the eve of the conflict to the British government's suppression of the Rising. Certainly, so long as Irish sovereignty and devolved government had not been delivered in some form, it was impossible to introduce conscription—as the British government discovered in 1918.[36] The

11

war effort in the eyes of many nationalists had been de-legitimised. But what matters here is that the mobilisation of Irish society for (and against) the war, and in particular the figure of the volunteer, helped determine the versions of statehood in contention and the credibility of British policies in Ireland.

How did this contested process of mobilisation for the war relate to the soldiers' experience and the impact on society of death at the front? The idea of mass death needs qualification in the case of Ireland. Without conscription, casualties remained lower in relation to the overall population than in most combatant countries, including Britain. Out of a population of 4.4 million, 30,000 military dead represented 7 per 1,000 people, compared to 16 per 1,000 for the United Kingdom as a whole. This was less than a quarter of the German or French figures (30 and 34 per 1,000 respectively). Ironically, Belgium, which had been occupied and was only able to field a small army, lost even fewer (5 per 1,000) whereas Serbia, which resisted three invasions before the Serb army retreated into exile, topped the table at 57 per 1,000.[37] The best comparison is with Australia—because it was a dominion and because it, too, rejected conscription. From a similar size population (4.9 million), 413,000 volunteered of whom 60,000 (or 12 per 1,000) died. This shows the limits of the Irish voluntary effort.

Yet Irish soldiers were exposed to the same risk of death, shell shock and wounds from shrapnel or machine-gun fire as other men. The losses of the 36th and 16th divisions in the Battle of the Somme, with the Ulstermen sustaining 5,482 casualties and the 16th Division losing 4,330 men, were comparable to those of other British divisions, and of course many Irishmen fought in non-Irish regiments.[38] 'I have seen war, and faced modern artillery, and know what an outrage it is against simple men', wrote Tom Kettle in his last letter to his brother.[39] A young Aran Islander, Liam O'Flaherty, who joined the Irish Guards, was wounded and shell-shocked at the Third Battle of Ypres (or Passchendaele) in 1917. He later drew on the experience to write *Return of the Brute*, one of the most powerful literary depictions of the brutalising effect of the war in any language.[40]

As for the home front, even if the national death rate in combat was at the lower end of the scale, it was beyond anything in contemporary Irish experience. Some circles were especially hard hit the losses, like the recruitment, were sufficiently widespread for Ireland as a whole to answer Freud's description of a society faced with collective mourning. Ordinary families from North and South, Catholic and Protestant, were left to find consolation, and if possible a meaning, for the death of loved ones at the front.

By the end of the conflict this task had become harder for families in nationalist Ireland, owing to growing British suspicion of southern loyalty (which culminated in the withdrawal of the 16th (Irish) Division from service in France, whereas the 36th (Ulster) Division continued to be lionised) as well as republican hostility to the British uniform. If Irish soldiers had initially felt outrage on hearing the news of the Easter Rising, by 1918 the logic of volunteering for nationalist motives was compromised by British policy and changing attitudes at home. Michael Moynihan, from a middle class Catholic family in Tralee, who joined the British civil service from University College Dublin (UCD) and fought in the Irish battalion of a Liverpool regiment, displayed this tension in letters to his brothers and family friends who held advanced nationalist opinions. While not renouncing his engagement, he expressed 'the fullest sympathy for the new men and the new teachings' (meaning Sinn Féin) and a bitter disillusionment with Redmond.[41] Returning from patrol in June 1918, he was accidentally killed by one of his own sentries.

Making sense of such deaths, however, became even more conflictual in the Ireland that emerged from prolonged strife in 1923.[42] Northern Ireland quickly established its title-deeds as a self-governing province within the union by an essentially Protestant and unionist myth of heroism at the Battle of the Somme. Completed in 1921, the Ulster Tower at Thiepval, near the heart of the battlefield, associated the 'other men of Ulster' with those of the unionist 36th Division, and was fully the equivalent of the national memorials built by Australia, Canada, New Zealand and South Africa. Armistice Day ceremonies came to be dominated by unionists and were endorsed by the province's new elites.

Ambivalence, by contrast, reigned in the Free State. While republicans openly contested the rituals of remembrance, the state was anxious to exclude neither former unionists nor Home Rule nationalists. It supported the National Irish War Memorial, completed at Islandbridge, Dublin, just before the Second World War, though the inauguration had to wait until 1988. Yet no national memorial was raised on the Western Front, and only modest Celtic crosses commemorated the Irish divisions abroad. Ceremonies took place between the wars but these were the acts of groups in civil society (nationalist veterans, former officers), not the state. Memorials were built, but they were sparse by comparison with Australia where they are found at the heart of every city and township across the country—and the same is true of Canada and New Zealand.[43] The Irish state could extend civic tolerance to Irish war veterans and their ceremonies. What it could not do was endorse the war as a foundation-stone of the

13

state. This was the task of the growing commemoration of the Easter Rising and its heroes and martyrs. From the Second World War the memory of the Great War was increasingly denied in the public life and self-understanding of independent Ireland.[44] For 40 years, the National War Memorial was a ghostly ruin. Even the war memorial library in Trinity College Dublin became known (after the date of its opening) as the '1937 Reading Room', as if the war that occasioned it had never taken place—a situation that still exists.

Such contested and marginalised memories were not unique. Three million Poles fought as conscripts in the opposed armies of Tsarist Russia and Germany and Austria–Hungary, so the new post-war state sought its founding myth (and 'unknown soldier') in the victorious war against Bolshevik Russia of 1919–20. Likewise, the minority of Czechs who fought as volunteers with the Allies supplied the myth of the 'legionaries' for the new Czechoslovakia, most of whose men had been Austro–Hungarian conscripts, while the alienated Sudeten German minority had its own counter-myths of the war.[45] In these cases, and in independent Ireland, the question of whether the absence of an official discourse of sacrifice affected how families and local communities came to terms with their war dead remains to be answered. Likewise, it is unclear whether the explicitly political uses of war-time 'sacrifice' in Northern Ireland militated against the rejection of the horrors of industrialised warfare that was discernible in inter-war France and Britain.

In every sense the Great War was 'our war'. While never the sole determinant, it contributed decisively to the major turning-point of twentieth century Irish history, 1913–1923, which saw a polarisation and realignment of national and political identities that has lasted to the present. Since divergent versions of the war experience lay at the heart of those opposed identities, it is not surprising that the war's legacy should have proved so contested nor that Irish war experiences—North and South, male and female, military and civilian, unionist and nationalist—should so rarely be placed in a common framework. The chapters that follow seek to do just this.

14

PAX IN BELLUM; or, UNITED KINGDOMERS.

JOHN—"My dear Edward, if you and I ever fight, it will be shoulder to shoulder against any outsider who ventures
to attack these islands sacred to both of us."
EDWARD—"My dear old friend, there's my hand on it."

'Pax in Bellum; or, United Kingdomers', *The Lepracaun*, August 1914. Edward Carson (left) and
John Redmond (right) are shown united in a fight against a common enemy.
Reproduced by permission of the Board, Trinity College Dublin.

WHAT HAVE <u>YOU</u> DONE FOR IRELAND?

What have you done for Ireland?
How have you answered the Call?
Are you pleased with the part you're playing
In the job that demands us all?
Have you changed the tweed for the khaki
To serve with the rank and file
As your comrades are gladly serving,
Or isn't it worth your while?

Can you meet the eyes of soldiers?
Or have you to turn away?
When they talk of the stay-at-home slacker,
Have you never a word to say?
When you read the roll of honour
Of living and dead—what then?
Does the voice within approve you
As one to be ranked with men?

For if in Ireland's glory
Each soldier may claim his share,
So he who would shirk his duty,
His burden of shame must bear.
You who are strong and active,
You who are fit for the fray,
What have you done for Ireland?
Ask of your heart to-day!

'What have you done for
Ireland?' recruitment poster, *c.*
1915. © Royal Irish Academy.

Right: NLI, Ephemera
Collection, POL/1910-20/10:
'Ireland demands Home Rule',
c. 1912. Sepia-coloured label of
Home Rule leader, John
Redmond. Courtesy of the
National Library of Ireland.

(3336.)Wt.P.591— .10,000.3/15.   ALEX. THOM & CO., LTD., DUBLIN.

IRELAND DEMANDS HOME RULE

IWM, Q 10683: Men of
the 12th Royal Irish Rifles
washing at Essigny, France,
7 February 1918. Taken by
T.K. Aiken. © Imperial
War Museum.

NLI, Ephemera Collection, WAR/1914-18/9: 'Farmers of Ireland:
join up and defend your possessions', *c.* 1915. It is interesting to
note that the CCORI recognised the need to target farmers.
Courtesy of the National Library of Ireland.

Farmers of Ireland
JOIN UP & DEFEND
your possessions.

A memorial service held at Delville Wood, 1916. It illustrates how men of the cloth had to improvise in the conditions and the importance to the solemn men in the background of such religious rituals. © Popperfoto/Getty Images.

Christmas card, 16th (Irish) Division, 1917. Courtesy of the National Irish War Memorial Records at Islandbridge.

Survivors from the *Lusitania*, a passenger
liner, hit by a U-boat torpedo killing
1,198 people off Kinsale Head, standing
outside the town hall in Cobh,
Co. Cork, May 1915. Recruitment
posters are visible on the wall behind
them. © 2007 Getty Images.

CHANGING HIS FRONT.

KAISER—"I'm pretty well tired of Cathedrals and Universities; they don't pay. I'll try looting this sort of 'National Treasure' in future."

'Changing his front', *The Lepracaun*, October 1914. Kaiser Wilhelm II, imagined leading the charge on the Bank of Ireland, College Green. Underfoot are documents from towns already sacked by German forces. Reproduced by permission of the Board, Trinity College Dublin.

Daily News(Letter to the Editor)

September 26th 1914

UCDA, LA34/374: Tom Kettle writes to the editor of the *Daily News*, London, 26 September 1914. He argues that the Great War is 'without parallel' and calls for a 'people's peace' once it is over. Courtesy of UCD Archives, School of History and Archives.

Historic Parallels

' A Grand memory for forgetting.'

Sir:-

Will you permit me, with all the respect due to two great names, to

beg the Chancellor of the Exchequer and the Right Hon. G.W.E. Russell to abstain

from "historical parallels"? This war is without parallel.   Britain,France

and Russia enter it, purged from their past sins of domination.   France is as

right now as she was wrong in 1870.   England is as right now as she was wrong

in the Boer War.   Russia is as right now as she was wrong on Bloody Sunday.

Mr. Lloyd George's reference to Napoleon   3's respect for Belgian

neturality was singularly unhappy.   Did he ever hear   of the Benedetti Treaty?

Or of Napoleon's design to protect Belgium by annexing it?   And does Mr.

Russell really suggest that in the events that led up to the unchaining of the devi

in India in 1857 the occupiers and governors of that ancient land were blameless

and radaint Knights of the Holy Ghost?

At all times it is well to have at the back of one's head what

Stevenson's Highlander calls "a grand memory for forgetting."   Let this war go

LOST ON THE LUSITANIA

Sir Hugh Lane.

Height about 5ft. 11in.

Build—very slight.

Hair dark brown, slightly turning grey, rather bald, small pointed beard, chest hairy.

Forehead very high, deep set eyes, large nose.

Wore cellular underclothing marked " H. Lane" and Jaeger cholera belt.

Usually wore plain gold signet ring with lion crest as shown below.

When last seen was wearing pearl tie pin.

Communicate by Wire with

CHARLES LANE,

26 South Mall, Cork.

32

Shocked survivors of the *Lusitania* disaster, brought ashore
at Cobh, Co. Cork, May 1915. © 2007 Getty Images.

RECRUITS REQUIRED

AGE

18 to 41

'Recruits required. Age 18 to 41'. Irish recruitment poster, *c.* 1916. A soldier marches by with a sprig of shamrock on his cap. Reproduced by permission of the Board, Trinity College Dublin.

FOR INFORMATION

Apply to any RECRUITING OFFICE or POLICE BARRACKS

CHAPTER 2

Going to war

C A T R I O N A   P E N N E L L

Intelligence Corps.

Instructions as regards Uniform Equipment, Field Kit, etc.

You should provide yourself at once with uniform, equipment, etc., on the following scale :-

2nd Lieut

Uniform.

1 Cap, service dress with G.S. badge, *General Service*
1 Field Service Jacket, open at neck (Buttons G.S.)
1 pr." " Breeches
1 " " " Trousers
1 Coat, warm, British (or Greatcoat)
Sam Browne Belt, (Waist-belt, 2 shoulder-belts,
~~Revolver (for .45 ammunition (if unobtainable application should be made at Room 226).~~
~~Ammunition pouch~~
Putties,
2 Khaki Shirts.
2 Collars,
1 Khaki tie,
2 boots (Pairs)
~~Field Glasses~~
~~Haversack~~
Water bottle and sling,
~~Folding knife, fork and spoon.~~

NAI, 1096/10/20: Kit list for a 2nd Lieutenant of the Intelligence Corps.
Courtesy of the National Archives of Ireland.

Note - A second suit may be taken if considered necessary.

Camp Kit.

~~Valise (sleeping)~~
~~Waterproof sheet (optional)~~

~~3 blankets will be provided free, and will be issued later.~~

The total weight of baggage and field kit allowed for each Intelligence Officer is 135 lbs. which must not on any account be exceeded. Of this 100 lbs. will be left at the Base, and 35 lbs. only taken into the field. The 100 lbs. should be packed in a strong bag or trunk and labelled.

You will present yourself in uniform at Room 226 War Office, at *10 o'c* on the *09th January* prepared to leave this country at short notice.

Outfit

allowance of £50 will be credited to you.

HO5A
13/1

R.Page

Ireland, July 1914: as the Home Rule Bill edged towards ratification both the Ulster Volunteer Force (UVF) and Irish National Volunteers prepared for an armed response. Gun-running into Larne by the UVF and the threatened mutiny at the Curragh Camp in Kildare, when British Army officers refused to enforce Home Rule in Ulster, convinced nationalists that they could not expect impartiality from British rule in Ireland, and they intensified their own paramilitary mobilisation. On 23 June the Government of Ireland (Amendment) Bill had been introduced in the House of Lords. Proposing that the six temporarily excluded counties in Ulster would be controlled by a makeshift administration under the Lord-Lieutenant in Dublin, for unionists, it was tantamount to Home Rule by stealth. Five days later, on 28 June, the heir to the dual monarchy of Austria–Hungary was assassinated in Sarajevo.

On 21 July at the opening of the Buckingham Palace Conference convened to 'settle the Irish question',[1] King George V warned that 'the cry of civil war [was] on the lips of the most responsible and sober-minded of my people'.[2] Two days later the Austrian government, backed by Germany, issued a harsh ultimatum to Serbia in response to the assassination of Archduke Franz Ferdinand. This was designed to be rejected and thus allow the Austrians to crush Serbia. In Britain and Ireland, however, eyes would soon be firmly focused on a domestic tragedy. On 26 July, confirming the king's worst fears, a detachment of the King's Own Scottish Borderers fired on a crowd of Dublin civilians (suspected of nationalist gun-running) on Bachelor's Walk, killing four and wounding up to fifty. The killings were denounced across the country and on 29 July (the day that Austro–Hungarian forces began to bombard Belgrade) the funeral of three of the victims became a day of national mourning on which shops and businesses closed. The funeral procession was over a mile long, watched by 200,000 people, and ended with Volunteers firing a volley over the graves. The funeral was filmed and screened at cinemas across the country. The tragedy again encouraged brisk recruitment to the Irish National Volunteers; anyone who did not answer the call was 'not for but against Ireland'.[3] In the wake of the murders, John Redmond, nationalist leader of the Irish Parliamentary Party, bluntly told the House of Commons: 'Let the House clearly understand that four-fifths of the Irish people will not submit any longer to be[ing] bullied, or punished, or shot, for conduct which is permitted to go scot-free in the open light of day in every county in Ulster by other sections of their fellow countrymen'. The incident was relayed to people in Britain under frightening headlines like 'Slaughter in Ireland' and 'Fighting in Dublin'. This, then, was the Irish political situation at the end of July 1914 as the great powers in Europe declared war and started invading each other until, on 4 August, the United Kingdom was obliged to intervene when German troops stormed into neutral Belgium *en route* to Paris. While in Britain, the outbreak of war in Europe led the labour and suffragette movements to suspend their causes temporarily and rally behind the national effort, such loyalty was not guaranteed in Ireland. Would civil war erupt as seemed inevitable? Would Germany replace Britain as the enemy for nationalists? Would the population of Ireland respond to Britain's rallying cry to unite behind the war effort?

THE OUTBREAK OF WAR

As late as 31 July the European situation was still less important in Ireland than the shootings on Bachelor's Walk. As in Britain, opinion only changed over the Bank Holiday weekend (Saturday 1–Monday 3 August). Military precautions, such as mobilisation orders and the mass movement of troops, fuelled speculation about the war, and anxiety over the future. Kevin O'Sheil (who went on to become legal adviser to the provisional Free State government), in Dublin, recalled how 'by the first week of August, events that we had hardly noticed had plunged Germany, France, Russia, Austria and Serbia into war'.[4] However, no evidence exists to suggest that war was desired amongst the Irish population. According to Dr Charles Dowse, the Church of Ireland Bishop of Cork, the war 'was not of our asking. It was thrust upon us'.[5]

Prior to its official declaration, the majority of British and Irish people hoped that war would be avoided. Tuesday, 4 August was therefore a momentous day across the United Kingdom. A variety of emotions were felt: shock, despair, panic, a thirst for news and a sense of stoic necessity, among many others. There was, however, one distinctive feature of the Irish response: war abroad meant peace at home. It is one of the paradoxes of modern Irish history that the outbreak of war in Europe may have prevented conflict in Ireland in 1914. In consequence, the war was greeted with a short-lived sense of relief. On 4 August Captain George Berkeley, an Irish National Volunteers commander in Belfast, confided in his diary that the outbreak of war 'meant *peace*'.[6]

As in Britain, the war caused immediate changes. Soldiers were sent to protect coastal areas, and towns and bridges were put under police guard. The army commandeered football and cricket fields. Perhaps the most visible evidence of war was the departure within three weeks for England and the Continent of some 40,000 British soldiers who had been stationed in Ireland. On 15 August as ships departed for France down the River Liffey in Dublin, Thomas King Moylan, a mental asylum clerk in Dublin, recorded how 'the fog horns and sirens of every vessel were blown, making a most heart rending wail [...] Last night the hooting was kept up almost continuously between 6 o'clock and 9'.[7]

Eye-witness accounts of the send-off that British troops received as they left Ireland during the first weeks of war contradict later myths about indifferent or hostile Irish reactions to the outbreak of the conflict. Cheering crowds were common. In Dundalk, local man, Thomas McCrave, watched as the local British military garrison left for the war. 'They were conducted to the railway station by the Dundalk Emmet Band, and they got an enthusiastic send-off from the townspeople.'[8] None other than the King's Own Scottish Borderers were given a 'rousing send-off' by Dubliners as they marched to the docks to embark for France.[9] On 6 August an estimated crowd of 50,000 people accompanied reservists to the North Wall at Dublin Port and was 'most enthusiastic for England, singing and playing "God Save the King", an unheard of thing hitherto among [...] nationalists'.[10] Charles Arnold left Dublin with his regiment on 13 August: 'What crowds there were to see us off! The Dublin people went mad, flags were flying, bands playing, in fact we got a right Royal [*sic*] send off (including a packet of fruit, cakes and cigarettes for each man)'.[11] Percy Whitehouse, who was serving with the Royal Field Artillery in Kildare, recalled how people cheered as his brigade left for Dublin on 15 August.[12] These scenes were not the displays of an occupied people willing British soldiers off Irish soil. Yet, neither could they be described as a population enthusiastic for war. When troops departed from Cork, the *Cork Free Press* described how 'a vast crowd filled the spacious station yard, and the scenes full of pathos, tinged at times with humour, have never been equalled in the memory of the oldest inhabitant'.[13] As in Britain, France and Germany, there was a sense of giving soldiers a good send-off in the knowledge of the hardships they were about to face.

The economic impact of the war was felt immediately. As in Britain, banks were closed until 7 August and food prices rose during the first weeks of war. This led to protests in some areas. In Mallow, a crowd of local labourers gathered at the town square to protest about the 'sudden and [...] unwarrantable increase in the prices of provisions and coal, already dear enough'.[14] Others panicked and began to stock up on food and provisions, with some shopkeepers 'delighted to get a chance of increased profit'.[15] The *Western Nationalist* wrote of 'shivering' bank accounts and 'food traitors' increasing their prices.[16] The Irish tourist industry was also badly hit. Jobs were affected just as quickly and severely as in Britain, with unemployment peaking in September. Belfast shipbuilding, which flourished later in the war, suffered dislocation as reserve soldiers were called up and workers left for industrial districts in Britain. Employment in the city's engineering industry was badly affected by the loss of Continental demand for textile machinery. Linen workers were put on short-time in Belfast, Lurgan, Antrim and Drogheda. 'Nonessential' trades felt the greatest impact and as a consequence in Dublin, unemployment was high among cabinet-makers and seamstresses.[17]

THE DUST SETTLES

Across the United Kingdom, by late August–early September, the shock of the outbreak of war was beginning to lift, assisted by a stabilising economy. However, while people tried to carry on as before, the best they could achieve in these unprecedented circumstances was a gradual acceptance of the new situation and a 'settling down' to life in war time.

Many Irish women responded by offering assistance to soldiers who they believed were 'now fighting for our rights and liberties'.[18] Voluntary work in Ireland drew support from all classes, religious denominations, and political affiliations.[19] By 13 August Ulsterwoman Helen Duffin and her Aunt Charlotte, in Newcastle, Co. Down, were furiously knitting socks for the soldiers.[20] Combatants were also cared for via fund-raising events, letter-writing and the sending of comforts. Local businesses sponsored their work, such as the Cork Steam Packet Company, which sent Red Cross goods free of charge.[21] Soldiers' dependants were also looked after under the auspices of the Prince of Wales' National Relief Fund; in Cork alone, by 28 September £2,610 18s 10d had been raised. Intense feeling for Belgium and sympathy with her sufferings were manifested in a practical way when the refugees began to arrive in Ireland. Associations and organisations sprang up to help these 'victims of the monstrous barbarity of the enemy'[22] and as representatives of a Catholic nation, Irish people had a moral obligation to answer the call and look after them. When Belgian refugees were entertained at the Palace Theatre in Cork the 'house was specially decorated for the occasion, prominently displayed being the Irish and Belgian flags entwined, and surmounted by the Union Jack'.[23]

As in Britain, striking the right moral tone for the home population in the momentous circumstances of the time was a preoccupation. This particularly concerned the war's impact on women. Vigilance committees, like those established in Britain, were set up in Ireland in army towns and major ports. Unease regarding women's immorality and intemperance led to a public meeting in Dublin to establish an Irishwomen's League of Honour in November 1914, the purpose of which was to uphold 'the standard of women's duty and honour during the time of war [...] and to combat some of the social and moral dangers emphasised by the war; to deepen amongst women and girls a sense of their responsibility for the honour of the nation, and by their influence to uplift manhood'.[24] The Dean of St Patrick's Cathedral, Dublin, also proposed that Irishwomen shun those who did not volunteer for service: 'Visit them with the severest disapproval, and when they expect a smile just look them straight in the face and turn away'.[25]

Whilst practical support was a key characteristic of entry into war, less positive emotions also appeared. Here, too, Ireland manifested similar reactions to those of societies across Europe that were swept up in the war. To construct a figure of the enemy involved feelings of fear, anger and hatred. As in Britain, people in Ireland felt that Germany was the enemy and that the allied cause was just. Germany's aggression, her tyrannical rule and, in Catholic Ireland, her Protestantism, were all denounced. On 11 September Desmond Ryan, a boarder at St Enda's College, Pádraig Pearse's bilingual school in Rathfarnham, Co. Dublin, described to his father the anti-German attitude of the staff and priests at the school.[26] Stories of German atrocities in Belgium fuelled the outrage. Though discredited after the war as allied propaganda, it is now clear that invading German soldiers treated Belgian and French civilians with considerable brutality, a reality that was exaggerated by the feverish atmosphere of the early months of the war rather than by deliberate mistruths.[27] Thus, Thomas Moylan, in Dublin, recorded in his diary on October 1914:

> Many tales of brutality of the Germans have been circulated [...] I have heard it said that a Civil Servant out of one of the Dublin offices, who joined the Army was invalided to Netley with his hands and ears cut off, and so otherwise mutilated that his doctors think it better for him to die. A little girl is said to have been in Dublin a week or so ago, a refugee from Belgium, whose hands were also cut off [...] Belgian girls have [...] been outraged, their breasts cut off, and other indignities inflicted on them.[28]

On 15 and 16 August a series of attacks on German pork butchers' shops occurred across Dublin. Led by a soldier who had recently enlisted and wanted to start fighting the 'barbarians' immediately, the most serious attacks were on the premises of Frederick Lang on Wexford Street and George Reitz at Leonard's Corner on the South Circular Road, Portobello.[29] Another attack occurred on Thomas Street. According to the *Freeman's Journal* the crowd involved in this attack were 'principally of youths' who 'completely wrecked the shop' and 'threw all furniture, fixtures and meat stocks out onto the street'. No reason for the attacks could be ascribed 'except that the proprietors of the premises were believed to be German'.[30] Further smaller attacks also occurred in Dublin following the destruction of Louvain by the German Army on 25 August. In these instances, hapless locals were the scapegoats for crowds unable to vent their hatred against the real enemy. Such events were commonplace across the towns and cities of belligerent European countries.

As elsewhere, too, the lack of official news about the progress of the war produced spy-mania, which betrayed deep fear and anxiety about the outcome of the war as much as anger against the enemy. On 4 August a gentleman of 'foreign appearance' and two ladies who accompanied him were arrested in Crosshaven, Co. Cork, on charges of espionage. On his arrest, sketches and photos of the harbour were found in his possession evidence only of a tourist's souvenirs.[31] Shortly after war broke out, a leading Cork chess-player, F.U. Beamish, was arrested for suspicious behaviour after being seen 'studying a position on a pocket chess board' in a local park.[32] Some people even believed that German spies in Ireland had caused the outbreak of the war, having conveyed to the Kaiser the extent of domestic discontent within the country which suggested to the Germans that this was the optimum moment to start a war.[33]

It was but a short step from spy-mania to fear of actual invasion. Although it must have seemed remote to many, invasion certainly appeared to be a possibility to some in Ireland. On 15 August the *Sligo Champion* published a 'Call to Arms to the Manhood of Sligo' arguing that 'County Sligo as a coastline is liable at any time to be raided [...] It is the bounden duty of every man fit to bear arms [...] to protect his home and family from the foreign invader'.[34] Moreover, the arrest in Ireland of enemy aliens (that is, German and Austrian nationals) matched the graph of invasion anxiety in the United Kingdom as a whole, with 60% occurring between 3 and 9 August, during the initial surge of anxiety surrounding the outbreak of war, and the remainder in October–November, when the Germans, defeated at the Battle of the Marne, retreated towards the English Channel before the stalemate of trench warfare set in.[35]

And as elsewhere, the vacuum of official news was filled by rumour and speculation. On 26 August Thomas Moylan recorded in his diary that the British Army had been annihilated in France—a rumour that was exaggerated, but founded in the reality of the retreat of the BEF from Mons. However, adding a local twist based on the involvement of Irish regular soldiers in the fighting, he also believed that Irish regiments had been wiped out as well.[36] In response to this horrific news, the main compensating myth of an all-powerful ally made it to Ireland, in the form of morale-boosting tales of Russians with 'snow on their boots'. On 28 August Helen Duffin, still in Newcastle, wrote to her mother, in Belfast, how there was 'no doubt' that 'a strong body of Russian troops' had been transported from Russia to Scotland and 'through England by train and are now in France and probably in Ostend which is a startling move and a good one'.[37] She was far from alone in spreading these tales in Ireland.

The industrialised killing and horrendous casualties were revealed from the outset. Indeed, the mortality levels of 1914 were never to be surpassed on the Western Front, even in 1916, the year of Verdun and the Somme. Although the BEF (with 100,000 men) was at this stage only a small component of the allied forces, it was decimated. Opinion and the media in Ireland were exposed to these horrifying and upsetting realities from the outset. For the *Roscommon Messenger* on 8 August, the conflict would be the most appalling in history.[38]

43

For the *Leitrim Advertiser* it was 'the Armageddon',[39] particularly powerful language in a religious country. High casualties reported in the British press at the end of August were widely circulated in Ireland along with Kitchener's prediction that the war would last for two to three years. The violence of war was soon visible. On 26 October a hospital ship arrived at Queenstown (Cobh), and a train brought the wounded to Cork. By the time it reached the city 'an immense crowd had gathered in the precincts of the station, the Lower Glanmire Road being almost impassable'.[40] Crowds waved handkerchiefs and cheered as the men were taken to hospitals. Around the same time, in Sligo, a steamer was sunk by German mines, causing the deaths of fourteen men. Via refugees, casualty lists, and communications with the front, Irish towns and villages became aware of modern warfare and the horrors that lay ahead.

All Irishmen who enlisted left families behind. Parents, siblings, family and friends were frightened and anxious. People knew from an early stage that they might not see their loved ones again. According to contemporary accounts such as that by Timothy Healy, low levels of recruitment amongst the farming classes were not due to 'pro-Germanism' but because 'the farmers don't want their sons to leave their work, and perhaps return cripples, or not at all'.[41] Farewells and separation had to be endured. On 7 August Thomas Moylan described an emotional scene which he had witnessed in Dublin:

> Many moving sights are to be seen in and around the City these days ... [I] saw an officer hurrying up the steps of a house in Mount street [sic] as if he were just rushing to say 'goodbye' ... The officer paused, then went down the steps slowly, wiping his eyes and walking with lagging steps. Then he braced himself up and set off at the same rapid pace at which he had arrived. Evidently he had come to say goodbye to some friend and found them out. These [actions] seem to [highlight] the grimness of this war.[42]

On 23 November Rosamond Stephen, an Englishwoman living in Belfast, described a woman she had seen whose husband had departed to the front: 'Poor little thing she was almost crying, and I told her the women were very often the real heroes, because they had all the hard part'.[43] Death and grief did not discriminate politically or by class. Captain George Berkeley, in Belfast, first encountered death in the war on 2 September when he heard news of a fellow nationalist colleague killed in action.[44] In October Shane Leslie, the diplomatic aide and writer, heard the ominous sound of the Chapel bell tolling 'for whose death I knew not' at Glaslough, Co. Monaghan. The following month Leslie visited a friend whose son had been killed in the war. He 'kept me an hour talking of his dead boy. He read his letters aloud but broke down. At this rate everybody in a year will be mourning. I can think of half a dozen already'.[45]

DISSENT

It is a myth that in 1914 Ulster was in complete support of the war, while nationalists saw 'England's difficulty as Ireland's opportunity'. In reality, when war was declared both Edward Carson, leader of the Ulster Unionist Party, and John Redmond offered the support of their constituents to the war effort. For Irish unionists, support for the war was based on their political ties with Westminster. Germany's aggression was a threat to the integrity both of the United Kingdom and the British Empire; as proud supporters of both, Irish unionists rallied to the British effort. Irish nationalist support for the war is perhaps more surprising. Yet even Redmond, in his celebrated intervention in the House of Commons on 3 August, pledged nationalist Ireland's support for the Allies and urged the government to leave the defence of the Irish shores to the Irish National Volunteers and the Ulster Volunteer Force. Edward Grey, British Foreign Secretary, was moved to describe Ireland as 'the one bright spot' in the whole 'terrible situation'.[46] Even after Redmond's controversial statement extending the commitment of Irish nationalists in the war beyond Ireland[47]— famously repeated to a nationalist crowd at Woodenbridge, Co. Wicklow, on 20 September—the majority of Irish nationalists continued to support Redmond and the war effort. A rational assessment that turning their back on Britain in a terrible war would do nothing to help secure Home Rule afterwards was accompanied by feelings of a moral duty to participate in the war and to protect the rights of small nations like Belgium. In effect, in 1914 both unionists and nationalists took advantage of the new situation created by the war rather than opposing it outright; both made certain demands, jockeyed for position and attempted to extract every ounce of political advantage.

This is not to say that dissent amongst Irish nationalists evaporated entirely. Officials in Dublin Castle, under orders from Westminster, were wary of the possibility of Germany exploiting pre-war anti-English feeling in Ireland.[48] Redmond's extension of Irish support for the war to its foreign battlefields split the Volunteer movement, the majority (between 150,000 and 170,000 men) staying with Redmond. Between 9,700 and 11,000 of the more extreme members broke away to form their own force, retaining the name of Irish Volunteers, led by Eoin MacNeill.[49] Although this number was small, the split would have serious ramifications. A revolutionary conspiracy began to take shape to which the whole concept of Home Rule was irrelevant.

Advanced nationalists could not temporarily suspend their political beliefs and support the war. In their opinion, 'Ireland cannot, with honour and safety, take part in foreign quarrels otherwise than through the free actions of a national government of her own', and they denied 'the claim of any man to offer up the blood and lives of the sons of Irishmen and Irish women to the services of the British Empire'.[50] Their enemy was England, and Ireland needed its men to protect its shores from the British, not the Germans. As a result this minority engaged in anti-war activity in 1914: speeches by Redmond and his supporters were condemned, National Volunteer assemblies were interrupted, anti-war meetings were convened and military recruitment was opposed.

However, in 1914 their impact was limited. The authorities followed Redmondite advice not to make martyrs of the dissidents. But more generally the United Kingdom in 1914 allowed room for controlled dissent as was shown by the example of the labour disagreement in Glasgow in 1914–15. This was only the case provided the broad population could be counted on to limit anti-war and especially anti-recruitment feeling. All the available evidence at the end of 1914 showed that this was still so in Ireland. Large numbers of Irishmen enlisted in the British Army from both North and South. By February 1915 over 50,000 volunteers had come forward.[51] Lower recruitment in Ireland, as compared to England, Scotland and Wales, had more to do with occupational status—more specifically the proportion of the population involved in agriculture—than political or religious affiliation and was not so different to other parts of Britain and the empire.[52] Ironically, the Irish Transport and General Workers' Union (ITGWU), one of the most fervent opponents of recruiting, had contributed 2,700 former members to the British Army by May 1915.[53] Francis Ledwidge, who had supported MacNeill in the split in the Meath Volunteers and had been accused of being pro-German by his local Board of Guardians, enlisted with the Royal Inniskilling Fusiliers on 24 October 1914. On 27 September one anti-recruitment campaigner wrote to Hanna Sheehy-Skeffington, the Irish suffragette and pacifist, explaining that newsagents in Dublin were refusing to display anti-recruitment posters produced by the *Irish Citizen*.[54] In late September the *Freeman's Journal* described the negative reaction of the crowds at one of Francis Sheehy-Skeffington's anti-recruitment meetings in Dublin. According to the journalist, he was 'jeered and hooted by the crowd' and arrested for his own 'protection'.[55] Parents of schoolboys attending St Enda's College showed their distrust of Pearse's political opinions by withdrawing their sons from the school in autumn 1914. On 26 September Pearse wrote 'we have fewer boys than last year. My political opinions are looked upon as too extreme and dangerous and parents are nervous'.[56] Thomas Hynes, a MacNeillite Volunteer in Galway, recalled how 'we tried to break up recruiting meetings but we generally got beaten up ourselves as at least 80% of the population were hostile to Sinn Féin, for a number of their husbands and sons were in the English army and navy'.[57]

The essential point is that advanced nationalist dissent was limited in 1914. The bulk of security concerns related to the German enemy rather than dissident nationalists. Around 41% of registered correspondence to and from the Chief Secretary's Office in Dublin between 4 August and 31 December was concerned with enemy aliens and their incarceration, compared with only 10% of correspondence discussing the activities of the Volunteer movements and 8% concerned with dissent amongst advanced nationalists.[58] By November advanced Nationalist opinion was felt to be of little significance. On 28 November John Dillon, Irish Parliamentary Party MP for Mayo East, wrote to Matthew Nathan, under-secretary for Ireland since that July: 'I do *not* believe that the Sinn Féiners and pro-Germans are making any headway against us in Ireland'.[59] By the beginning of 1915 Dublin Castle felt that the threat of sedition in the press had all but disappeared.[60]

47

CONCLUSION

Placing Ireland in an all-UK and international context, rather than projecting back onto 1914 the polarisation of responses to the Easter Rising two years later, suggests that the ways in which the Irish went to war were akin to those of Britain and other countries. The particularity of the Irish experience was the complicated politics of national and imperial unity. However, nationalist Ireland *did* enter the war and believed that by endorsing the aims for which the United Kingdom stood—honour, freedom and the liberty of small nations—Ireland would benefit in practical terms as well as fulfilling a moral duty. Nationalist Ireland contributed almost equally to unionists with volunteers and charity, and had parallel encounters with fear, rumour, anticipation and emotion. British fears of dissident nationalist reactions were vastly exaggerated. In the view of the Redmondite publication, *Lepracaun*, the relationship between unionists and nationalists could be renegotiated within the national identity of 'United Kingdomers'. Rather than being a looming dark cloud, a cartoon published in the August issue of the magazine showed the war as a ray of light that shone over John Redmond and Edward Carson as they shook hands, marking a new atmosphere of co-operation—'Peace in War'(see p. *15*). This may have been wishful thinking. But a short, successful war ending in 1915 would have left the configuration of Irish politics and Ireland's relationship with Britain in a very different (more positive) position to that following the 1916 Rising. The Redmondite strategy might well have governed nationalist policy and Redmond might have retained the leadership. It is clear that the kingdom of Britain and Ireland was much more united in 1914 than has previously been appreciated.

'"I'll go too!"'. Irish recruitment poster produced by the CCORI, *c.* 1915.
Reproduced by permission of the Board, Trinity College Dublin.

Next page: TCD, OLS L-1-540 no.3: 'Appeal to the people of Ireland' by John Redmond,
1916. In this letter dated 17 February 1916, Redmond acknowledged the great response
made in answer to the call for volunteers and called for more men, 'we have to stand by
and maintain the Irish Army at the front'. Reproduced by permission of
the Board, Trinity College Dublin.

APPEAL FROM

JOHN REDMOND, M.P.

To the People of Ireland.

At the very commencement of the War I made an appeal to the Irish people, and especially to the young men of Ireland, to mark the profound change which has been brought about in the relations of Ireland to the Empire, by whole-heartedly supporting the Allies in the field.

I pointed out that, at long last, after centuries of misunderstanding, the democracy of Great Britain had finally and irrevocably decided to trust Ireland, and I called upon Ireland to prove that the concession of liberty would, as we had promised in your name, have the same effect in our country as in every other portion of the Empire, and that Ireland would henceforth be a strength, instead of a weakness.

I further pointed out that this was a just war, provoked by the intolerable military despotism of Germany; that it was a war in defence of the rights and liberties of small nationalities; and that Ireland would be false to her history and to every consideration of honour, good faith, and self-interest if she did not respond to my appeal.

I called for a distinctively Irish Army composed of Irishmen, led by Irishmen, and trained for the field at home in Ireland.

I acknowledge with profound gratitude, the magnificent response the country has made.

For the first time in history, we have to-day a huge Irish army in the field. Its achievements have covered Ireland with glory before the world, and have thrilled our hearts with pride.

North and South have vied with each other in springing to arms, and please God, the sacrifices they have made side by side on the field of battle will form the surest bond of a united Irish Nation in the future.

We have kept our word. We have fulfilled our trust. We have definitely accepted the position, and undertaken the obligations of a self-governed unit amongst the nations which make up the Empire.

One more duty remains to be fulfilled. We have to stand by and maintain the Irish Army at the front.

We must not, and will not, tolerate the idea of our Irish regiments being reinforced by any but Irish soldiers. Ireland must maintain the Irish regiments until victory has been won. The gaps in the ranks of our Irish army must be filled, not by Englishmen or Scotchmen or Welshmen, but by Irishmen.

Our gallant fellow-countrymen at the front commissioned me to make this appeal.

They appeal to-day through me from the trenches to the farmers, the labourers, the artisans, and to every class of our people not to desert them.

In your name I promised them in France and Flanders that Ireland would stand by them.

Will you fulfil that promise ?

The task is not difficult. Fill up the reserve battalions. Your brothers in the trenches are not only upholding the honour of Ireland before the world, they are defending Ireland itself from ruin and destruction, from murder and sacrilege, from the confiscation of the lands of the Irish farmer, and the wrecking of the property and prosperity of every class of our population.

You are under no compulsion save that of duty.

In the name of honour, justice, and religion, in the name of common gratitude, and in their own highest self-interest, I appeal to the young men of Ireland who are still available to join the Reserve Battalions, and to commence their training so that, in the event of the war not speedily ending, they may be ready to fill every gap in the ranks of " **the Irish army at the front.**"

Signed,

JOHN E. REDMOND.

17TH FEBRUARY, 1916.

SEALY, BRYERS & WALKER, PRINTERS, DUBLIN.   7380. 3/16.

from field kitchens in the Ancre area. Chalk dust and mud are clearly visible on the troops. © Imperial War Museum.

Following page: 'Australia has promised 50,000 more men', *c.* 1916. Australian men like Irishmen joined up on a voluntary basis with conscription not being adopted by either country. However, from a similar sized population, 413,000 Australians volunteered (60,000 died) in comparison with 200,000 Irishman volunteering (30,000 dying). Courtesy of John Horne

Australia has

romised Britain

0,000

MORE
MEN

WILL YOU

HELP US KEEP

THAT PROMISE

THE GREAT WAR

THE DEPLETION OF IRISH REGIMENTS

HE vast majority of the Irish race are proud—and justly proud—of the magnificent achievements of our Irish Regiments during the Great War. On many occasions our brave and gallant soldiers, especially those attached to the 10th and 16th Divisions, have lost a large proportion of men, and it is now up to Ireland to see the gaps are filled up. We cannot see why Scotchmen, Englishmen, and Welshmen should be requisitioned to replete our noble Connaughts, our Leinsters and Munsters, and many other famous Regiments of Irishmen who have practically won the many victories for our Empire. It is needless to go into figures, but it is a well-known fact that the depletion of Irish Regiments has been of a very severe character. The

matter is a serious one, and we earnestly
trust that Irishmen, and especially Irishwomen, will assist in gaining recruits
to fill up the gaps made by the bar-
barous and brutal Huns in months gone
by. It is a matter of Irish honour that
our brave formations should be upheld
and strengthened, and the dearth of
recruits in Ireland must be saddening to
the brave Irish boys who are doing such
magnificent work at the Front. What
a number of insults will be hurled at
the available young men in Galway and
the district who have failed in their duty
we shudder to think of. When the boys
"come home" what will *they* say to
the shirkers? What will they think of
the mothers and sisters who daily say,
"Stay at home, don't fight for your
country?" Every Irishman and every
Irishwoman should remember that their
fathers, brothers and relations are fighting to repel a German invasion of this
country—that once Ireland became a
German dependency all hopes of freedom
would cease to exist, and that half the
population of our dear land would be
dragged along the streets and roads like

Soldiers rest with their rifles (undated). Taken by Fr
Frank Browne. He volunteered for service as a chaplain
to the Irish Guards in 1916. © Irish Picture Library/Fr
F. M. Browne S.J. Collection.

Detail from *Ireland's memorial records 1914–1918*
(Dublin, 1923) vol. VII. Illustration by Harry Clarke.
Courtesy of the Royal Irish Academy Library.

IWM, ART 3027: *South Irish Horse,
a Dubliner resting on his way to
Arras Front* by William Orpen, 1917.
© Imperial War Museum.

CHAPTER 3

200,000 volunteer soldiers

PHILIP   ORR

64

Four pals from the 7th Battalion, Royal Dublin Fusiliers, before heading off to the front, *c.* 1914.
© English Collection.

It is hard to be exact about the number of Irishmen who served with the British armed forces in the Great War, given that many non-Irish troops served with Irish regiments and numerous Irish-born men fought with other military units raised in places as varied as Canada and Australia. However, the figure of 200,000 is a useful approximation and as the majority of these men were in the infantry, it is their experience on which this chapter will focus.

At the beginning of the twentieth century the British Army no longer held the huge proportion of Irishmen that it did in the 1830s when 40% of its men were from this island. However, close to 30,000 Irishmen were in the regular forces by 1914 and another 30,000 were reservists. Irish soldiers were stationed in locations across the empire, in units known as battalions, approximately 1,000 strong. Each battalion belonged to one of the historic regiments that recruited in Ireland, usually on a regional basis. Every regiment had its store of military traditions, going back in some cases to the seventeenth century and including participation in famous battles such as Waterloo. As well as the long history of Irish foot-soldiers, there was an officer tradition among Anglo–Irish gentry with twelve of the generals in the British Army being Irish in 1914, including Henry Wilson, from Ballinalee, Co. Longford, who was assasinated by the IRA in 1922.

The Irish military heritage, however, also included men who had fought in the armies of Europe and America, not least the 'Wild Geese' who had given the support of 30,000 soldiers to the French in 1691. There was also the radical, insurgent army which had striven to overturn British rule in 1798 and the long tradition of the Gaelic chieftains and warriors, stretching back into the mists of early legend. More recently, as the third Home Rule Bill passed through Westminster, citizen armies seemed to have sprung up everywhere. In the North there was the UVF, arming itself with smuggled weapons to resist a Dublin parliament. In opposition was the INV, equally determined to ensure that Home Rule was not thwarted. As European war-clouds gathered in the summer of 1914, thousands of Irishmen were 'playing soldiers' at home where civil conflict loomed.[1]

When war was declared in early August, some regular Irish soldiers, such as the 2nd Royal Irish Rifles, were swiftly transported from their barracks in England to France. There, they fired some of the earliest shots of the conflict at the Battle of Mons. A sister battalion of the Rifles was in the colonial outpost of Aden, on the Arabian Peninsula, and was shipped back to Britain to prepare for battle. A battalion of the Royal Dublin Fusiliers had further to travel, being stationed in Madras, south-west India, while a Royal Munster Fusilier battalion made the longest voyage of all, coming from Rangoon, south-east Asia.[2]

Men in the reserve forces were also told to rejoin their regiments. John McIlwaine had been a Connaught Ranger but was now working for the postal services in the north-east of England. Bidding farewell to his wife, he made his way by train and boat to Ireland, and then headed west to the regimental depot in Galway, meeting men whom he had last seen in far-off outposts of the British Empire.[3]

But regular and reserve soldiers would never be enough to help the French take on the mighty German infantry. New volunteers were needed—thousands of them. All across these islands recruiting posters adorned with the picture of the War Secretary, Lord Kitchener, announced the formation of battalions in a 'new army' to be filled with ordinary citizens each being promised training, a uniform and a gun. In Ireland, as elsewhere, recruiting began and although the tensions of the Home Rule crisis, the predominance of agricultural workers and the impact of immigration on the young men of this generation meant that enlistment levels were lower than across the Irish Sea, none the less, by autumn three Irish divisions had been formed, each taking up to 17,000 men who were organised into thirteen battalions, based on the historic regiments.

The 10th Division was the first to be formed, within days of the outbreak of war. Following this, the 36th Division was created, mainly in the North, which provided a 'home' for the men of the Ulster Volunteer Force, many of whom were recruited directly into the new division. Although the War Office was wary of giving similar endorsement to Irish nationalism, a 16th Division was created, sponsored by the leadership of the Irish Parliamentary Party. It offered places to John Redmond's National Volunteers. The controversial Home Rule Bill was finally passed but its application was suspended until after the war. Ironically, voluntary military service put an end to paramilitary tensions in Ireland, in the short term, although unionists and nationalists understood their military contribution in terms of their opposed and mutually exclusive goals—retention of the union as opposed to Home Rule. Meanwhile, it was up to every fit young man in Ireland, no matter what his politics, to enlist in the armed forces and 'do his bit'.

Into the 10th Division came restless young men such as Joe O'Leary from Skerries, who boarded the train for Dublin and went into a recruiting office to 'take the King's shilling', searching for adventure. Working-class recruits from Dublin included dockers who had lost their jobs owing to pre-war labour disputes. Some families sent several brothers into the forces, such as the Protestant commercial Dublin families, the Lees and the Findlaters. Academics such as the Reid Professor of Law in Trinity College Dublin, Ernest Julian, and the gifted writer of legal textbooks, Joseph Lee, joined up, motivated by camaraderie and duty, as did a group of rugby players known as the 'Dublin Pals'. Aristocrats, like Bryan Cooper from Sligo, and men from prosperous Catholic families such as Ivone Kilpatrick from Kildare, also joined. A young working-class recruit from Co. Meath was Francis Ledwidge. He was an Irish Volunteer and budding poet. Ledwidge was motivated in part by romantic disappointments but also by a sense that nationalist Ireland must stand against German imperial tyranny, sentiments which were distilled into the verse that he wrote.[4]

The 36th Division closely reflected the make-up of Protestant Ulster. It drew in young men from Queen's University Officers' Training Corps who found themselves as junior officers in charge of working-class men imbued with unionist politics and often possessing little aptitude for discipline. Tommy Ervine joined up with his mates on Belfast's Newtownards Road, in the shadow of the shipyard gantries, keen to abandon parents who drank and fought. Too small to be a soldier, he persuaded the recruiting officer to bend the rules. My own great uncle, working as a bicycle mechanic in Co. Down, had been in the UVF. Now, in 1914, he walked 40 miles to join up in Lurgan, where he was soon digging practice trenches with new colleagues in the countryside south of Lough Neagh.[5]

Meanwhile, the 16th Division was making headway despite the lack of Catholics in the officer corps which was 85% Protestant, while the ranks were

98% Catholic. Some National Volunteers did get officers' positions, such as John Wray, a solicitor from Enniskillen, who brought along to his enlistment interview a statement from his parish priest regarding his 'moral character'. He also convinced his interviewers of his knowledge of the British infantry training manual, which the National Volunteers used for drill purposes. Wray brought into the division 200 Fermanagh men who had been under his command. The prestige of the 16th was helped by the inclusion of the nationalist MPs, Stephen Gwynn and Willie Redmond, younger brother of John, as well as that of Tom Kettle, who was a poet, journalist and former Home Rule MP. Kettle, a leading nationalist intellectual who was a professor at the National University of Ireland in Dublin, had been buying arms in Belgium for the Irish National Volunteers when the Germans invaded in 1914.[6]

By winter all three divisions were training in barracks across the island, from Finner in Co. Donegal to Kinsale in Co. Cork. There was endless route-marching, parade-ground drilling, undertaking of assaults with dummy rifles on sandbags filled with straw and practising raids on enemy trenches with 'grenades' made from tin cans filled with stones. Good behaviour was not easily achieved and a bunch of Belfast men headed homeward after tents collapsed in the rain at their camp near the Mourne Mountains. They had to be persuaded to return by vexed officers. However, a relaxed atmosphere often prevailed in the evenings. One officer arrived in Galway to find most of the Connaught Rangers drifting into town in the evening to drink beer. For Irish soldiers who were already in France, it was a different story. They had witnessed the emergence of trench warfare. Irish troops arriving home with injuries spread rumours of horrors that awaited the fresh recruits who by the end of December had still not left Ireland.[7]

For the 36th and 16th Divisions, 1915 was a year of transition, leaving Ireland for completion of training in the south of England and then moving to France and 'into the line' for a first taste of the Western Front. However, there was much frustration in the 16th at being 'held back' from military duties, a delay they felt might be due to British scepticism about the nationalist ability to fight with conviction. It was December before they got to France, where Tom Kettle would record his observations.

> There are two sinister fences of barbed wire on the barbs of which blood-stained strips of uniform and fragments more sinister have been known to hang ... a figure in khaki stands as he peers through the night towards the German lines ... His watch is over. The trench has not fallen. As for him he

has carried his pack for Ireland and Europe and now pack-carrying is over. He has held the line.[8]

Christmas 1915 saw no repeat of the famous fraternisation of 1914. On 25 December the first casualty in the 16th Division occurred.[9]

The 36th Division had arrived in France in early October 1915 and by Christmas some men felt they were 'old hands', used to duty in the line and periods spent resting in billets in French villages. Many Ulster Orangemen were shocked by the Catholicism of their French allies and intrigued by the articulate English with which the—often Protestant—Germans greeted them across no man's land. General Oliver Nugent, the Ulster Division's commanding officer, was keen on raiding parties, which were sent out under cover of darkness to break through enemy wire and bring back prisoners. Ulster casualties occurred, so they were an unpopular contrast to the amateur warfare in which the UVF had engaged during the Home Rule crisis.

Gradually, however, the men got used to raids, foul-smelling dug-outs, rats that fed on unburied corpses and the 'foot rot' that left men crippled after hours spent standing in deep water. They developed the habit of black humour. In one trench where a half-buried Frenchman's arm stuck out of the wall, Ulstermen would hang their kettle on the limb as they brewed up their cup of tea.[10]

For the 10th Division, 1915 had been infinitely more serious—as it had been for several regular Irish battalions. All of these men had sailed across the Mediterranean to a base on the Greek island of Lemnos, where they were to play a part in the allied invasion of the Ottoman Empire at the rocky peninsula of Gallipoli, guarding the gateway to Constantinople, in European Turkey. The strategic idea was to offer an alternative to the stalemate in France and Flanders by knocking the Turks out of the war and directly supporting Russia.

Along with a number of other 'regular' troops, two units of Munster and Dublin Fusiliers landed at Cape Hellas on 25 April, disembarking from the transport ship the *River Clyde*. They struggled through the surf and entanglements placed beneath the water, exposed to machine-gun and artillery fire as they floundered towards the beach. The Dubliners lost 670 men in the next 36 hours and the Munsters were also devastated, exact figures being unknown.

Tim Buckley of the Munster Battalion described how 'I was coming ashore talking to the chap on my left when a lump of lead entered his temple … I turned to the lad on my right, his name was Fitzgerald from Cork, but soon he was 'over the border'. The one piece of shrapnel had done the job for two of them'.

Sergeant J. McColgan was bringing 32 men ashore, of whom 6 survived: 'One fellow's brains were shot into my mouth as I was shouting for them to jump for it. I dived into the sea. Then came the job to swim ashore and one leg useless, where I had been shot. I pulled out a knife and cut the straps and swam ashore. All the time bullets were nipping around me ...'. The assault on Cape Helles had been a disaster and the sea was red with blood. Today the grave-yards in this part of Turkey are filled with tombstones that read like entries from an Irish street directory.[11]

An Australian and New Zealand assault on the coastline of Gallipoli also ran into deep trouble. The 10th Division was then sent, with a number of other units of Kitchener's new army, to launch an amphibious attack on Suvla Bay, several miles to the north, in an attempt to rescue the campaign. This led to even greater tragedy, as the division lost almost half of its 17,000 men, killed, sick, injured or missing, in two months. Joseph Lee, the lawyer from Dublin, died within hours of landing, as did Ernest Julian, the Trinity professor. The 'Dublin Pals' who had assembled at Lansdowne Road a few months before, were shot to pieces on a mountain ridge overlooking the blue waves of Suvla Bay. Many 'Pals', lacking the grenades that the enemy had in such abundance, would catch the Turkish missiles and throw them back before they exploded, in a bizarre and deadly game of cricket.

In a monumentally ill-organised campaign, the Allies sustained over 140,000 casualties before withdrawing at the end of 1915, while the Turks lost even more heavily, with 250,000 men dead, wounded, captured or missing.[12] Many 10th Division Gallipoli victims died of thirst, sunstroke or dysentery on bare slopes where, in the fierce sunlight of a Turkish summer, fresh water was scarce and flies lit on every mouthful of food. Many who lived shrank to two- thirds of their body weight. Those who managed to survive named their trenches 'Grafton Street' and 'Patrick Street', before the remnants of the division were evacuated in late September and sent to the Macedonian theatre of war to 'recover'. Back in Ireland, the obituary columns filled and recruitment slumped.[13]

Those who survived Gallipoli with the 10th Division spent 1916 in the dreary sideshow of the Balkans, in a war against the Bulgarians, who were allies of Germany, Turkey and Austria. The men fought at Kosturino on icy mountain slopes where their uniforms froze to their bodies and they caught malaria in the mosquito-ridden swaps of the Struma Valley. Joe O'Leary was evacuated with infected wounds, tuberculosis and the psychiatric condition known as shell-shock. Those who were luckier enjoyed leave in the street cafes of Salonica. Today a Celtic cross stands on the hillside at Rabrovo in Macedonia, a monument to all who died so far from home.[14]

On the Western Front, 1916 brought big changes for the 16th Division. At Easter Dublin was convulsed by insurrection but the focus of attention at the

16th and the 36th were moved northwards to Flanders and their ranks were replenished with conscripts, meaning that these divisions became less Irish in character.

Numerous other Irish battalions experienced losses and recruitment problems. Suffering and death were a regular occurrence. As Rudyard Kipling pointed out in his histories of the Irish Guards—in which his own son had served and died—the roles of doctor and chaplain were particularly trying. He described how in one incident:

> the regimental doctor appeared out of the darkness wounded in the arms and shoulder, his uniform nearly ripped off him and very busy. He had been attending a wounded man in a house near the HQ when a shell-burst at the door mortally wounded the patient, killing one stretcher bearer outright and seriously wounding two others. The padre, dodging shells en route, dived into the cellars of the house where he was billeted for the Sacred Elements then went back to the wayside dressing station ... it was the mildest of upheavals but it serves to show what a priest's and a doctor's duties are when the immediate silence after a shell-burst is cut by the outcries of a wounded man.[22]

In 1917 the 10th Division moved from Macedonia to begin the business of helping chase Ottoman Turkey out of Palestine. Meanwhile, in Flanders, just south of Ypres, the 36th and 16th divisions fought side by side for the first time, although by now the former was only 50% Irish and the latter even less so. At 3.10am on 7 June the Battle of Messines commenced as 500 tons of explosives in underground mines blew the German lines to pieces, enabling the British troops to make progress through the murk, dust and debris, which did not settle for hours. The two units went forward at Wytschaete, supported for the first time by tanks. By mid-morning all objectives had been taken but stalemate would resume in the days that lay ahead.

The symbolism of these two divisions, which represented opposed traditions, engaging at Messines in a common cause, was not lost on political commentators at home in Ireland. However, the battle was marred by the death of Willie Redmond, brought in from the battlefield by members of the Ulster Division. Respected by many unionist soldiers, the nationalist MP and army officer was

73

buried in the grounds of a nearby convent. A sealed message was found at his home which said: 'I should like all my friends to know that in joining the Irish Brigade and going to France, I sincerely believed, as all Irish soldiers do, that I was doing my best for the welfare of Ireland in every way'. But when the by-election was held in his East Clare constituency, the victor was the Sinn Féin candidate and senior surviving commander of the Easter Rising, Eamon de Valera—an indication of how opinion had changed in nationalist Ireland.

Within weeks the successes of Messines were left behind as the two divisions continued to fight in proximity to one another in the infamous Third Battle of Ypres, known as Passchendaele. Once more, the British High Command sought a breakthrough in a major onslaught close to the Belgian coast.[23] Conditions were dire, with many men drowning in muddy shell-holes as well as succumbing to enemy gunfire. As one 16th Division officer wrote: 'No decent language can express it. The country is a marsh: horses up to their breasts in mud ... one pair of puttees has simply rotted on my legs'.[24] Some battalions which had stood up admirably to the horrors of the Somme, were to be found retreating in the face of enemy machine-guns, their morale utterly shaken.

Between 1 and 20 August the 16th Division incurred over 4,000 casualties. The awfulness of modern warfare continued to manifest itself. Willie Doyle found 'one Irish soldier burnt by mustard gas ... his hands and face a mass of blue phosphorous flame, smoking horribly in the darkness'. Another man observed an officer as he 'blew his brains out in front of him ... with a revolver, the pain from a severe stomach wound proving unbearable'.[25] Passchendaele ended in November 1917. The war had dragged on for over three years and thousands of Irish troops were still in the firing line, albeit in decreasing numbers as fatalities and injuries mounted.[26]

By 1918 the 10th Division had been 'Indianised' as colonial troops replaced most of the remaining Irishmen who were moved to France and Flanders where the war was reaching its end game. After abortive plans to amalgamate the 16th and 36th Divisions, the decision was made to push many of the regular Irish battalions into these larger units, to preserve some of their Irish character.[27] The first great test of that year was the German offensive of March, which smashed the British 5th Army along the old Somme battlefield, forcing a precipitous retreat that was only stopped short of Amiens. The Germans captured numerous troops in the process, Irishmen among them. The prisoners included my own great-uncle, John Martin, who having served with the Ulster Division for nearly four years, had been nicknamed the 'old man' by his younger colleagues despite the fact that he was just 21. John was forced to work long hours with meagre rations in a cook-house, a dangerously short distance behind the German lines, in contravention of the Hague Convention's rules concerning the protection and well-being of prisoners of war.

Stories went around in British circles of the 'inadequate' response of the Irish soldiers to the German attack of March 1918, which was thought to be due to political disaffection in the Irish ranks and the 'fact' that 'Celtic troops' did not have the temperament for defence. This was all the more ironic in that the 36th Division put up the same kind of fighting retreat as the 16th Division only a few miles distant from it, and with similar results in terms of the number of prisoners taken. But whereas the 36th Division survived with its prestige intact, within weeks the 16th Division's life on the Western Front was at an end. It moved to England in the summer to be reconstituted while the 36th stayed on in France and took part in the final allied breakthrough, which reversed earlier losses and brought an exhausted Germany to its knees in the autumn.

By 1918 Irish soldiers, recuperating at home or on leave, were shocked to discover antipathy to them—at least in many strongly nationalist areas. One officer, returning to Limerick, found it to be 'a nest of Sinn Féinery', saw soldiers being stoned and heard pro-German slogans. Another officer, returning to Cork, found it to be a city where any girl who befriended a serviceman got labeled and abused as a 'British soldier's moll'. From January 1918 onwards Irish soldiers on leave were no longer allowed to bring their rifles with them owing to the suspicion that guns might fall into the hands of rebels. There was also official suspicion that seditious thoughts were surfacing among nationalists in the army. The Home Rule MP for West Belfast, Joe Devlin, told the House of Commons that he regularly got letters from soldiers who said that they had not enlisted for an Ireland 'under the military governorship of General Maxwell'.[28]

When the armistice came in November, there was little euphoria—more an exhausted sense of anti-climax common among soldiers of all nationalities along the Western Front. Noel Drury, serving with the Royal Dublin Fusiliers, felt only 'a sort of forlorn feeling'. Major Guy Nightingale of the Royal Munster Fusiliers, who survived the hell of Gallipoli, could write in his diary only that there was 'no excitement'. Captain Hitchcock in the Leinster Regiment would later recall that 'most men in the battalion merely discussed their dead comrades and the likelihood of their battalion being sent to India'.[29]

For men who had gone to war on behalf of Home Rule within the empire, it was an uneasy time as they speculated about the reception they would receive on landing in an Ireland where separatism was now the dominant philosophy.

As Stephen Gwynn put it: 'When the time came to rejoice over the war's ending, was there anything more tragic than the position of men who had gone out by the thousands to confront the greatest military power ever known in history, who had fought the war, and won the war, and who now looked at each other with doubtful eyes?'[30]

With deep understanding, Rudyard Kipling would convey the feelings of alienation and deflation felt by his beloved Irish Guards as they looked back in later months on their experience of the armistice. He believed that 'in some inexpressible fashion … they themselves appeared to themselves the only living people in an uncaring world'. He imagined the men reflecting that 'there was nothing real to it all except when we got to talking and passing round the names of them we wished was with us. We was lonely in those days. By God, we Micks was lonely!'[31]

For northern Protestant veterans, returning to a community that at least accepted what they had done, the journey home was easier than for nationalists. As one Inniskilling Fusilier put it:

> I arrived in Larne and sent a telegram to my mother telling her I was on my way. When I arrived at the Waterside station, there was no one there to meet me so I started my long walk to Drumahoe. As I walked down the brae in my uniform, someone must have spotted me in the distance. The bell of Clarke's mill started to ring as a signal to my mother. When I got home the house was filled with my friends, relations and neighbours. They were overjoyed.[32]

The UVF donated to Belfast City Hall a painting by an English artist, James Beadle, which only a few months after the battle recorded the heroic exploits of the 36th Division on the 1 July 1916. It was to provide a potent image in the years ahead of the value of the men's sacrifice for unionist Ulster.

For many families, Protestant as much as Catholic, there was no happy ending. Among the 30,000 to 35,000 Irishmen who had died was my great-uncle John, blown to pieces, just weeks before the war's end, by 'friendly fire' from French aeroplanes that bombed the German canteen where he had been compelled to work. Thousands of Ulster veterans, like their southern counterparts, came home to unemployment and disability. They returned to an island divided by civil strife. Some nationalist ex-servicemen joined the IRA and eventually had two sets of war medals to show their children. Some unionists joined the Ulster police and helped maintain the stability of the new Northern Ireland. Others, of both camps, just kept their heads down and tried to rebuild their lives.

The three Irish divisions of 1914 were disbanded at the war's end and, shortly after, so too were the regiments that recruited in the territory of the new Irish Free State, ending several centuries of military heritage. The citizens' armies of the pre-war era—the Ulster Volunteer Force and the Irish National Volunteers, which had all but disappeared in the era of the Great War—were supplanted by new militias and constabularies as new jurisdictions arose out of the conflict.

The most costly period in Irish military history was over. However, a battalion of the Royal Irish Rifles—which, recruiting in the North, was spared disbandment—sailed for Mesopotamia and was soon engaged in quelling the 'Arab Rebellion' of 1920–1.[33] Years later, British troops are back on service in Mesopotamia in a 'war against terror', fighting in a country now named Iraq, For although the Great War has receded into the distant past and Ireland's own era of rival domestic militias seems to be at an end, fierce global conflict is still taking place. It remains to be seen whether the Irish nation will be drawn into an international conflagration in the twenty-first century, as it was over 90 years ago, incurring such a truly heart-breaking cost.

On Active Service

WITH THE BRITISH EXPEDITIONARY FORCE

Address Reply to :

Corporal H Waterman Nfelb 18/210.
12 Batt WSR. 18. A camp 36 ulster Div
Base Dept Le Havre.
France. 4th December 1915

Dear Sister Maggie.

An answer to your nice letter which I
receieved last night ~~————————~~ and was very
glad to hear from yous as I thought my letter had
went astray. tell mother I dont think any long at all
+ likes this place alright but we are having very wet
weather here. well I dont think there is any thing else
that I want but what I told you in the last
letter. Willie John is alway here yet but his feet is
very bad with him he is going about on his heals.
I was talking to Dan Mc hedee he is down here for a
few weeks next. mother will think long after me every
week end now but she will soon get used with it
I am sure you + Minnie felt dressed geting to the
Melvin with Alfie. you dont see any girls asking for
me in Belfast. well I think this is all at present
as it is near bed time. tell mother & Father + Minnie

78

m 1 994/160-13

SOM, 1994/160-13: Ronald Waterman (12th Battalion, Royal Irish Rifles, 36th (Ulster) Division) to his sister, Maggie, 4 December 1915. He has just arrived in France and mentions friends from home who were with him. He also enquires after his disconsolate mother: 'Mother will think long after me every week end now, but she will soon get used with [sic] it'. Courtesy of the Somme Heritage Centre.

(2)

+ Cameron + Andy that I send my best love to them all. Hope to hear from you soon.

I remain your loving Brother Ronald.

excuse bad writing + short letter as the ymca will soon be closed.

Write soon. soon x x x x x v v x

79

80

IWM, Q 10655: Soldiers in Ham, Germany, during the taking over
of part of the French line, 15 January 1918. Taken by T.K. Aiken.
© Imperial War Museum.

IWM, Q 10685: Men of the 12th Royal Irish Rifles fetching rations from the limbers (the detachable fore part of a gun-carriage) at night near Essigny, France, 7 February 1918. Taken by T.K. Aiken. © Imperial War Museum.

Battle of the Somme, the attack of the Ulster Division by J.P. Beadle, 1918. The officer shown leading the unit, Lieutenant Francis Bodenham Thornley, was wounded in the battle and advised Beadle on the painting while recuperating. In the background, a soldier carries a battalion marker, which was used to show the battalion's progress. The troops are of the 5th Battalion, Royal Irish Rifles, a supporting unit to the 108th Infantry Brigade. The painting subsequently became an icon of Ulster unionism's sacrifice in the war. Reproduced by kind permission of Belfast City Council.

27 June 1916.

Dear Sister Maggie

an answer to your
~~kind~~ two kind & welcome letters
to hand a day ago, hoping
these few lines findes yous all
well as this leaves me the same
at present. I am glad to hear
that the weather is good in
Ireland. we are having rain
here every day. I had a letter

SOM, 1994/160-78: Ronald Waterman to his sister, 27 June 1916. 'I am sure mother will think long for me [sic] ... but I hope it won't be long till I [sic] be home.' Four short days later, on the first day of the Battle of the Somme, he would be dead. Courtesy of the Somme Heritage Centre.

from Aunt Susan yesterday &
also one from May McClean she
was asking me for a Photo but
I have not got any to give
her. she sent me one of her.
Brothers Photos. he seams to be
a nice looking chap. I wont
for get to tell that other
chap that you were asking
for him. yes Maggie I am sure
Mother will think long for me
on Saturdays. but I hope it
wont be long till I be home
again. I have not saw Jim

Armstrong (3) long time. I dont
know where he is. I surpose
Tomey Harland will soon be
out here I have not saw
Alfie since but I see Dan
every day, does Alfie Bell
ever be in now. I surpose he
is still swinking it round
yet. has he got any girl now.
well I think this is all at
present hope to hear from
you soon tell Mother Father
Minnie Cameron & Andy that
I send my best love till

them all. also tell Tomey
Harland I was asking for
him.

I remain your loving
Brother Ronald

good bye till yous all

Write soon xxxxxx

89

IWM, Q 1213: Hauling an 18-pounder gun into a new position near Delville Wood taken by Ernest Brooks, 15 September 1916. © Imperial War Museum.

Following page: IWM, Q 1256: Wounded troops wearing German helmets outside a CCS at Heilly. Taken by Ernest Brooks, September 1916. © Imperial War Museum.

"Fed up" Ulster Division

'Fed up' Ulster Division by
William Conor, 1916. Courtesy of
the Royal Ulster Rifles Museum.

CHAPTER 4

The Politics of War

PAUL BEW

Who Will You Follow ?

The Men Who Fought for You in Dublin

DURING EASTER WEEK,

Or. the men who would have you sent to **MEET GERMAN GUNS:**

John E Redmond, M.P., Thos F Smyth, M.P.
F E Meehan, M.P., Joseph Devlin, M.P.,
T O'Donnell, M.P., and Thirty other M.P.'s
who stumped the Country TO GET RECRUITS FOR the BRITISH ARMY.

When they appeal for your Votes Ask them when and why they stopped Recruiting.

Issued for the Limerick Sinn Fein Committee and printed at the
City Printing Co., Rutland st., Limerick.

'Who will you follow?', c. 1917 This piece of Sinn Féin propaganda was seized on 17 June 1917 at a time
when the level of enlistment had fallen very low and the political tide was turning in favour of the party.
Reproduced by permission of the Board, Trinity College Dublin.

John Redmond's support for the British war effort cost him the political leadership of nationalist Ireland. One can go further with this statement. It can now be said that, like David Trimble in the early years of this century, Redmond's trust in the promise of the British political elite led to the electoral humiliation of a great Irish political party. Like the Ulster Unionist Party in 2005, Redmond's Irish Parliamentary Party lost almost all of its seats in the election of 1918. No wonder that when de Valera contemplated Winston Churchill's seductive offer of apparent Irish unity in exchange for an end to Irish neutrality in 1940, he is said to have remembered the fate of Redmond and kept Ireland out of the war.

There can be no argument about the scale of Redmond's eclipse. None the less, one of the tasks of the historian is to question the history of the victor. As John Mitchel once put it, to be the 'historiographer of defeat' is not always a pleasant task but it is sometimes a necessary one.[1] More recently, Reinhard Koselleck has observed: 'in the short run history is made by the victors. In the long run the gains in historical understanding come from the defeated'.[2]

In September 1914 Redmond offered Irish support for the British war effort in exchange for Home Rule being placed on the statute book. He was well aware that London intended to make special arrangements in an amending bill which would lead to some form of partition; but the total area to be excluded from the operation of a Dublin parliament was still open to question, as was the style of government of that excluded area. Redmond was operating from within the tradition of constitutional nationalism which had always assured Britain that, in the face of an international crisis, a self-governing Ireland would be a loyal ally. As a man of honour who had often repeated that promise, he found it difficult to escape the obligation when put to the test.

Redmond's strategy, however, was not based simply on a sense of honour but also on calculations about the future. He was convinced that in the final debate about the Irish settlement which would come at the war's conclusion Irish nationalists would be seriously disadvantaged if it was perceived in London that only the Ulster unionists were prepared to make great sacrifices for the British war effort. In a worst case scenario—but one actively articulated in the press at the time—Britain would refuse to implement Home Rule altogether. While separatists sincerely believed that Redmond was responsible for the blood sacrifice of tens of thousands of Irishmen at the front in pursuit of a will-o'-the-wisp which the British would in the end tear away, Redmond believed that Home Rule was in his hands and that only egregious Irish disloyalty could endanger it. He hoped also that a Westminster parliament with remaining Irish members—possibly in the Cabinet—would ensure fair play for Catholic minorities in any excluded area in the north-east corner of Ireland. More romantically, he hoped that a common sacrifice at the front would bring together Irishmen of different creeds. Such a strategy was plausible but ultimately ineffectual, and we have certainly paid a heavy price in Ireland for its failure. To explain its failure, however, it is necessary to look at the unfolding events throughout 1915 and early 1916, paying attention to some neglected moments.

For Tom Kettle, leading light of the nationalist intelligentsia and formerly the MP for East Tyrone, speaking at Cookstown, Co. Tyrone, there was no doubt: 'The nation is engaged in a terrible war'. He added: 'This was for Britain a just and holy war, and they were engaged in it to defend their independence'.[3] Does this statement mean that Kettle, the son of a celebrated Land League activist, considered that the Irish were part of the British 'nation'? Possibly not—but many separatists will have read this remark as meaning just that. One fact is that in public and private, many senior constitutional nationalists no longer thought in terms of 'us' and 'them' in the way they once had. It was not inconceivable in such sections to think in terms of 'we' and 'our objectives', when thinking of British and Irish affairs. The population as a whole, however, was rather Anglophobic in outlook.[4]

Old sectarian habits also died hard. Mainstream Ulster unionism was slow to concede that Redmond was sincere and was persistently contemptuous of the relatively low rate—as compared with their own community—of nationalist recruitment. No allowance was made for differential historical experience. No allowance was made either for the simple fact that the imagined community of Britishness—so alive and meaningful for Ulster unionists—had only a partial and limited appeal for Irish nationalists.

In Easter 1915 20,000 young men filed respectfully past Redmond in Dublin.[5] The rhetoric was exciting: a year from now, it was said, these men would be the honour guard for a new Irish parliament. But the following Easter, it would not be Redmondite loyalists who would be leading the drive for a new Irish parliament. The Ulster unionists, however, took little comfort from the still existent strength of constitutional nationalism in 1916; instead, they pointed out how little talk there was of recruitment. There was always a not-so-latent fear that while the Ulster unionists made their sacrifice on the front, the military balance within Ireland itself would shift against them. In fact, some of John Dillon's rhetoric seemed almost designed to intensify that fear.

As British anxiety intensified about a war that was dragging on far longer than expected, talk turned to a necessary reconstitution of the Cabinet to enhance the war effort. On 18 May 1915 it was publicly rumoured that both Edward Carson, the leader of the Ulster unionists, and John Redmond, leader of the Irish nationalists, were to be offered places in the Cabinet. The rumours were true. In a rather striking and revealing example of Anglo–Irish misunderstanding, when messengers from Dublin Castle arrived at Redmond's Wicklow country abode saying they 'wanted Mr Redmond', the door was slammed in their faces by Redmond's cook, who feared they had come to arrest the Irish leader. Redmond dined out on the story, but it was a bad omen, revealing the depth of mistrust of British intentions among ordinary Irish people.[6]

At first, it seemed that both Redmond and Carson would decline the invitation to join the Cabinet. Over the next week to ten days, however, it became clear that Carson would accept and that Redmond alone would refuse. There was nothing inevitable about Redmond's refusal. On 20 May the Press Association reported that Redmond's appointment, though at 'the present moment unlikely is still not regarded as absolutely outside the range of possibilities'. Redmond's ally, T.P. O'Connor, the Irish Parliamentary Party (IPP) MP for Liverpool (Scotland Division) and head of the party organisation in Britain, pointed out that Redmond's appointment would have been 'a guarantee for the future of Home Rule of the most valuable character, for nobody would be foolish enough to believe that if Mr Redmond were fit to be a Minister of the Empire in war he would not be fit to be Prime Minister of his own country'.[7] On 25 May the British Liberal organ, the *Daily Chronicle*, insisted it would accept Carson in the new Cabinet only if Redmond were also there. But the debate was now closing; the IPP met and confirmed its adherence to the policy of non-participation.

Redmond's refusal was based on the classic Parnellite principle of 'independent opposition' that had been at the core of nationalist parliamentary politics since the 1880s. But circumstances had changed, with Home Rule, for instance, on the statute book. In a 1912 interview, Redmond had declared: 'After Home Rule was granted [...] there will be no reason why Irish members elected to Westminster should not join British cabinets'.[8] At a minimum, if Redmond had accepted, he would have been acting in a consistent logical fashion rather than a selfish opportunistic one. In the end, Redmond got the worst of both worlds— responsibility for a British war policy that imposed heavy burdens on Ireland without the ability to influence it in ways that might have made it more acceptable. D.P. Moran, the editor of the *Leader*, was not the only shrewd nationalist commentator who believed a mistake had been made.

Redmond was much more of an insider than the Irish public knew: after September 1914 he had moved closer to Carson, Andrew Bonar Law and Walter Long, chastened as they all were by war. He did not, however, wish to advertise this fact; his natural discretion and conservative political style dictated his approach. But the question remains whether Irish popular politics—always troubled by a sense of powerlessness and exclusion—might have been mollified, rather than infuriated by the sight of an Irishman running the British state. Instead, what they saw was Irishmen being asked to make the supreme sacrifice by a British state that did not seem to respect their basic political rights.

Warre B. Wells, in his biography of Redmond published in 1919, argued that the reconstitution of the Cabinet in May 1915—more particularly the inclusion of Edward Carson as attorney general—was the decisive negative tipping point in Redmond's fortunes. Was not Carson committed to treating the Home Rule act as a 'scrap of paper' to be repealed when the war was over? This was to treat Carson rather too seriously, although the fears were understandable, as John Dillon later declared, adding that 'from that hour our men left us by tens of thousands'.[9] The British Liberal press was inclined to agree. At a by-election in College Green, Dublin, in June 1915, an associate of the revolutionary James Connolly, Thomas Farren of the Irish Neutrality League, scored a respectable 1,816 votes against the party's official candidate, John Dillon Nugent, who none the less won with 2,445 votes. The *Daily Chronicle* insisted that the relatively poor result was due to nationalist Ireland's hostile reaction to the new Cabinet in London.[10] Others were unimpressed by this argument: in Belfast, the *Northern Whig* pointed out that the IPP's performance was lacklustre in King's County (Co. Offaly, and specifically Tullamore) in December 1914—long before the changes in British high politics.[11]

Carson's resignation from the Cabinet over the Balkans issue in October 1915 generated a sense of political crisis on both islands. Setbacks on the front encouraged wild speculation about political change in London. At a public meeting in October 1915, Redmond warned that there was every possibility of an election: well aware of the decline of the United Irish League's political organisation, he called for it to be perfected. A voice called out, 'what about Carson's army?' In fact, as Carson's astute biographer, Alvin Jackson, has pointed out, by September 1914 Carson had turned away from any notion of an Irish dirty war—'violence was the politics of suicide'.[12] Redmond replied with statesmanlike dignity:

> Pray, don't introduce that now. I will answer it.
> Carson's army is in Flanders at the present moment
> and for my part I am certain that they will acquit
> themselves like brave Irishmen (applause) and my only
> hope is that they may find themselves fighting
> shoulder to shoulder with their nationalist and fellow
> countrymen.[13]

In fact, it might have been better for the IPP if there had been an election: while the party would have received a lively challenge, it would surely have triumphed. The war-time freeze on electoral politics did the Redmondites no favours, making their last mandate from 1910 seem all the more irrelevant and lost in time. None of this in itself quite justifies the refusal of the separatists to exploit democratic opportunities to challenge Redmond. In November 1915 the main journal of constitutional nationalism was correct to assert that the separatist radicals had failed the challenge of electoral tests: 'there were vacancies in the South, in the West, in the East and in the North. They could have tested their views in Tipperary, in Galway, King's County or Derry but they did not budge'.[14]

The tone of recruiting posters managed to imply—against all objective evidence—that the war was drawing to a close. On 11 November 1915 all the Irish journals carried this advertisement for recruitment to Irish regiments:

'Irishmen, you may object that if you join at this stage of the war you may never reach the firing line. However, that may be you will have the satisfaction of knowing that you have released a trained soldier, now in this country, for service at the front'. The effect of such misleading propaganda on Irish separatists is easy to guess: it encouraged the belief that it was necessary to strike quickly before the war was won, before the Irish heroes returned from the front and claimed their justified place in the affection of the people.

The separatists were, however, beginning to receive encouragement from elements in the Catholic hierarchy. In November 1915 after Irishmen travelling to America to escape the war were turned back forcibly at Liverpool, the Bishop of Limerick insisted in a public statement that what he termed the 'cosmopolitan considerations' of the IPP were 'too high flying for uneducated peasants': so much for Redmond's efforts to encourage sympathy for the plight of Catholic Belgium.

At the end of November 1915 some 2,000 Irish Volunteers turned out in Cork to celebrate the Fenian Manchester Martyrs of 1867 and demonstrate the cruelty of the English crown, which had resulted in their execution. There were only 100 Redmondite National Volunteers present. Seán MacDermott chose to find nothing patronising in the Bishop of Limerick's words, and thanked him for his support. Crippled by polio, but still an active republican organiser, MacDermott was now well set on the path which would lead to his execution in May 1916. The eccentric Herbert Pim assured the crowd that Ireland would soon be independent with its own navy and army, and that Englishmen would shortly require a passport to visit the country.[15] It was a correct prediction; though before it was fulfilled, Pim, originally a member of the northern branch of a prominent Quaker business dynasty, had in 1918 reverted to his earlier unionism and, indeed, became a vigorous supporter of conscription. Pim's giddiness needs to be set alongside MacDermott's steadiness of purpose: it was not always obvious to the Redmondite elite that their new political opponents were entirely serious or credible.

The war in the meantime had taken a turn for the worst. The newspaper headlines in December 1915 covered the retreat from Suvla; with only 'Irish bayonets' preventing disaster.[16] Many in Ireland insisted that the country's natural honour was at stake. If Ireland flinched from her duty to support the Allies in a just cause, she would be forever discredited. At the beginning of 1916 the unionist *Northern Whig* in Belfast published a poem entitled 'Sinn Féin': 'Rise up young lusty Irishmen and spare your country shame!/If not for justice, not for right, then for our own land's good name'. Very few Sinn Féiners read the *Whig*, but we can be sure that those who did had a different conception of what constituted 'national shame' and a different perception of what sort of 'rising' would vindicate Ireland's 'good name'.

In January 1916 all public discussion centred on conscription as a possible solution to the British manpower crisis which was emerging on the front. The Asquith government had felt compelled by the exigencies of war to introduce a conscription bill and by the exigencies of Irish politics, to exclude Ireland. Redmond wished simply to abstain on the conscription bill; but John Dillon, true to his left-liberal instincts and left-liberal British allies, persuaded the party to vote against the second reading. But the British Liberal revolt on the issue, such as it was, collapsed—leaving the party in a seriously exposed position at Westminster.[17]

As with the offer of a place for Redmond in the Cabinet, the IPP contrived to garner the worst of both worlds during the conscription crisis. 'Old Fogey', the pen name of a Belfast columnist, imagined Redmond saying to his party that 'we have made a disaster', only to be told by MPs from Kerry, Limerick and Dublin that Sinn Féin was growing. Redmond none the less replied—in the imagination of 'Old Fogey' anyway—'we have made a holy mess of our chance to remain neutral and now it is better for us to go the whole way with Britain'. 'Old Fogey' imagined Redmond's final words to the party: 'on your heads, not on mine, be the responsibility. But if your short-sighted providence results in your obliteration as a party or as a power, do not blame me'.[18] The 'Old Fogey' articles represent the beginning of awareness in unionist Belfast that Redmond, personally, was sincere in his support for the war effort, combined with an insistence that the party, as a whole, was not.

The conscription bill fiasco definitely weakened the Redmond's party at Westminster. At the beginning of February the *Saturday Review* asked whether 'British soldiers returning from the trenches will generally be in the humour to secure Home Rule for Ireland even with Ulster left out'.[19] This was not mainstream British opinion but it was precisely Redmond's darkest fear.

Relentlessly, the Ulster unionist press hammered out a message. We are loyal; we join up while nationalist Ireland sulks in a corner. Why would Britain reward that group for their disloyalty? In April 1915 the *Whig* declared 'we have given 35,000 against the rest of Ireland's 15,000'. On 4 June 1915 the paper was back again on the same claim: nationalists represented three-quarters of the population, but had given one-quarter of recruits from Ireland. In January 1916 the *Westminster Gazette* was attacked for exaggerating nationalist recruitment. In the *Whig's* view, the Ulster unionists' recruitment rate was one in sixteen men, the overall British rate one in seventeen, while the nationalist rate was one in ninety.[20]

Redmond's brother was to make one brilliant and effective intervention against such polemics. On 16 March 1916 Major Willie Redmond appeared in the House of Commons in his British Army uniform. He spoke movingly about the low morale and moaning over strategic issues that he found at home. Walter Long, a key Tory and unionist, was moved to acclaim the debt owed by the empire to Ireland. The *Northern Whig*, though, remained unrepentant: on reflection, it noted, Long would realise that he had been rather too generous.[21]

On St Patrick's Day, 1916, the day after his brother's stirring performance, Redmond went with King George V and his royal family, along with Lords Kitchener and French, to visit the reserve battalion of the Irish Guards stationed in East Anglia. The men were all presented with a sprig of shamrock by the monarch, and there was much talk of Irish heroes like Michael O'Leary, VC.[22] Redmond then visited the Irish war-wounded at King Edward Hospital in London. He said that he had recently visited Belgium and Flanders, and felt that the tide was turning in favour of the Allies. But in Ireland itself, the tide was turning against Redmond. Eoin MacNeill inspected 1,600 anti-Redmondite Irish Volunteers in Dublin, whilst in Cork, the same force was 2,500 strong— one-quarter of them armed with rifles, another quarter carrying pikes. The Redmondite counter-mobilisation was much smaller, though they gaily advertised on their banners that their best men were at the front.

In late March the separatists issued a statement saying they would react aggressively to any government attempt to disarm them. They operated even more aggressively—taking Dublin Castle in a form of 'mimic warfare'. Unionist opinion regarded all this a little contemptuously; few outside the rebel ranks believed that they would be capable of any serious military assault. The Irish Parliamentary Party—many of whose MPs even in 1916 had Fenian backgrounds—feared above all an incompetent bungling episode that would damage the whole nationalist cause.

At the beginning of April Karl Liebknecht, the German socialist deputy who was to be murdered alongside Rosa Luxemburg by the Freikorps in 1919, protested in the Reichstag against Germany's militarism. He drew attention to one attempt to turn allied prisoners-of-war to fight against their own side, and stressed the role of Roger Casement in this operation.[23] The effect of such public reports can only have encouraged separatists in Ireland to gain an exaggerated sense of the likely German support for a rising.

How did Redmond view the separatist threat? Michael MacDonagh, a close ally, has recorded:

Redmond looked upon this playacting by nobodies—a
manifestation of the histrionic side of the Irish
character by persons of no consequence. Had not his
influence over the coalition saved Ireland from the
threatened disruption of its civil life by conscription? And, had not the South and West voluntarily
joined the colours to the number of 45,000? That,
indeed, was a remarkable response, everything considered. Looking to the future, Redmond saw the reconciliation of North and South, and Home Rule
established by general consent, at the victorious conclusion of a terrible war, out of which all came
softened by suffering.[24]

With a sharp insight, Stephen Gwynn, a Galway nationalist MP and serving
British Army officer, expressed the flaw in his leader's thinking. Redmond,
Gwynn noted, could only see 'empty vanity' in the separatist platform. But
Gwynn pointed out there was something rather abstract about the very real
physical heroism of those Redmondites who served abroad.

Irish regiments after all, could only do what other
regiments were doing; their deeds were obscured in
the chaos of war from which individual prowess could
not emerge. Pearse and his associates offered to
Irishmen a stage for themselves on which they could
and did secure full personal recognition—the complete
attention of Ireland's mind.[25]

The *Northern Whig's* reaction to the Easter Rising was nonplussed: it had
confidently predicted at the end of March that the separatists were incapable
of a serious challenge. While Robert Emmet in 1803 had in the words of a
Belfast newspaper, the *Irishman*, at least managed to 'organise thousands of
poor countrymen' and besieged 'the government in its strongest position',[26] the
Whig noted correctly that Young Ireland in 1848 and the Fenians in 1867 had
not produced 'a challenge which could not have been handled by a corporal in
the infantry'. Easter 1916 was clearly different. The rebels had held their

ground for some days and tied up 10,000 troops—it had the appearance, at least, said the *Whig*, of a 'formidable show'.[27] For the Redmondites it was the beginning of the end.

Between the outbreak of the Great War in 1914 and the outbreak of the Easter Rising in 1916 there elapsed some twenty months. In a famous article published in *Studia Hibernica* in 1967 entitled '1916—Myth, Fact and Mystery', Father F.X. Martin asked the question, 'Was there any perceptible change in public opinion in Ireland towards the parliamentary party and the British government during those short twenty months, or did a lightning change occur after the Rising?' Father Martin answered his own question. 'A cursory glance at the facts corroborates the view that Redmond and his party had no serious challenger in Ireland (except for Carson and the Orangemen) before 1916.' Put as baldly as this, Father Martin overstated the Redmondite case. The Irish Parliamentary Party's organisation was admitted on all sides to be in decay. The agrarian issues which had for so many years helped to sustained enthusiasm and participation had in many cases been resolved. Redmond was out of touch with working-class Dublin in a way that Charles Stewart Parnell was not. Nevertheless, the conclusion of any analysis of the by-elections in nationalist Ireland between the outbreak of the war and the Rising is unavoidable—the Irish party won all five of the contested seats. Redmond had the confidence of the majority of the Irish people on the eve of Easter week; after the fighting he never had that confidence in the same way again.

The implications were profound. A substantive form of Irish self-government was inevitable but its nature and scope were not predetermined. It now took a different form, leading eventually to the declaration of the Republic. The North remained lost, and in the sense understood by the separatists of 1916, remains lost till this day.

Might things ever have been different? What about Redmond's hope that a common sacrifice might have softened nationalist–unionist enmity? Death at the front was non-sectarian and apolitical in its targeting. With some poignancy, the first MP to die at the front was the Ulster unionist Arthur Bruce O'Neill; the second was W.G.C. Gladstone, the great Home Rule hero's grandson. In the early morning of 7 June 1917 the Catholic and nationalist 16th (Irish) Division advanced side-by-side with the Protestant and unionist 36th (Ulster) Division to take the Messines Ridge, south of Ypres. Major Willie Redmond, MP, of the 16th Division died of his wounds in an Ulster Division field hospital.[28] The last clergyman that devout Catholic Willie Redmond talked to was a Belfast Church of Ireland chaplain, the Reverend John Redmond, who later published a dignified account of the episode. There is no doubt that Willie Redmond won the respect of the Ulsterman he served with, but in the years that followed the same Reverend John Redmond, as vicar of Ballymacarrett, found himself at the centre of the bitter sectarian conflicts of 1920–2. As a consequence of which he even felt it necessary—for fear of something more undisciplined—to play a role in the setting up of the B Specials (Ulster Special Constabulary).[29] Context is everything. The violent circumstances that attended the formation of both Irish states marginalised the better impulses of men of good will. Ireland in the end got the worst of both worlds—an unavailing mass sacrifice of Irishmen of both traditions at the front and a brutal and bloody civil war at home.

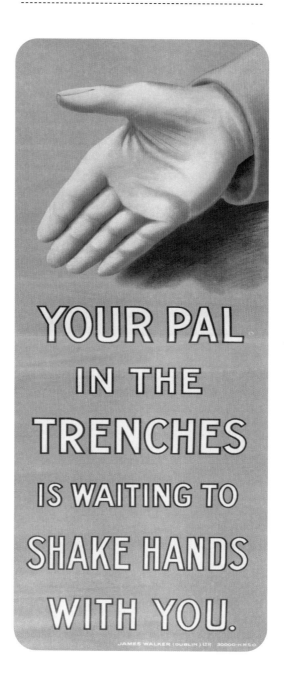

YOUR PAL
IN THE
TRENCHES
IS WAITING TO
SHAKE HANDS
WITH YOU.

•

NLI, Ephemera Collection, WAR/1914-18/59: 'Your pal in the trenches is waiting to shake hands with you', 1914–18. Courtesy of the National Library of Ireland.

Following pages: NAI, 98/43/19: Extract of a letter from John (Jack) Duggan, Lieutenant in the Royal Irish Fusiliers, to his sweetheart, Beatrice Seymour, c. May 1915.
Courtesy of the National Archives of Ireland.

•

Mother and Father managed
to fight their way down to
the boat at the North Wall,
but I was so busy I only saw
them for about five minutes.
Once we got on board we
were not allowed off. Three
of our Longford dogs followed
us, and then are still with
us here. They are marvellous
animals. We crossed on the
mail boat Connaught and had
a very nice crossing, but
had to wait three hours on
Holyhead pier.

My brothers regiment crossed
on Thursday on the Connaught also.
They apparently were not quite so
well treated as we were. They
came down to the ship with all
their luggage but were told by
the skipper that no luggage of any
sort could be allowed on board as
the Royal Irish had brought over

about 100 tons which was altogether
too much! As a result it had
to wait a day in Dublin.

When they got on board they asked
for dinner, but were told by the
head steward that the Royal Iris
had refused their food, so they
would not serve any more.
As a matter of fact when we got
on board our, the mess waiters
immediately laid our own dinner
and we did not hear about any
being prepared for us at all.
As a result of all this we seem
to be getting rather popular. The
regular toast in the Fusilier's mess
now is "Gott Straffe the Royal Iris"

Well, I have told you all
we have done or seen of
interest (or not as the case may be)
so don't forget to give me the news
from Longford.

I suppose you have

...ed Tennis now. I wish I
could get a set. Tell Laurice
that I am sure Father Jephson
would like to go out on the Canlin
in that boat. Why didn't I
think of it before?

I expect you wish the hunting
season was round again. Have
you had that horse you used
to ride out lately. It seems
to be your favourite.

Give my best love to all the
family. (Also ask Katie if she has
any message for my nice young
sergeant)

Yours ever

Jack. M. Duggan.

P.S.

Excuse this paper. It is from
my field note book.

16

Sunday
10/7/15
(not sure if the date is right)

There is nothing to report since my despatch of the 9th inst! Land has been sighted and we are now near a strongly fortified rock in the South West corner of Europe — that ought to suit the most exacting censor.

Every third day our battalion finds all the duties on board. Last night Beard, Kerr & I were officers of the watch from 8 a.m. yesterday till 8 this morning. We took it in four hour stretches. I was on from

twelve till four in the day and
at night. There are no less than
seventeen sentries on board which
one has to visit twice during the
four hours. This takes up about
an hour of the four.

We have certainly had
beautiful weather so far. Today
is very warm. Every day feels
hotter. We are still in the
khaki we wore at home as no
order has come out about wearing
drill yet.

My dear Bee,

        We are now on an island forty miles from the firing line, being the main base for it. We arrived last Wednesday. There is a splendid natural harbour full of Russian, French & British battleships and transports. While we were at anchor in the middle of the harbour about a dozen destroyers and small steamers left for the front full of troops.

        On Thursday we came ashore about two o'clock in the afternoon in battleship's cutters drawn by steam pinnaces, and marched about three miles to our bivouac. There are no roads at all, and very few tracks even. Our way here from the landing stage which is on a sort of peninsula lay across a hill on the peninsula and round an inlet of the sea on this side of the peninsula. That was about three miles round, but we have since discovered that the inlet is never deeper than your knees, so we always ford it now.

Harbour

Landing stage

Inlet

Village

Bivouac

        All our transport vehicles with Mr Harding and Mr Stanley have been left at the last place we called, probably permanently as the country is too rough. As a consequence we have to carry everything by hand. Some of the boxes too

eight men to carry them, so you can imagine the job
it was as the ford has a greasy bottom and the
land where it is not ploughed (so called) is composed of
rushes and loose stones. The ploughed land is worse
to walk on as it is all hard clods of earth.

I have not seen a vehicle except two motor
lorries belonging to the A.S.C and some water carts
since I came on the island. Donkeys and little
ponies are universally used.

The day we arrived on the island we
started about six hundred men to carry the
baggage to the bivouac at 2 p.m, and we did not
finish till 9.30 p.m - by moonlight. It is a distance
of about two miles.

You ought to see the Royal Irish officers now
with all the hair off our heads and about half of us
wearing smoked goggles. I have got a pair, but
have not used them yet as I don't notice the
glare much.

We are in quite the best place in the island
with a well for washing water and a spring for
drinking water about twenty yards from where I am
sitting now. The well, the same as everything else,
is absolutely primitive.

98/4/17

The bathing is splendid. The best bathing place is at the jetty where we landed, but it is too far away, so we bathe just near here, but ~~half~~ have to walk out a long way before it is deep enough to ~~swim~~.

My brother has not arrived yet as far as I know but expect he will be here shortly. His regiment had not left Basingstoke when we left.

Some of the men's letters are really rather amusing although one feels like a criminal reading them. In "A" Coy one of Mr McAndrew's men said "B Coy are in the firing line and A Coy in support. We will soon be going forward to join B and show the Turks what stuff we are made of. The night is dark, the flash of the ~~shell~~ is blinding and the din awful etc etc". Isn't it alarming. His people will spread the news a bit, and at least publish his graphic letter in the paper. As I said we are only forty miles from the firing line! Fifty per cent of their letters are taken up with the strange device of crosses, representing kisses I don't know why they don't keep them till they get home, like sensible fellows!

My servant Callaghan and I have just been manufacturing a wash stand made of canvas, sticks and string — What a life! My spare clothes are all hanging on a tree. At my head is a large stone exactly the same as a tomb stone. Several fellows passing including Costello, who is awfully funny, have knelt down in the end of my valise and prayed for my soul to rest in peace.

This morning we were manufacturing a dinner table which consists of two trenches which a table of earth in the centre. Our legs fit in the trenches so we are quite comfortable.

This seems to me a most selfish letter, being all about my doings. Do let me have the news from Ireland. We get the war news on a slip of paper entitled the "Peninsula Press" which is composed of the most important news. It is issued one to each company.

Love to all

Yours

Jack.P.Duggan.

NAI, 98/43/7: Jack Duggan to Beatrice Seymour, 23 July 1915. He tells her 'you ought to see the Royal Irish officers now, with all the hair off our heads…'. Courtesy of the National Archives of Ireland.

98/43/7

119

IWM, Q 13315: Gallipoli taken by Ernest
Brooks, 1915. Royal Fusiliers returning from
the trenches through Gully Ravine.
© Imperial War Museum.

Gallipoli

18.8.15

Dear Mrs Seymour,

I am afraid I have only got the worst possible news. Jack Duggan is reported killed + I have done all I can to disprove it, but I am afraid it is beyond doubt. His Mother will know by the time you get this, from the casualty lists, so I will tell you the whole thing so as you might soften it for her a bit. On the night of the 15th there was the start of a big fight, + very soon "D" Coy was called on to provide volunteers to act as Stretcher bearers. Practically the whole company went, but they would not let any officers go. Then "A" Coy was turned out to bring up ammunition. + later on "B" (Jack's Company) + "C" were sent up to act as reserve. It was their turn to go, we had been doing it 2 Coys at a time since we were here. In the morning what was left of "D" Coy was split up on various jobs + I heard nothing further till about 2 P.M. when I was recalled in a hurry + told that "A" Coy had gone up to reinforce "B" + "C" in the firing line + that we were to go too. We started but were so short of men that it was a farce + they recalled us + at the same time the other 3 coys were ordered to come back. We heard that Jack was slightly wounded + gone to hospital. Fulda was brought in very bad + More slightly wounded, + presently

---

NAI, 98/43/9: Mervyn Pratt, friend of Jack Duggan to Beatrice Seymour, 18 August 1915. He breaks the news to her of Jack's death 'I am afraid I have only got the worst possible news'. On the same day, Jack's elder brother, George also died in Gallipoli. Courtesy of the National Archives of Ireland.

an order came to Capt Scott to detail
a "D" Coy officer for duty with "B" Coy
as they had no officers left & the
Adjutant was in command. We all
volunteered & it fell to me by right of
seniority, but when I got up to them
they were being relieved by the Dublins
& were coming back. I had the roll called
in the morning (we only got to our bivouac at
eleven oclock) & the wounded were straggling
in all night) & when I put Jack down
as wounded some of his men corrected me
& told me he had been wounded in the face
& wrist & still carried on & that they saw
him killed afterwards. I was busy all
day but Scott went round all the hospitals
& he had not been through any of them.
There is just the bare chance that if he
was not dead he might have got to the shore
& been taken off in a boat or that he
might have been taken prisoner after by the
Turks, but I don't think that would be possible.
I can't tell you how I feel about it, it has knocked
me out. Macandrew & Costello are also killed or
& wounded. The 10th Division is practically
non existant now. All is quiet to-day but 98/43/9

121

On the night of Aug: 15th — "B" & "C" companies were up. & there was a big attack going on, so "A" coy: was sent for. "D" was called on to provide 40 stretcher bearers. The whole company volunteered, & we did not see the 40 men for 3 days. The morning of the 16th the company was split up into the usual working parties. & at 2 P.M. a messenger brought me an order. to bring the my parties as the other companies were getting a hammering & we were to go to the firing line. We got in what could be collected of the company, & started off with them. but when we got half way were ordered to return as they had too many men up there & were over crowded. So we could do nothing but sit & watch the wounded coming back. I asked any "B." coy: men I saw about Jack, & they said he was wounded & gone to hospital.

Later in the evening a messenger came to say "B" coy: had no officers left, & for "D" coy: to detail an officer for duty. it fell to me by right of seniority. — As I was starting

NAI, 98/43/17: Mervyn Pratt's diary, 15 August to 10 September 1915. In it he recounts to the story of Jack's death.
Courtesy of the National Archives of Ireland.

to go up I met. T.J.D. going down wounded.
he was awfully cheerful & perfectly conscious
the only thing he seemed to mind was keeping
his being wounded out of the papers. So as
not to worry his people.   When I got up
I met "B" coy: under command of the
Adjutant. returning to bivouac. having being
relieved by the Dublins.   When I called the roll.
next morning I was told by 2 of his men that
Jack had been wounded in the wrist & mouth
& had got it dressed & come back again &
been shot throught the head.   I only hope it is
a mistake, he was one of the very best. he
& Jonny.   We lost 10 officers (3 killed)
(McAndrew. & Costello.). & about 200 men in
that show.

          About Aug: 25th - Shifted over to tata
Baba. by night.   a terrible trek along the
soft sand. carrying all our tools & grub.
          25th to Sept: 10th

Entrenching the whole of Laba Baba. & well
sinking, to the tunes of the Hymn of Hate
morning & evening from the Turkish guns.

IWM, Q 13447: 'Gallipoli: 1915' taken by Ernest Brooks.
A Faugh-a-Ballagh (Royal Irish Fusilier) teasing a Turkish
sniper by holding his helmet above the trench on his rifle.
© Imperial War Museum.

124

TWO BROTHERS KILLED.

The death is announced on August 17th of Captain George Grant Duggan, 5th Royal Irish Fusiliers, as the result of wounds received at the Dardanelles on August 16th. Captain Duggan was buried at sea. His residence was 12 St. Kevin's Park, Rathgar, and he was the third son of Mr. George Duggan, 5 College street, Dublin. He was aged 29.

Lieut. John Rowswell Duggan, 5th Royal Irish Regiment, killed in action at the Dardanelles on 16th August, was the fifth son of Mr. George Duggan.

TO JACK.

You have fought your one great fight
In the glory of your youth,
Died for freedom and the right
You have battled for the truth.

To the God who made your frame
So fair, so lithe, so strong,
You have given it back the same
Without spot unstained by wrong.

From his Treasure-house He gave
Us one Jewel and you kept
A child-like heart, a spirit brave
And joyous. Now our eyes have wept.-

Wept for soaring courage gone,
For your blithesome laugh now still
For a future still unwon,
For a past death cannot kill.

X X X X X X X X

In the lonely star-lit night
You lie sleeping . Far away
Up the valley comes a light,
Comes a song on winds astray.

'Tis the angels of the slain
Silver-wighed with silence shod,
Come to bear you home again
To the keeping of your God.

G.C.D.

Sept. 1915.

Top: NAI, 98/43/14: The death notice for Jack Duggan and his brother George, August 1915. Courtesy of the National Archives of Ireland.

NAI, 98/43/14: 'To Jack', September 1915. Poem in memory of his dead brother by George Chester Duggan. Courtesy of the National Archives of Ireland.

+as a matter of fact we
98/43/12

are very well off & comfortable
& there is really very little
danger and a lot of
amusement to be got out it.
Some people have got awfully
"nervy" + with the shells coming
along at odd times.

Scott + I got great value
out of one of my sergeants
King by name, who got
into such a state that
he would not come out
of his trench or put his

NAI, 98/43/12: Mervyn Pratt to Beatrice Seymour's father, 5 September 1915. He
discusses their desensitisation to the horrors of war including shell shock and suicide.
Courtesy of the National Archives of Ireland.

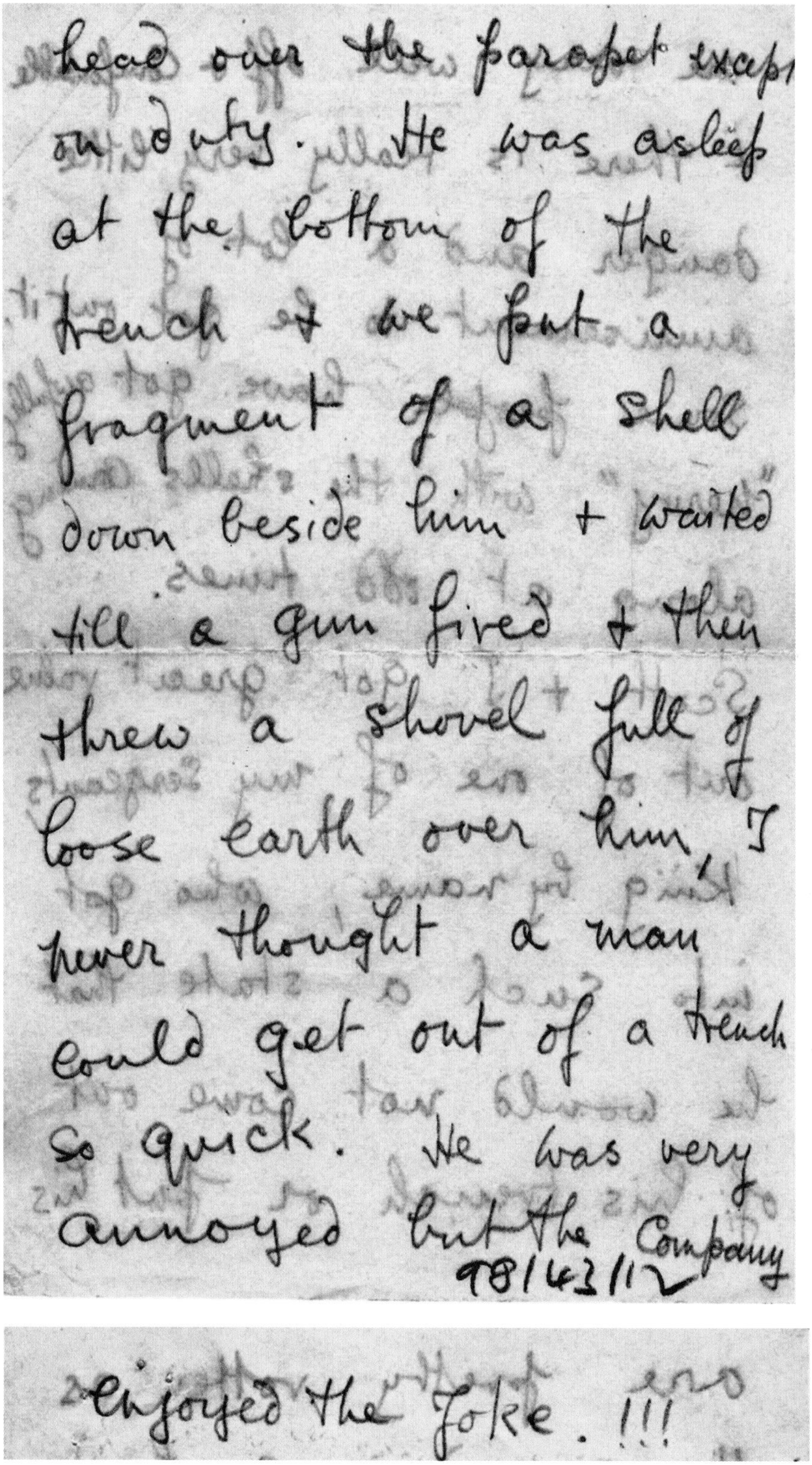

head over the parapet except
on duty. He was asleep
at the bottom of the
trench & we put a
fragment of a shell
down beside him + waited
till a gun fired + then
threw a shovel full of
loose earth over him, I
never thought a man
could get out of a trench
so quick. He was very
annoyed but the Company
98/43/12

enjoyed the joke. !!!

Scott's servant shot himself a couple of days ago with Scott's pistol & scared the life out of me. I was asleep beside him when it went off. I didn't wake up properly but heard it all sort of subconsciously, & thought it was a shell

that had burst & killed the whole expeditionary force?

FORERUNNERS
of a Successful Day.

To surmount all obstacles and get through the most trying conditions, physical fitness is a *sine qua non*.

Fry's PURE BREAKFAST COCOA

contains the very ingredients to ensure this to those who drink it regularly. Easily Digested. Economical.

Contractors to the Allied Forces

Fry's

Basham

CHAPTER 5

Home front and everyday life

DAVID FITZPATRICK

The Shamrock, 8 March 1919. Cartoon by 'Geo Monks'. Image scanned by the IURLA (UCD).

'Grand-Da! What did you do during the Great War?'

'I have remained a member of the Ballyclattery Urban Council, my child.'

This exchange decorated the cover of the *Shamrock*, an illustrated magazine published shortly after the armistice, with the caption 'A Propheteer-Oh! who has neither fought nor fled for us'.[1] It reminds us that the Great War brought gains as well as losses to Ireland, touching every aspect of Irish life, whether personal, social, economic or political. Its most obvious personal impact was on the lives of over 200,000 men (and a few 100 women) who joined the war-time services in Ireland, in addition to tens of thousands of expatriate Irishmen who joined British, colonial or American forces.[2] No war or conflict had ever involved so many Irish participants, making the revolutionary events of 1916–23 appear as minor skirmishes by comparison. Think of the 1916 Rising, involving 1,600 rebels, or the War of Independence, fought with about 3,000 rifles and 80 sub-machine-guns.

The majority of Irish participants in the Great War were Catholics, even though enlistment was always sluggish from the farming sector and from the impoverished 'Atlantic fringe'. Recruitment was most intense in the industrialised north-east, among Catholics as well as Protestants. Admittedly, recruiting fell well

short of British levels, even before the gap was widened by the exclusion of
Ireland from conscription. Less than a quarter of Irishmen with non-agricul-
tural occupations actually joined the forces. Yet there was not a parish in
Ireland untouched by the call to arms, regardless of its political, religious or
social make-up.

One of the most perplexing questions facing any historian of the war is
why normally sane, sensible people should have thrown themselves into
something so dangerous and unrewarding. Since Ireland was one of the few
combatant countries never to experience conscription, every decision to join up
was personal and voluntary. Few were swept up by the alleged 'war hysteria'
of August 1914, and enlistment rates were much higher during 1915 when the
dreadful human cost and uncertain outcome of the war were universally understood. Unqualified loyalty to king and country cannot have been a major factor,
since hundreds of thousands of unionists as well as nationalists had been
preparing before the war for possible confrontation with the forces of the
crown. While most recruits would have had a strong sense of civic duty and
patriotism, the decision to translate sympathy for the allied cause into personal
participation required something stronger than sentiment. Nor was poverty or
unemployment the major impulse. Whereas in peacetime the armed forces were
an attractive option for young men without means or prospects in civil life, it
made no economic sense to exchange poverty at home, however severe, for the
misery of life in the trenches and the strong likelihood of death or disablement.
In fact, the groups most likely to join up were not the unskilled or unemployed,
but those with relatively secure, well-paid jobs such as skilled workers, clerks
and professional men.

What drove most recruits into the war-time forces, apart from a desire for
adventure and subsidised international tourism, was loyalty to their friends
and families. It is, therefore, not surprising that so many recruits had belonged
to paramilitary organisations, fraternities, sporting clubs, schools or universities, where each member felt under strong psychological pressure to conform
to group expectations. Once the UVF and the Orange Order had fallen in line
behind Edward Carson, it was easier for individual members to join the new
Ulster Division than to stay at home. Likewise, John Redmond's support for the
war effort soon impelled thousands of National Volunteers and members of
the Ancient Order of Hibernians to join the 10th or 16th (Irish) divisions. Most
recruits were influenced more by the behaviour of their peers than by self-
interest, preferring to face massive personal risks rather than lose the esteem of
those they admired.

The fact that most Irishmen did *not* join the forces was likewise due in part to pressures applied by family, friends or fraternities. In early 1916 a recruiting canvass in Charleville, Co. Cork, revealed that most men attributed their recalcitrance not to politics or conscience but to family and business commitments. Only a few refused information 'with violence' or declared there was 'nothing to fight for'.[3] As republican organisations multiplied in 1917 and 1918, young men faced ridicule from their peers and even social ostracism if they joined the forces of the crown. These factors help to explain why Australia, with a population similar to Ireland's, dispatched 330,000 men overseas in the Australian Imperial Force, not to mention 85,000 on home duties. In Australia, as in Ireland, Catholics were only slightly less likely than Protestants to enlist, and Irish emigrants showed no hesitation in serving his imperial majesty. Nearly 60,000 Australian servicemen died overseas, about twice the number of Irish fatalities.[4]

For the great majority of participants, this was their first experience of the privations (and fraternal compensations) of military life, though the fight against the Boers had given a foretaste at the turn of the century. For one in six Irish soldiers, the adventure ended in death, often caused by accidents or illness rather than enemy fire. Irish servicemen, contrary to myth, were neither more nor less likely to die than their British counterparts. Few of the survivors escaped physical or psychological mutilation; and few Irish families were untouched by the excitement, anxiety and often personal loss aroused by the enlistment of a father, son, brother, cousin or husband. The Irish, therefore, did not escape the trauma that afflicted Europe in the wake of the war, though its collective expression was muffled by the upsurge of emotion occasioned by the conflicts of 1916 to 1923.

From an early stage of the war, injured and disabled soldiers were to be seen in every Irish town, mutely or loudly reproaching those who had stayed out of the conflict. Even before the Battle of the Somme, which tore the heart out of the 36th (Ulster) Division in July 1916, the rector of Carrickfergus in Co. Antrim, Frederick MacNeice, had begun to count the cost:

> In the days to come there will, all through the land, be
> many memorials of the sacrifices made in this agonising
> conflict. For a generation or more there will be living
> memorials—men who have suffered loss in their bodies—an
> eye, a hand or leg—men who will all their days on earth bear
> the marks of the terrible struggle in which they had been

*engaged. And there will be other memorials, too. In oldest
castle, in humblest cottage, in every kind of home in town
and country there will be material things—a cap, a sword,
a scroll, a medal, a something that will have a dearness, a
sacredness, because it belonged to the brave dead.*[5]

The war's social and economic impact was equally significant, though here
too the Irish experience was in some respects muted by comparison with the
dramatic transformation of everyday life in Britain, France, Russia or Germany.
The shortage of available men had a stultifying effect on social events, as Olive
Armstrong (later a lecturer in political science at Trinity College Dublin)
remarked in her diary on 2 August 1915:

*We are back here again, and it is a very different Ballycastle.
Hardly any of the people we know are here and everything
is very dead. The dearth of men is awful, but for the last
fortnight I believe they have had a wildly gay time as the
9th Inniskillings were here. They had picnics, tennis & even
dances. Why weren't we here!* [6]

The absence of men was also reflected in slightly fewer marriages and
births; but the most obvious impact of the war on family life was the virtual
stoppage of emigration to America after early 1915. For generations, Irish
couples had been producing twice as many children as could expect to gain a
livelihood in Ireland, in the knowledge that some would be able to emigrate to
make a living. Suddenly, would-be emigrants were faced with the options of
enlistment, working in munitions factories or trying to scratch a living at home.
In the more urbanised east and north, the stock of frustrated emigrants was
easily absorbed by war-time demand, so that industrial unemployment was
virtually eliminated by 1916. In the rural south and west, however, there were
fewer recruits and more disappointed emigrants, creating a surplus of restive
young men and women who were to contribute so crucially to Sinn Féin and
the IRA in the years after 1916. Without the war, it may be argued that, most
of the manpower driving the revolutionary movement would have been absent
without leave in America.

In the early months of the war, it was universally expected to have cata-
strophic economic consequences. While it is true that 'inessential' industries

were severely disrupted, this was soon outweighed by the insatiable demand for munitions and essential goods (such as linen for aircraft). After a few weeks of severe unemployment, as workers were laid off in industries such as construction and textiles, it became clear that civilians in most parts of Ireland had brighter job prospects than in peacetime, provided they had the versatility to adapt to radically changed conditions. Even in construction, unemployment rates fell far below those of summer 1914.[7] Wages kept pace with inflation, while earnings and working conditions improved sharply for those employed in the munitions sector. Industrial unrest, which had brought Dublin to a standstill in 1913–14, was negligible until the last year or so of the war. Even Larkin's ITGWU, whose leaders were strongly anti-war, was virtually inactive. A senior union official revealed after the Rising that as many members had joined the forces as the number of persons currently enrolled in the organisation in Ireland.[8]

In one respect, the war had a more positive impact in Ireland than in Britain. By 1916 the German submarine campaign and the naval requisitioning of most merchant vessels had cut Britain off from many of its traditional food suppliers, providing Irish farmers with an irresistible opportunity to 'do well out of the war'. Ireland, still overwhelmingly agricultural, was only lightly affected by food shortages and rationing, while the entire rural economy prospered in the course of sating British appetites. Rural Ireland's prosperity drew sneers from British patriots and Irish nationalists alike, but it gave Ireland a solid economic stake in the war, and a reason for avoiding personal participation. Demand for farm labour increased along with enlistment, and poverty was virtually eliminated in many regions. Urban wage-earners and those on fixed incomes, faced with the doubling of food prices between 1914 and 1918, did not fare so well. The agricultural boom lingered until 1920, its subsequent collapse coinciding precisely with the most destructive phase of the Civil War.

The costs and benefits of the Great War for Irish civilians are more difficult to assess, once we broaden the discussion from income and employment to personal 'welfare'. The 'welfare state' was greatly extended after 1914, as more workers qualified for insurance or gained statutory protection by working in 'controlled' industries and state factories. Yet those who worked in munitions also accepted restrictions on their freedom to move jobs or to campaign for collective benefits through trades unions. Even in Ireland, basic commodities such as bread and beer became scarcer and more expensive, though some food prices were capped, and rationing introduced, in order to protect poorer consumers. By early 1918 there was only one shop in Belfast still selling butter

137

over the counter.[9] Anxiety about the future of the human race led to important advances in Irish child and maternal welfare, with provision of free milk for school-children, clinics for mothers and babies, and encouragement of breast-feeding in order to diminish infant mortality. Nutrition actually improved through the enforced substitution of wholemeal for wheaten breads, margarine for butter, and vegetable products for meat.

Yet consumers undoubtedly suffered from unprecedented restriction of choice and the unavailability of 'luxuries', except to the rich and well-connected. Even liquor became a luxury through curtailed licensing hours and increased excise duties, though the political clout of the liquor lobby (unionist as well as nationalist) ensured that it was still easier to get drunk in Ireland than in Britain. Housing conditions, already appalling in the urban inner cities, deteriorated alarmingly as the building trade declined. Rapid inflation and higher interest rates made it difficult for borrowers to meet their obligations, and fuel prices soared because of a shortage of imported coal. Recreational travel, sport and public entertainments were all hard hit, though the cinema flourished as civilians flocked to watch battle films and newsreels. A shortage of trains for Sunday excursions became a major problem, making it difficult to organise Gaelic matches and monster meetings. Life should, therefore, have been less fun than before the war.

Even so, privations and sacrifices unthinkable in peacetime were widely accepted as not just inevitable but life-enhancing. For Frederick MacNeice, this response showed that the war had conferred a deeper, moral benefit. Speaking eleven years after the armistice of November 1918, he recalled the years of rationing and self-sacrifice as 'a glorious interval. The spirit of that brief period must be recaptured'.[10] The feeling, stronger among Protestants, that the war had overwhelmed all normal preoccupations was well conveyed by Olive Armstrong in September 1915:

> There is a queer strained feeling about everything now. It is the war, it has cast an awful gloom over everything. When you take up the paper in the morning, it is with a sort of dread, for you don't know whose name may be in the Roll of Honour. Then on Sunday we have the national Anthem in Church and of course special prayers & hymns. 'God the All-Terrible' to the Russian National Anthem is the nicest I think. Absolutely everyone is doing war work from knitting

to Munition Factories & nursing, in France if possible. It is perfectly splendid.[11]

Gloom and splendour coexisted in Olive's vision of the war, reminding us of Yeats's notion of the 'terrible beauty' engendered by the 1916 Rising.

War-time mobilisation had indeed drawn women into the mainstream of economic life, as they temporarily took over jobs once monopolised by men. Irish 'munitions girls', in Irish, as well as British, shell factories and engineering plants, were the most obvious tokens of the new order. As in Britain, men were taken aback, even thrilled, by the novelty of female bus conductors or ambulance drivers. Through a scheme of 'national service' introduced in 1917, women were deployed in heavy farming work and encouraged to take the place of male clerks and 'shop-walkers' (department store supervisors). Though the number of women at or near any front line was small, many Irishwomen (including Maud Gonne) became nurses or occasionally doctors in Irish, British and French hospitals. There were also thousands of 'separation women', notorious for drinking away the maintenance payments sent on behalf of their husbands on active service. Their novel access to cash caused resentment on the part of wives still hampered by the presence of husbands. This could erupt into violence, as was apparent in a case brought before Ennis petty sessions court in May 1915, in which Patrick Mahony was charged with breaking Mrs Rynne's window with a stone:

> Jane Mahony [Patrick's wife] deposed that on Sunday morning Mrs Rynne cursed her and her ass because the ass went into her yard. Because she [Mrs Rynne] was getting a separation allowance she wanted to look down on [the] witness. Mrs Rynne caught [the] witness by the hair of the head, and she ([the] witness) caught Mrs Rynne's, and they wrestled around and could not kill one another (laughter). Butler (defendant's brother) came out and gave [the] witness a black eye. That was the wholly all of the fight.[12]

In addition, women dominated the innumerable charities providing comforts for servicemen and support for those who were injured, widowed or orphaned. So massive was the supply of clothing that one Dublin charity announced in April 1915 that 'no more socks or woollies are required at the front'. As a Wexford writer remarked: 'This is really a calamity to many women, to whom the resource of knitting has been a God-send, helping to take from their minds the terrible strain of the war, and giving them the feeling that they were doing their "bit" in this great national upheaval'.[13] The effect of the war was to extend something approaching full citizenship to women, a change reflected in the extension of the franchise in 1918.

The imprint of the war on Irish life is best understood through the trivial details recorded in newspapers and personal diaries or letters. Particularly, in the first year or so, terms and phrases associated with the war were the stock-in-trade of advertisers, music hall performers, and even (in a twisted form) republican prisoners when running rings around the censor. Phrases like 'Business as usual', 'It's a long way to Tipperary', 'The call to arms', or 'The one bright spot' were endlessly quoted, jokily misapplied and parodied. Scrap albums were cluttered with cuttings and photographs relating to the war, and children drew sketches of toddlers with rifles or union flags rather than dolls. School magazines were crowded with reports of the heroic doings and deaths of old boys, as well as facetious essays or verses about the quality of war-time cooking or the hazards of taking a cross-channel ferry. Even sport became entangled with war, as recorded in the magazine of a Dominican convent school in Blackrock, Co. Dublin. In November 1917 Sion Hill drew two-goals-all against a hockey team composed of volunteer nurses from the Linden convalescent hospital for officers, six of whom were old girls: Hilda O'Reilly, Agnes and Hilda McDermot, Una Minch, Pearlie Stein and Edie Lemass. Who remembers those names?[14]

Artists, writers and musicians all applied their skills to war themes, sometimes as official propagandists or contractors but more often as entertainers responding to war-time demand. Even William Butler Yeats, though famously refusing to contribute a war poem to an anthology edited by the American novelist Edith Wharton, was moved to write a profound meditation on the psychology of enlistment, 'An Irish Airman Foresees His Death':

> Nor law, nor duty bade me fight,
> Nor public men, nor cheering crowds;
> A lonely impulse of delight
> Drove to this tumult in the clouds;
> I balanced all, brought all to mind,

The years to come seemed waste of breath,
A waste of breath the years behind
In balance with this life, this death.[15]

The political impact of the war was far-reaching, but difficult to disentangle from the consequences of the failure to achieve a constitutional settlement before August 1914. Its most obvious immediate effect was to transform potential rebels, both unionists and nationalists, into advocates of a common cause. Britain and France were almost universally regarded as champions of liberty and democracy facing a brutal and despotic adversary. Despite lingering anti-English sentiment among nationalists, most admired the workings of English democracy everywhere except in Ireland. The former 'settler colonies' in North America, Australasia and South Africa were particularly extolled as models for a free Ireland within a free Commonwealth. At the outbreak of war, Carson, as well as Redmond, was keen to commit his armed supporters to coastal defence, and to use the deeper loyalties reawakened by the war to defuse tensions within Ireland. Despite ill-feeling over the manner in which Home Rule was put on hold for the duration of the war, both sides believed that common sacrifice, both in the field of battle and on the home front, might break down the ancient walls of partition between Protestant and Catholic, unionist and nationalist, northerner and southerner.

These hopes faded as the war continued, partly because of perceived discrimination against nationalist units by the War Office and the government. In the wake of the 1916 Rising, the crude application of communal penalties, such as, mass internment, suspension of common-law rights and banning of fairs and markets, unravelled the progress made by a succession of reformist governments. How could one trust a country whose government, in emergency, cast aside the basic tenets of democracy and justice in order to assert control by brute force? Despite Lloyd George's attempts to reach a compromise settlement after the Rising, through bilateral negotiations and then the Irish Convention, the pursuit of reconciliation had lost most of its appeal for both unionists and nationalists. Irish politics emerged from the war more bitterly polarised than at any time since the Land War of the 1880s.

Though retrospective sympathy with the rebels of 1916 was far more important in radicalising nationalists than any aversion in principle to the allied cause, the Rising would have been inconceivable in the absence of war. The instigation of a rebellion without popular support or any prospect of military success, justified by the specious cliché that 'England's war was Ireland's opportunity', was essentially an expression of frustration on the part of several small cliques of anti-Redmondites. The subsequent coercion, also inconceivable in peacetime, undoubtedly undermined recruiting as well as accomplishing the redescription of millions of constitutional nationalists as (often nominal) republicans. Yet, despite the apparent triumph of Sinn Féin and anti-war propaganda, there were notable upsurges in military enlistment immediately after the Rising and even at the height of the anti-conscription campaign in 1918. It would probably be futile to follow fashion by conjecturing whether Redmondism would have triumphed in the absence of European war, or what sort of civil war might have emerged from the impasse of 1912–14. Yet, if the world had remained at peace between 1914 and 1918, the Irish would surely have been poorer, less employable, and more troubled by class and sectarian conflict. To that extent, Ireland fared well from the Great War.

A cartoon from Oonagh Carroll's sketch-book, 17 January 1918. The public's preoccupation with the availability of food is still evident four years into the war. Reproduced by permission of David Fitzpatrick.

Princess Patricia Hospital in Bray, Co. Wicklow. The hospital was run by the Red Cross
and St John's Ambulance during the war period. Year and photographer unknown.
Reproduced by permission of David Fitzpatrick.

Photograph from a postcard captioned 'The Soldiers'
Rendezvous, Dublin No.2', postmarked 8 April 1917.
Reproduced by permission of David Fitzpatrick.

THE SOLDIERS' RENDEZVOUS, DUBLIN   NO. 2.

145

1914-16 **REDMON**

180,000 PRIME YOUNG IRISHMEN PURCHASED BY THE ENGLISH GOVERNMENT

Printed on Irish Paper by P. Quinn, Belfast

NLI, Ephemera Collection, POL/1910-20/9: '1914–16 Redmond & Co. Butchers to HM Government', 1916. This handbill (printed on 'Irish paper') shows John Redmond dissecting Ireland, which is hung from a butcher's hook. Courtesy of the National Library of Ireland.

Denying the right of the British Government to enforce compulsory Military service in this country, we pledge ourselves solemnly to one another to resist conscription by the most effective means at our disposal

Oath taken in R.C. Chapels, one Sunday after mass during the Great War — by both men & women —

The Irish Railway Workers Trade Union

Reg. No. 288.

7 St. Vincent Street, South Circular Road, Dublin.

A PUBLIC MEETING

Will be held

On Wednesday, 11th September, 1918
At 7 p.m.

AT THE BLACK LION, INCHICORE.

Fellow Railway Workers and Electors :

On the 15th January 1915 you re-elected me to support the wise and patriotic policy of the late lamented Mr. John E. Redmond, M.P., viz.—to support Voluntary Recruiting. This I have done, and I will continue to do so until the termination of this sad war, as the unchanged and unchangeable constitutional Nationalist and Trades Unionist. It is the only means to achieve my life-long aspiration " Colonial Home Rule for all Ireland."

For the last three and a half years I have day after day looked after the social and financial welfare of thousands of our Irish soldiers' and sailors' families. Any person who visits my happy home any evening from 7 to 10 p.m. will realise the good work that I am doing to help on the noble cause of Voluntary Recruiting against " Conscription " for I cannot forget how generously Kilmainham Ward responded to Mr. John E. Redmond's Call to Arms in 1914-15 and the early part of 1916. The same response was made throughout Dublin and Ireland. For my part I will not desert the brave Dublin Fusiliers and the other Irish Regiments in the trenches or neglect their families while I have a tongue to speak or a pen to write, for I plead for the young and old, and will do so to the end.

Captain Stephen Gwynn, M.P., a member of the Irish Recruiting Council, will be present at the meeting, and will speak in support of Voluntary Recruiting against Conscription.

Yours faithfully,

JOHN SATURNUS KELLY, T.C. (C.R.A.)
Orgainser and General Secretary.
Chairman of the Municipal Old Age Army
and Navy Committee, Court House,
William Street, Dublin.

Wt. 4572 5/9/18 3 000 R.T.W.

NAI, 3/493/5-6: Notice of a public meeting to be held by the Irish Railway Workers Trade Union, September 1918. The union while opposing conscription affirms its support for the war. Courtesy of the National Archives of Ireland.

NLI, INDH 211: Children play Red Cross, *c.* 1918–23. Courtesy of the National Library of Ireland.

151

MINISTRY OF FOOD.

FOOD CONTROL COMMITTEE FOR IRELAND.

SUGAR (FOR JAM) DISTRIBUTION

BOTH the enclosed Forms are to be filled up by applicant for Sugar for domestic jam preserving.

The Certificate on the back of the BUFF Form should be signed by the Sergeant in charge of the nearest police station.

BOTH Forms must be handed to a registered Sugar Retailer NOT LATER THAN 18th MAY, 1918.

(646).Wt. —G.114,2.60,000.4/18.A.T.&Co.,Ltd.*
(843.)Wt.651— 60000.4/18.

This page: NAI, 1096/10/20: Instructions on how to fill out the application form to obtain sugar to make jam. Courtesy of the National Archives of Ireland.

Next page: NLI, Ephemera Collection, POL/1910-20/11: 'Irish girls', *c.* 1914. Handbill issued by Inghinidhe na hÉireann discouraging Irishwomen from associating with members of the British Army. The organisation lamented the 'sad sight of Irish girls walking through the streets with men wearing the uniform of Ireland's oppressor'. Courtesy of the National Library of Ireland.

IRISH GIRLS!

Ireland has need of the loving service of all her children. Irishwomen do not sufficiently realize the power they have to help or hinder the cause of Ireland's freedom.

If they did we should not see the sad sight of Irish girls walking through the streets with men wearing the uniform of Ireland's oppressor.

No man can serve two masters; no man can honestly serve Ireland and serve England. The Irishman who has chosen to wear the English uniform has chosen to serve the enemy of Ireland, and it is the duty of every Irishwoman, who believes in the freedom of Ireland, to show her disapproval of his conduct by shunning his company.

Irish girls who walk with Irishmen wearing England's uniform, remember you are walking with traitors. Irish girls who walk with English soldiers, remember you are walking with your country's enemies, and with men who are unfit to be the companions of any girl, for it is well known that the English army is the most degraded and immoral army in Europe, chiefly recruited in the slums of English cities, among men of the lowest and most depraved characters. You endanger your purity and honour by associating with such men, and you insult your Motherland. Hearken to the words of Father Kavanagh, the Irish Franciscan Patriot Priest, who pronounces it a heinous crime against Ireland, for Irishmen to join the forces of robber England. Do you think it is less a crime for Irish girls to honour these men with their company. Remember the history of your country. Remember the women of Limerick and the glorious patriot women of the great rebellion of '98, and let us, who are their descendants try to be worthy of them. What would those noble women think if they knew their daughters were associating with men belonging to that army, which has so often wrought ruin and havoc in Ireland, and murdered in cold blood thousands of Irishwomen and children. What English soldiers have done in Ireland in the past they would do again if ordered to do so. They would slaughter our kith and kin and murder women and children again as unhesitatingly as they hemmed in the helpless Boer women and children in those horrible concentration camps, where ten thousand little Boer children died from want and suffering.

Irish girls make a vow, not only that you will yourselves refuse to associate with any man who wears an English uniform, but that you will also try and induce your girl companions to do the same.

Women's influence is strong. Let us see, fellow-countrywomen, that we use it to the fullest for the Glory of God, and for the honour and Freedom of Ireland.

Inġiniḋe na héireann.

Inġiniḋe na héireann are very anxious to get the co-operation of any girl who reads this handbill and feels she would like to help in working for Ireland's freedom and trying to save innocent country girls from the great danger which their thoughtless association with soldiers exposes them to. The Secretaries are always to be seen on Thursday evenings between 8 and 10 o'clock at Dún Inġiniḋe, 22 North Great George's Street, Dublin, and we appeal to all Irishwomen to help us in this great social and national work.

NLI, INDH 211: Troops search a bread-van for arms in Dublin, 1916. While Irish soldiers were at the front protecting the freedom of small nations, their own country was virtually under martial law following the Easter Rising. This caused some discontent among troops at the front when news filtered through. Courtesy of the National Library of Ireland.

Sketch of an Irish woman by
Margaret Phelan, 8 February
1917. Drawing taken from
Ooonagh Carroll's sketch-book.
Reproduced by permission of
David Fitzpatrick.

Margaret Phelan

8-2-'17

CHAPTER 6

Fewer ladies, more women

CAITRIONA CLEAR

‘Every fit man needed attest to-day’, cartoon by Lulu McAuley, 20 February 1919(?). The use of the word ‘attest’ references the Derby Scheme in which men registered their willingness to go to the front if called upon. The scheme was ultimately a failure and caused Lloyd George to introduce conscription from which Ireland was excluded. Reproduced by permission of David Fitzpatrick.

'Men must work but women no longer weep', declared a correspondent to an Irish women's magazine in March 1915 during a debate about women's role in society. Women—and men—certainly wept bitter tears in Ireland, as in other countries, in the four devastating years of the Great War; what the writer meant was that women did not confine themselves to weeping. In all the belligerent countries—and Ireland must be considered as such—women engaged in many kinds of war work, paid and voluntary, harrowing and dangerous, boring and humdrum. This particular war mobilised civilian populations on a scale never seen before, and looking at the changing social scene it is often easy to imagine that it was the war itself which brought women into public view.[1]

Irish women, however, had long been active outside the home. At the turn of the century they were nurses in hospitals and rural communities, itinerant cookery instructresses, secretaries, telephonists and telegraph operators, and they made up over half of all national school-teachers. They served behind the counters in the new department stores and the older grocery and drapery shops, and worked in the offices of these and other businesses. A growing number were drapers and grocers in their own right. In the north and north-east of the country, thousands filled the shirt factories, spinning mills and weaving factories. In other cities, factories and workshops employed smaller numbers of girls and women. The joyfully raucous females who shocked onlookers by 'following' rival bands in Cork and Limerick in the 1890s and early 1900s obviously had money in their pockets, as did the more sedate working girls who went to Irish and drama classes. A growing number of women held positions of authority, with nuns making up the majority of managers of institutions and hospitals, and women of the leisured classes prominent in organisations like the Women's National Health Association and the United Irishwomen, a forerunner to the Irish Countrywomen's Association. Even domestic servants were achieving a new independence in the early twentieth century, buying bicycles on hire purchase and insisting on more time off.[2]

New organisations and clubs—cultural, religious and political—attracted women, and suffrage organisations drew attention to their claims for political rights. When Christabel Pankhurst came to Galway Town Hall in 1912 the full-to-capacity attendance included the business, landed and academic elite of the locality.[3] 'Feminism is one of the burning questions of the day', wrote Father Michael O'Kane in 1913, in a pamphlet on women's role in the modern world, and he apologised to women for seeming to know more about them than they did themselves.[4] The advice he gave was traditional—women's most important role was the domestic one—but his apology, and his carefully neutral use of the term feminism, shows a recognition of women's heightened public profile before the outbreak of war.

Most historical accounts and biographies of women for this period in Ireland have concentrated on suffragists, nationalists, unionists or trade unionists. Women from the high-profile Hanna Sheehy-Skeffington and Mary MacSwiney to those who made up the Irish Women Workers Union have been given due recognition. The efforts of the social and political elite, such as those of Lady Aberdeen to improve public health and Lady Dudley's crucial sponsorship of district nurses, have also been restored to the historical record, as has the relentless campaigning of Ulster unionist women's organisations which meant that a majority of the signatories to the Solemn League and Covenant in 1912 were female.[5] Although Eileen Reilly has done some valuable research on women's voluntary work in these years, women and the Great War remain in the historical shadow. Thus, while we have an image of Cumann na mBan member, Nurse Elizabeth O'Farrell, carrying the surrender flag at the end of the Rising, we do not hear about the Voluntary Aid Detachment nurses who came to the aid of the dying and wounded Sherwood Foresters who were sent to Dublin to put down the Rising. While there are many photographs of Maud

Gonne MacBride in widow's weeds after 1916 campaigning on behalf of Sinn
Féin, we can only imagine what she looked like in her Red Cross uniform in
Argelès in France in 1914.[6] Yet, while the suffrage movement brought together
nationalist and unionist women (at least until 1912), and the nationalist and
unionist movements each brought together women of all social classes, war
work brought thousands of Irish women of all classes, religions *and* political
affiliations together.

NURSING AND THE MOBILISATION OF CHARITIES

Nursing was the most obvious and visible way in which women took part in
the war. One suffragist was not happy about this:

> Women have been asked to knit, to nurse, to collect
> tickets, to deliver letters, to make munitions, to do
> clerical work of any kind, but from any work in which
> they could utilise their intellectual gifts or show any
> powers of initiative, they have been and are [being]
> rigorously excluded.[7]

Many educated upper-class women were frustrated at being confined to
what they saw as women's traditional, supportive roles, but even a cursory
glance at diaries, letters and other accounts of women who nursed in this
conflict shows that their work gave plenty of scope for initiative and authority.

Nurses in the Great War were of two kinds, professionals and temporary
volunteers, the latter being known in Britain and Ireland as Voluntary Aid
Detachment (VAD) nurses.[8] The trained nurses usually had several years' experience in hospital and district work whereas the VADs' only training was a
three-month first-aid course with the Red Cross or St John's Ambulance. In
August 1914 a ship full of trained Irish military nurses set sail from Dublin
'amid scenes of the greatest enthusiasm'.[9] By the middle of the war, nurses
trained in Dublin's Mater Hospital were working in France, Britain, Salonika
and Palestine, some having come out of retirement to do so.[10] The Irish Local
Government Board reported a slight shortage of trained nurses in 1915, due to
nurses volunteering for the war. It is difficult to be precise about how many
Irish nurses served in military medical organisations abroad, let alone how

many tended to soldiers in Ireland. Because they joined British nursing organisations like the Queen Alexandra Imperial Military Nursing Service (QAIMNS), the First Aid Nursing Yeomanry, the Red Cross and others, it is difficult to count them, but the number 4,500 has been mentioned.[11] Certainly, Irish nurses were distinctive enough for one historian to identify them separately, even though organisations at the time did not do so.[12]

The experiences of two Irish nurses in the Great War, one a professional and one a VAD, give an idea of the kind of women who took up the challenge of overseas service. Catherine Black was a shopkeeper's daughter from Ramelton, Co. Donegal.[13] She went to England in 1901 to train as a nurse in The London Hospital in Whitechapel, and volunteered with the QAIMNS in 1916, at the age of 34. Marie Martin, the eldest daughter of a wealthy business family from Monkstown, Co. Dublin, was 23 when she was accepted to go to Malta as a VAD in 1915.[14] In Catherine Black's family, daughters, as well as sons, had to earn their living, but such economic independence was never expected of Marie Martin. Black was a Protestant and Martin a Catholic.

Black worked at various casualty clearing stations and general hospitals in France for the duration of the war, risking her life and health; one of her colleagues was killed and several others injured in a bombing raid. Marie Martin's account of her time as a VAD in Malta in 1915 describes with good humour her face swollen like putty from sandflies and mosquito bites and her arches fallen from so much standing that she had to have special supports fitted to her shoes. The work was anything but glamorous—dysentery and diarrhoea meant that sheets and linens were constantly being scrubbed. But most difficult of all was the emotional impact of seeing so many young men disabled and dying. Catherine Black said: 'you went into [a casualty clearing station] young and light-hearted. You came out older than any span of years could make you'. Senior nurses like Black had quite a lot of authority, and could influence the doctor on the all-important decision of whether a soldier was fit enough to return to the fighting. Nurses and matrons could also exercise their power in other ways. According to Westmeath soldier Edward Roe, of the East Lancashire regiment, some soldiers made themselves so obliging to matrons and nurses that they were allowed to stay in hospital, away from the fighting, indefinitely; convalescing in Basra, he lost his place in the hospital because a Scottish matron decided he was not swatting flies efficiently enough.[15]

Marie Martin, the only Irish VAD in her contingent in Malta, took a break in 1916, arriving home just after the Easter Rising; her mother sent out tea and stewed rhubarb to the British soldiers barricading their street in Monkstown. Shortly afterwards, Martin departed for a casualty clearing station at Hardelot, in northern France, finishing up around Christmas. She volunteered again for a Leeds hospital for war injured in 1918.

Rosabelle Osborne, another Donegal woman, and already a qualified nurse at the time of the Boer War, became matron-in-chief in Salonika in 1917, in charge of 26 hospitals.[16] Foreign service was so popular that a 50-bed hospital set up in Pau, southern France, under the patronage of the Duchess of Abercorn, wife of one of the leading unionist peers in Northern Ireland, had to turn volunteer nurses away, even though ability to speak French was one of the qualifications.[17]

More generally, the war required a massive mobilisation of the charitable activity that had become the particular domain of middle- and upper-class women. Catholic women proved as vigorous as Protestant women in this regard, and fund-raising, first-aid training, recruitment and provision of soldiers' comforts took place all over the island. A list of women who had aided the war effort, published towards the end of the war, contained as many Mrs and Misses as Ladies, a good mixture of Gaelic, Norman and 'New English' names, and a fair proportion of nurses, matrons and nuns.[18] Accounts of fund-raising and organisational meetings read like a roll-call of the landed and business elite of the country—Viscountess Powerscourt, Lady Arnott, Mrs O'Conor Donelan, the Marchioness of Headfort, Lady Clonbrock, Lady O'Connell, Lady Sophia Grattan Bellew, Mrs O'Grady (wife of The O'Grady, one of Limerick's oldest landed families) and many more.[19] Mary Donovan O'Sullivan, the first professor of history in University College Galway and president of the Galway Ladies Recruiting Society, declared in January 1916 that the 'only serious question before the country at present was the successful prosecution of the war' and urged women to encourage men to join. Her own husband and brothers were serving.[20]

There was plenty of war work to be done in Ireland itself. Soldiers wounded in Belgium and France who needed long-term care were usually shipped home to either Britain or Ireland, so new hospitals were set up, with a demand for nurses and VADs to work in them. Mr Pim, of the Dublin department store, Pim Brothers, gave Monkstown House for a military hospital, and similar donations were fairly common among wealthy people on the east coast.[21] There was a temporary hospital in Dublin Castle, despite the fears of 'Castle throat', a fatal infection put down to poor drainage; one bed was sponsored by the Irish Women's Suffrage and Local Government Association. Suffrage organisa-

163

tions, with the notable exception of the pacifist Irish Women's Franchise League headed by the Sheehy-Skeffingtons, supported the war. The Munster Women's Franchise League equipped an ambulance for France.[22]

Enthusiasm for war work seems to have been unbounded. Why would women in Ballygar, Co. Galway, for example, need to have been trained in first aid?[23] Yet trained they were, and when the Women's Emergency Committee in Cork City put on first-aid and invalid cookery classes in 1915, they were asked by women working in the city's laundries to run special evening classes for them. The Limerick City and County United Aid League was equally active in fund-raising and training. VADs from Trinity College Dublin 'helped to run a hostel for Belgian refugees' in Belvedere Place and worked in rotation for six-month stints in the temporary Mountjoy hospital. Comforts were also donated for wounded soldiers in Ireland. Gifts acknowledged by the Princess Patricia Hospital in Bray, Co. Wicklow, in October 1915 (which was run by the Red Cross and St John's Ambulance)—included (among many other things) weekly vegetables, eggs and honey from Miss Dease; vegetables and apples from the Countess of Carysfort; magazines from Lady Johnston; day and night shirts from the Tralee Women's National Health Red Cross Branch; tennis rackets from an optimistic Mrs Hewatt; and walking sticks from a more pessimistic Mrs Scales.[24] Kellett's drapers of Georges Street and Exchequer Street, Dublin, made the bizarre promise that one tenth of the purchase price of every 'cele-brated W.B. corset' would be handed to 'the War Fund': 'Ladies purchasing these much-appreciated Corsets will thus materially assist in the relief of distress now so prevalent'.[25]

Ladies, as we have seen, were able to help the war effort in ways that were far less passive than buying undergarments. Even the humble knitting of socks was one of the most important activities of all—soldiers' feet were woefully vulnerable, and washing and drying facilities were almost non-existent, so socks were, of necessity, almost disposable. They could never have enough of them. Knitting and sewing for the troops could also be carried on with the dual purpose of providing employment for those who needed it, as in the case of the Distressed Ladies Association of Dawson Street in Dublin: 'Good material is used and good making up is ensured. The patterns are authorised by the British Red Cross'. The kind of clothes made included shirts, bedjackets, pyjamas, nightshirts and 'helpless case garments'. Ladies were encouraged to order and pay for such articles, and thereby benefit both the distressed ladies and the soldiers and sailors.[26]

WOMEN WORKERS

Women from the urban working and lower-middle classes, and from the farming population, did not have much leisure to devote to organising war philanthropy, though as we have seen, some took an interest in first-aid classes and other war work, and many doubtless sent parcels to their menfolk who were serving. But the war affected them directly none the less. In other belligerent countries the Great War expanded jobs for women both in number and kind—the images of the smiling British bus 'conductorette' and the 'postie' (postwoman) are probably the most familiar.

The changes were not so dramatic in Ireland. Traditional patterns of female employment were not affected; domestic service and female agricultural labour remained buoyant throughout most of the country. Because conscription was never introduced here, and because unemployment and underemployment were so chronic, the men who served in the British forces left jobs that were for the most part filled immediately by other men. A letter-writer to the newspaper in 1915 recommended that shoppers should refuse to be served by men in Dublin shops, arguing that those men should either be in uniform or doing men's work to free other men to join up, but most Irish people do not seem to have followed this advice.[27] None the less, the war affected women's employment in many ways.

Women in the textile and shirt factories of the North, after an initial period of adjustment, saw their workforce increase by nearly 20% in 1916 compared to 1912 owing to the heightened demand for textiles generally and for items such as tents, haversacks and aeroplane cloth specifically.[28] This, along with the increased demand for shipbuilding and ancillary industries, meant that the north-east boomed, although high prices for basic foods and lengthened working hours meant that life was not easy, and health suffered.[29]

On the island as a whole, luxury trades were depressed and women were thrown out of work to the extent that two central committees on women's employment were set up, one in Ulster under Lady Aberdeen, and the other catering for Munster, Leinster and Connacht under the patronage of Lady Dufferin and Ava. A glove-making enterprise gave continuous work to about 250 women by 1917, while a toy-making business set up by the Women's Emergency Suffrage Council in 1915 was widely reported and applauded. The Women's National Health Association also set up relief work-rooms.[30] It is hoped that these women earned more than those in Donegal relief workshops in 1915 who were earning 10d per piece (in goods from the company shop)

165

plus a 'dinner' of bread and tea, for a piece of work which would have earned 15s in Dublin City before the war.[31] The Congested Districts Board encouraged people in the west to keep up their seasonal migration to Britain, so as to free British male labour for the war effort, but did nothing to guarantee wages or working conditions. Young women from Achill continued to go off on the harvest with their menfolk and to live in barns; 'There they eat, there they sleep, close and packed, there they sit if too wet to work …'.[32]

Irish people criticised the government for concentrating most of the munitions manufacturing in Britain. It was only after extensive negotiations and lobbying by John Redmond, for example, that a munitions factory was set up in Galway in 1917. The factory, which made 18-pounder shells, employed about 40 women or 'girls' who worked three eight-hour shifts.[33] The munitions factory on Parkgate Street, Dublin, which worked on a similar shift routine, had a nurse on full-time duty and a canteen staffed around the clock by lady volunteers.[34] But compared to Britain, France or Germany, the most distinctive war-time female worker, the *munitionette* who entered the male world of the arsenal and engineering factory to produce guns and shells on a vast scale was relatively rare, being a tiny minority of working women, especially outside the north-east.

In countries that endured the full impact of the industrial mobilisation for the war effort, women moved out of domestic service to better-paid employ-ment elsewhere. In Ireland, this did not happen. Advertisements for domestic servants in the 'Situations Vacant' columns did not increase appreciably between 1914 and 1918, or take on any note of desperation at the later date. Female agricultural labour was in such demand at certain times of the year that women and 'quite young' girls in 1915 could command between 1s 6d and 3s for a day's agricultural work.[35] Of its nature seasonal, 30 or so days of this work a year could add almost £5 to the annual income, which, if £1 a week is taken as an average for the unskilled labouring family in 1914, made a differ-ence. Male labourers could, of course, command much more.

LIVING STANDARDS AND DAILY LIFE

The impact of the war on living standards and daily life is dealt with in Chapter 5. But women's experience in this regard was not exactly the same as that of men, because of their role as mothers. Those who were deprived of a male bread-winner by military service, like their counterparts in Britain, received separation allowances which relieved the direst poverty; this was evidenced by the drop in numbers receiving relief from the Poor Law authorities in this period which fell by 13% between 1914 and 1918.[36] Separation allowances in February 1915 were 12s 6d weekly for the wife, and it was recommended that they be raised to 5s for the first child, 3s 6d for the second, and 2s each for the third and subsequent children; there were slight variations between army and navy payments.[37]

Countrywomen shared in the general wave of rural prosperity created by the war economy (see Chapter 5), whereas urban women had to balance increased wages (whether their own or those of their menfolk) against intense war-time inflation. Eggs were 2s a dozen in 1915;[38] a townswoman with three children on separation allowance could not have afforded enough of them to make a nutritional difference, while a family of rural labourers with the smallest cottage garden could keep hens and source milk locally. In the towns, milk was expensive—having increased over 66% in price between 1914 and 1915—and occasional convictions for the sale of adulterated milk ('nothing less than murder' according to a judge who sentenced a man to six months' hard labour for this offence) makes one wonder how many were never caught.[39]

Neither Irish nor British mothers and babies throve in war-time conditions. Irish infant mortality fluctuated between 87 and 88 per 1,000 births between 1914 and 1918, rising to 92 in 1915. (In England and Wales, infant mortality was higher, the numbers fluctuating between 110 and 97 in the same years.) Maternal mortality, a reliable indicator of poor female health and malnutrition, rose in Ireland from 3.23 per 1,000 births in 1914–15 to 5.51 in 1916, falling back to 4.80 in 1918. (In Britain the average maternal mortality for the years 1911–20 was not very different, at 4.7 per 1,000 births.) There were black spots around the country—Carlow, Donegal, Kilkenny, King's County (Offaly), Galway, Limerick in 1916, and in 1918, Armagh—where the death of mothers in childbirth was almost double the national figure. Women's increased vulnerability to puerperal fever, toxaemia and haemorrhage—the three major killers—can be attributed to poor nutrition, high blood pressure from anxiety and low iron levels.[40] The concern with working-class diet, living conditions and public health, which had absorbed the energies of many Irish upper-class and professional women since 1890, did not continue into the war years.[41] For example, the Omagh branch of the Women's National Health Association put its normal work to one side and sent its members gathering sphagnum moss for application to soldiers'

167

wounds.[42] How long this suspension of normal activity lasted we do not know, but it suggests that many maternalistic voluntary organisations may have turned their energies from mothers' and children's, to soldiers' and sailors' welfare.

Another diversion of female philanthropic and activist energy was the women's patrols. Set up with a strong feminist-suffragist input in 1915 on the grounds that there were no women police, these aimed to 'protect' young females by policing their behaviour on the streets. The patrollers, voluntary and paid, Protestant and Catholic, worked closely with the Dublin Metropolitan Police.[43] One patroller described the scenes around Dublin's north inner city on an evening in October 1915: 'the awful boldness of these men and girls appals one. They accost one another without, apparently, any shame ... I have turned my flashlight into dark doorways and corners in laneways and disclosed scenes that are truly indescribable'. Even though the writer went on to condemn the poverty that 'drove' girls into this kind of behaviour,[44] the strong message was that urban working-class girls and women were out of control. There was a similarly coercive attitude towards working-class women in war-time Britain.[45] The war years in Ireland did not see any rise in illegitimacy, infanticide, female drunkenness, child abandonment or other symptoms of social breakdown, and the patrollers seem to have been succumbing to a widespread moral panic.[46] While it emboldened women of all classes to participate in public life, the war did not challenge the authority of the 'lady' to shine flashlights on poorer women.

None the less, overall the war reinforced a sense of women's autonomy and maturity, albeit one still qualified by considerations of class and age. This was reflected in the changing female fashions of the war years. Gone forever, never to return, were multi-skirted, multi-petticoated, floor-length heavy clothes; a woman in the everyday clothes of 1918–19 seems a half-century rather than ten years away from the woman of 1908–09. From 1914 onwards the silhouette narrowed and skirts shortened, in contrast to the voluminous clothes of the previous decade.[47] Women wanted to be able to walk, cycle, get on and off buses, and hurry along crowded streets without making themselves conspicuous. Hair, still long, was swept back in a very simple style, hats were much smaller than the cartwheel styles of the first decade of the century, and the simple jacket-and-skirt combination became almost a uniform for the active woman.[48] Not by any stretch of the imagination pretty or frivolous, it conveyed serious intent and signalled competence.

THE LEGACY

At the end of the war, the Donegal nurse Catherine Black realised that because she had not spent any of her salary in France, she had saved quite a lot of money (this must have been true of many trained nurses). She kept on working, however, and by the 1930s acquired a job in the British royal household where she became known, predictably, as 'Blackie'. Dublin woman Marie Martin's experience of nursing abroad and her strong Christian faith led her first of all to Nigeria as a lay missionary with Bishop Joseph Shanahan, and then, after years of struggle, to the setting up of the Medical Missionaries of Mary. We know about these two women because each in her own way became famous, but there must have been many other Irish women whose untold experiences of work in the Great War led them to make unconventional or unusual life choices after it. All over Europe, the male mortality of the war years meant that more women then ever before had to adjust themselves to life without marriage and many of them managed to do this quite well. A debate in a woman's magazine in 1916 about whether love should be 'woman's whole existence' came down on the side that it should not. Women, it was argued, had gained their place in the world. Miss Maud White, from Holywood, Co. Down, gave her vision of women's future in 1915:

> The professional typist will take the place of the amateur pianist, and conducting a tramcar will be esteemed as maidenly as riding to hounds. The 10,000 women [in Britain and Ireland] who last week stretched forth willing hands to the Master of Munitions are the ancestors of a glorious race; they predict an age of fewer accomplishments and more achievements, fewer opinions and more convictions, fewer dilettantes and more scholars, fewer ladies and more women.[49]

This was gloriously optimistic, and with hindsight we can now see that it was premature. The legacy of the war for women has been the subject of much discussion by historians and feminists for countries such as Britain, France, Germany and the USA. Historians in Britain debate whether the 1918 Representation of the People Act, which gave the vote to women over 30 (with certain property qualifications) in the United Kingdom (including Ireland), was

169

due to their war service or the influence of the earlier suffrage agitation.[50] Women in the Irish Free State gained full political equality with men in the Constitution of 1922, six years before their counterparts in Northern Ireland and Great Britain; this had nothing to do with service in the Great War. In both jurisdictions, there was an increase in certain kinds of work for women—in independent Ireland alone in 1936, 18,000 more women in white-collar, retail, industrial and professional work than in 1926. Resentment of women 'taking men's jobs' was strong in Britain in these years, but it was stronger in Ireland where male unemployment was higher. Their extensive war work might have given individual women self-confidence and valuable experience, but its peculiar nature meant that the women who undertook it embarked upon the post-war years with the sense that paid work was either a privilege or an obligation, but never a right.[51]

While rights were under attack, however, women's new freedom of movement could not be taken away. Economic changes already in train before 1914 were reinforced by the exigencies of war to give women of all classes varying degrees of permission to operate independently of the family home. Young women in particular had never inhabited public space with such ease before, and this alarmed conservative commentators.[52] Whether the Great War was thanked or cursed for this social transformation, it played as much a part in the emergence of women's new freedoms in Ireland as in every other European country.

WOMEN

This page: Marie Martin, aged 23, in her VAD uniform, later foundress of the Medical Missionaries of Mary, pictured in Malta, 1915. Courtesy of MMM Image Library.

Following pages: NAI, 1096/10/20: Extract from letter to Mary Dyneley Vigors from her sister, Catie, 8 August (1916?). In it she details her duties nursing at the front, 'I think I am getting on pretty well & love it dearly, except the operations ... the Dr puts his hand inside the wound and brings out the interior by handfuls & lays it on the patient's chest!'.
Courtesy of the National Archives of Ireland.

Monday morning 3 AM
8 Aug. Coll. Cloisters

My Darling Mary

This is my third night running
on night duty! They have all been
full of excitement, but tonight especially, as we were rung up at 11 o'c
to say a new case was waiting in
a stretcher outside the gates! He
proves to be a "tommy" with a dis-
located elbow, but as he has been
tippling a bit he is very difficult
to manage, as it takes 2 of us
to hold him in bed, & we are rather
afraid he has put it out again in
his struggles! He is in great pain
poor fellow, & quite delirious. It is
simply delightful doing night duty
down here, as one is running about
in the open air nearly all night, & I
love watching the dawn as I take strolls
round the quadrangle & I enjoy doing
night duty very much & never feel in the
least drowsy, or done up the next

days. I think I am getting on at the work pretty well & love it dearly, except the operations which make me feel wretched. I go to the hospital for either night or day duty about 4 times a week: the day hours are from 7 till 12 in the morning, & 6 to 8 in the evening; the night hours are from 9 till 6. Six of us VAD's go a day & some of us are desperately keen — me, Maud Bambridge, the Mercers, Frends, & Myrtle. I've seen an operation for appendicitis which is pretty gruesome, as the Dr puts his hand inside the wound & brings out the interior by handfuls, & lays it out on the patient's chest! It is wonderful how neatly it is done, & also how little blood there is. I've seen about 6 others, but they all make me feel wretchedly ill, as I hate seeing the victim lying there being butchered, & not being able to do anything to help, & it is partly the atmosphere of the theatre too, as the warm temperature (70) & the

smell of the ether make it difficult to breathe

This page: 'Separation women' queuing for their allowance outside a post office on Aungier Street, Dublin, *c.* 1916. They were dependants of soldiers and were viewed with disdain for their perceived lack of morals (allegedly spending their allowance on alcohol) and after the 1916 Rising, their lack of patriotism. Courtesy of Keith Jeffery.

Right: TCD, OLS L-1-540: Separation allowance for wives and children of soldiers, 1 December 1915. Reproduced by permission of the Board, Trinity College Dublin.

46
————
1085

G.   R.

SEPARATION ALLOWANCE

FOR

WIVES AND CHILDREN OF SOLDIERS.§

WEEKLY RATES OF SEPARATION ALLOWANCE, INCLUDING THE USUAL ALLOTMENT OF PAY.

	Rank of Soldier.				
	Corporal and Private.	Serjeant.	Company Quartermaster-Serjeant.	Warrant Officer (Class II).	Warrant Officer (Class I).
	s. d.	s. d.	s. d.	s. d.	s. d.
Wife	*12 6	†15 0	†16 6	†22 0	†23 0
Wife and 1 child	*17 6	†20 0	†21 6	†27 0	†28 0
Wife and 2 children	*21 0	†23 6	†25 0	†30 6	†31 6
Wife and 3 children	*23 0	†25 6	†27 0	†32 6	†33 6
	and so on with an addition of 2s. for each additional child.				
Motherless child	5 0	5 0	5 0	5 0	5 0
Deduction if in public quarters with fuel and light	6 0	6 0	7 6	13 0	14 0

* These rates include an allotment of 6d. a day from the soldier's pay (*see* paras. 2 and 3).
† These rates include an allotment of 10d. a day from the soldier's pay (*see* paras. 2 and 3).

---

1. The total payment to the family, if the soldier makes the usual allotment from his pay, will be as shown in the above table. Any allotment above the usual rate which a soldier may make will be paid in addition.

ALLOTMENTS.

2. The rates of allotment are as follows :—
Soldiers not below the
rank of serjeant ... 5s. 10d. per week.
Other soldiers... ... 3s. 6d.   „

3. The allotment for the wife is compulsory in the case of a soldier serving abroad. In the case of a soldier serving at home, the allotment may be at a lower rate or withheld altogether if the wife's income without allotment reaches the amount in the table above. If the husband objects to making the usual allotment on the ground that his wife's income without allotment reaches the standard rate, the Paymaster will notify the wife and tell her what to do.

CHILDREN.

4. Separation Allowance is payable for children up to the age of 16 years.

It may also be paid for children up to the age of 21, suffering from mental or physical infirmity and, on the recommendation of the Local Education Authority, for apprentices receiving not more than a nominal wage, or children over 16 while in attendance as day pupils at Secondary Schools, Technical Schools or Universities.

LONDON ALLOWANCE.

5. In the case of wives of soldiers who at the date of enlistment were married, and

§ A separate pamphlet is published relating to separation allowance for the dependants of unmarried soldiers (and widowers).

(B 5012) Wt. w. 13321—6771 730M 12 15 H & S G.15/1421.

[P.T.O.

COMFORTS FOR TROOPS.

SOCKS

FROM IRISH FRIENDS.

——•••—— *Jan 6/15*

RECEIVED FROM

The Women of Leighlinbridge
& Mrs E. C Vigors
with very many thanks.

——————— *20* Pr. of Socks.

J. Currie
Hon Sec
M. J

12 Merrion Square,

•

This page: NAI, 1096/10/20: An acknowledgement of the receipt of socks for the troops sent by 'the women of Leighlinbridge and Mrs E.C. Vigors', 6 January 1915. This was one of the ways in which women could make a tangible contribution to the war effort. Soldiers' socks rotted on their feet in the waterlogged trenches causing these items to be virtually disposable.
Courtesy of the National Archives of Ireland.

Right: NLI, Ephemera Collection, WAR/1914-18/16: 'Have you any women folk worth defending?', *c.* 1915. Women symbolised the hapless victims of the enemy while at the same time acting as the voice of moral duty to men. Courtesy of the National Library of Ireland.

•

Have YOU any women-folk worth defending?

Remember the Women of Belgium

JOIN TO-DAY

THE IRISH WOMEN'S ASSOCIATION

(to aid Irish Regiments and Prisoners of War),

Telephone No.
Park 4139.

KENSINGTON PALACE, LONDON, W. 8.

10444 Per Mc Grath.

JUN 1918

Re _____

BRITISH PRISONER OF WAR,
KRIEGSGEFANGENENLAGER,

Limburg Lahn

c/o G.P.O. Mount Pleasant.

GERMANY.

DEAR {SIR, MADAM,

In reply to your letter of _____ received the name of the above-mentioned Prisoner of War was put on our books } on *to-day* from which will be put on our books }

date the maximum amount of food permitted by the present official rules will be {has been} sent to him; that maximum being 30 lbs. of food and 12 lbs. of bread per fortnight (see description of parcels marked A, B, C).

Each Grocery parcel costs   6/6 per fortnight.
,,   Bread   ,,   3/9 ,,   ,,
,,   parcel of extra smokes costs 2/6 ,,   ,,

If you wish, and can afford, to subscribe towards his parcels we shall be very glad. If you cannot afford the whole price of a parcel send us whatever you can afford, and the parcel shall be sent to him in your name, and he will acknowledge it direct to you. If you can afford to send a certain sum fortnightly (no matter how small the sum) a parcel shall be sent regularly in your name. The Prisoners greatly appreciate this personal touch, which forms for them a link with Home. If you cannot afford to subscribe anything the parcels will be sent from the Funds of this Association.

CLOTHING.—The following outfit is sent to each Prisoner of War when he is captured, and is renewed at stated intervals.

1 pair Boots.	3 pairs Socks.	1 Suit.	1 Kit Bag.
1 pair Canvas Shoes.	2 pairs Pants.	1 Cardigan.	Handkerchiefs.
1 pair Gloves.	2 Shirts.	1 Great Coat.	Towels.
1 pair Braces.	2 Vests.	1 Cap.	Needles and Mending.

PLEASE NOTE—According to official rules, NO EXTRA clothing of any description may be sent in excess of the above-mentioned outfit.

PLEASE NOTE for ALL future reference that, according to official rules, no Fund or Association may accept ANY PARCEL OR ARTICLE WHATSOEVER for transmission to a Prisoner of War. The contents of every parcel sent must be drawn EXCLUSIVELY from the stores of each Association or packing depôt.

The only parcel which may be sent direct to a Prisoner of War by a private individual is the "Personal Parcel" which may be sent to each man once in three months. Instructions regarding this parcel and the coupon for it will be sent from this Association to the NEXT-OF-KIN on their written application ONLY. The next-of-kin are strongly urged to send this most necessary and greatly appreciated parcel as soon as they have the Prisoner's definite address.

When a newly captured Prisoner writes on a dark blue post-card giving his address as LIMBURG, this must NOT be taken as the definite address, and the "Personal Parcel" should not be sent until the Prisoner of War sends some address other than that shewn on the dark blue post-card. Letters may be sent on chance to this Limburg address, but NOT the Personal Parcel.

If he followed any trade or profession before joining the Army please send me the name and address of his employers.

If he should ask for anything special let me know and we will always try and send it to him if possible, and please let me know every change of his address AT ONCE.

Each Prisoner of War is allowed to write four post-cards and two letters a month under normal conditions, but this privilege can be, and often is, stopped, so if you do not get letters for a few weeks there is no cause for anxiety. You can write to the Prisoner as often as you like, but one or two letters and one post-card a week is best. Post-cards get through quicker than letters, so we advise one being sent each week. When writing NO mention must be made of the War or of politics, or of the situation in England; no stamps are necessary, all letters must be left open and can be posted at your nearest post-office.

Please remember that you will not get an acknowledgment from a Prisoner of War, for any parcel, under six or eight weeks.

No current papers or magazines may be sent—all printed matter for Prisoners of War must be sent either from the publishers or from the—

CAMPS LIBRARY ASSOCIATION, 45, Horseferry Road, Westminster, London, S.W. 1.

It is ABSOLUTELY NECESSARY to mention the NUMBER, NAME and REGIMENT of the Prisoner of War in question every time you write to this Association.

I hope you will not be unduly worried or anxious about him, for we will look after him in every way possible. We take the deepest interest in all our men; they all write to us constantly, and we write to them, and are only too glad to help them to the utmost of our power.

Yours faithfully,
(Signed) ANNE MacDONNELL,
Hon. Secretary.

178

179

This page: Left to right: Misses O'Kelly, Murragh, O'Farrell, Roe and Johnson. Five female public servants in the styles of the later years of the Great War. Hair is pulled back and put up, and has not yet been bobbed or shingled, the skirts are high-waisted and probably near-ankle length, but the style is recognisably that of the modern 'white-blouse' office worker. Courtesy of Eithne McCormack.

Left: NAI, 1096/10/20: Letter re what to send to POWs from the Irish Women's Association (to Aid Irish Regiments and Prisoners of War) to Mrs Vigors, June 1918. The Honorary Secretary, Anne MacDonnell, closes with 'I hope you will not be unduly worried or anxious about him, for we will look after him in every way possible'. Courtesy of the National Archives of Ireland.

'Conscription! No woman must take a man's job', c. 1916. A banner hung from the offices of the Irish Women's Franchise League (co-founded by Hanna Sheehy-Skeffington) illustrates the fervent opposition to any introduction of conscription as well as concerns at feminine erosion of traditionally masculine jobs. © Getty Images.

CHAPTER 7

War, work and labour

NIAMH PUIRSÉIL

'Starvation', *The Leader*, September 1914. Courtesy of the Board, Trinity College Dublin.

In 1914 when it seemed that a Home Rule parliament was merely months away, the Irish Trades' Union Congress (ITUC)[1] added the words 'and Labour Party' to its title. The decision to establish a political wing had been made two years earlier, and but it was only in late July of 1914 that its leaders began fund-raising for the forthcoming election. The outbreak of war one week later put an end to Home Rule for the time being, and to Labour's entrance onto the political stage.

Far from hindering Labour's advance, however, the timing probably benefited the fledgling party, since it is difficult to exaggerate the problems faced by the trade union movement at this point. Established in 1894, the ITUC was no more than a talking shop, dominated by elite unions of craft workers with little or no political or industrial influence. New trade unionism, which saw unskilled and general workers organised into militant unions had grown in the years immediately prior to the war. The Irish Transport and General Workers Union (ITGWU), established in 1909, is the best example of such unions, but the Dublin lockout of 1913 had brutally and decisively ended this militant upsurge.

ECONOMIC IMPACT OF THE WAR

The war brought considerable economic gains to Ireland, but these were concentrated in certain geographical areas and industrial sectors. The British war economy was geared towards munitions, supplies and food. Thus, workers who were involved in these industries would have a 'good' war but those who were not would have a mixed experience. Naturally, in Ireland agriculture reaped immediate benefits, with the 1914 harvest receiving the highest prices since the 1880s.[2] But without rationing and caps on food prices, consumers soon found themselves at a loss. Only weeks into the war, the National Executive of the ITUC issued a manifesto to the workers of Ireland entitled 'Why should Ireland starve?' that called for controls of the food supply and castigated Irish farmers as 'profit-mongering crows'.[3] 'To the men of our class who are armed', it announced, 'we say keep your arms and use them if necessary. If God created the fruits of the earth He created them for you and yours'. The militancy of the manifesto was not reflected in any action at the time, however, and this was merely the first of many unheeded calls from the executive on the problem of prices and food.

Apart from food supplies, the main economic contribution to the war effort came from the shipyards of Belfast where Harland and Wolff not only built naval vessels but also converted passenger liners into military ships. War work saw the numbers employed in Harland and Wolff increase to around 25,000 while smaller yards also benefited to the point where 37,000 were employed in shipbuilding in Belfast.[4] Elsewhere in the North, the linen mills and shirt factories were fully stretched fulfilling military contracts. Between the industrial north-east and prospering farmers, the war ushered in an economic boom.

Yet the boom benefited only existing industries. From the summer of 1915, when the Ministry of Munitions was established, an effort to spur output resulted in national ordnance factories being established across Britain. Ireland, however, was largely overlooked. Home Rule MPs and local pressure groups called for Ireland to be given its 'share' of manufacturing armaments, but, in the short term, only a few 'minor contracts' were secured.[5] It has been suggested that this was because employers in Britain and in Ulster were determined to 'freeze nationalist Ireland out of lucrative contracts' to keep the south deindustrialised,[6] but when it came to munitions, northern firms fared no better.[7]

The truth is that there was no practical reason to situate munitions factories in Ireland and there were significant logistical and security reasons why it would be quite inadvisable. By the winter of 1917 only five state-run National Factories had been established in Ireland—in Dublin, Waterford, Cork and Galway—employing 2,148 people.[8] Most of these munitions workers were women since the government was determined that the creation of new jobs should not deter men from signing up. The contract signed by the Dublin Dockyard Company, for instance, stipulated that not more than 5% of the total staff could be men or boys.[9] In other factories, the proportion of men was greater, but women, doing the unskilled work, remained in the majority. It is hard to overestimate the comparative significance of the low level of munitions output in Ireland: what in many other war-time societies proved one of the most dynamic developments, affecting everything from gender relations (with the ubiquitous *munitionnette*) to the power and political clout of organised labour, was largely absent.

Yet Ireland did share in the wider phenomenon of economic uncertainty in the first few weeks of the war.[10] In most cases, the fall in demand was temporary, but the alcohol industry was hit more seriously. Excessive alcohol consumption was an issue that concerned most combatant states, and was a particular preoccupation of David Lloyd George who was Chancellor of the Exchequer in 1914–15. Believing that 'munitions and materials are even more important than men', Lloyd George felt that excessive drinking was diminishing their quality and output and he highlighted in particular the mischief caused 'in northern yards' by 'the drinking of raw, cheap spirits of a fiery quality'.[11] On 29 April 1915 he announced to the House of Commons that he planned to introduce supertaxes on whiskey, beer and wine in an effort to curb demand. In 1912 the brewing and malting sector was the largest industrial contributor to gross domestic output in the 26 counties, and distilling was also an important employer.[12] In Dublin, Guinness had a workforce of around 3,500. In any event, the supertaxes were shelved in favour of the compulsory bonding of all spirits under three years of age under the Defence of the Realm Act.[13] There followed legal efforts to curb alcohol consumption such as the reduction of opening hours in public houses and a 'no treat order' which prohibited buying rounds. There were also further restrictions on output, which included the Output of Beer (Restriction) Act in the autumn of 1916 and at its most extreme, the complete closure of pot distilleries such as Powers in 1917.[14] By 1918 Irish brewing output was half of what it had been in 1916.[15] These actions led to large scale redundancies not only in the breweries and distilleries but also in their suppliers. For instance, one round of restrictions introduced in 1917 resulted in 300 men being let go at the bottle works at Ringsend.[16] Those lucky enough to remain employed were left in a profoundly insecure position, only one food order away from destitution or the front.

Recruiters were quick to exploit this insecurity. The Director of National Service in Ireland assured the thousands of men threatened with the loss of their jobs that he was 'anxious to find employment for them' but was 'still unable to present any definite prospect of it'. Bryan Mahon, Lieutenant–General Commanding in Chief of the Forces in Ireland stepped into the breach and in a public letter to the *Irish Times* declared that 'their services will be gladly accepted in the ranks of any of our Irish regiments, or, if skilled workers, in [… the] technical corps'. He also brought their attention to increased separation and dependants' allowances 'which together with their pay, food, clothing etc., will be found to compare favourably with the amount they would receive in civil employment'.[17]

Of course, even without the additional push factors of the war, the economic impetus to enlist was very strong, not least since the conflict broke out only six months after the Dublin lockout had ended. The lockout had exacted a heavy toll on the ITGWU as an organisation but even more so on its members. The union, under the direction of James Connolly, was vehemently opposed to the war and waged a vigorous campaign against its members joining up. It was difficult to compete with the inducements that the recruiting officers put before them, which included the promise of a steady army income, along with separation allowances for their families. Amidst the efforts to appeal to men's patriotism in the enlistment campaign, the financial benefits for their families were prominent. By the spring of 1915 some 2,500 members of the union, amounting to nearly half its membership at the time, had enlisted and one officer in the 16th Division noted that many of the men signing up were 'real toughs […] Larkinites enticed to join the colours by the prospect of good food and pay, which was welcome to them after months of semi-starvation during the great strike of 1913 and 1914'.[18] The over-representation of working class soldiers in the ranks was noted unfavourably by Irish recruiters. They feared that the numbers of labourers enlisting was falling because they resented the failure of the farming and commercial classes to 'share the burden of the war', something that recruiters felt was due to the high ratio of working-class soldiers putting off middle-class recruits.

> We are satisfied that a much larger number of recruits could be obtained from the [farming and commercial classes] if it were not for their reluctance to enter upon their *training* with recruits from the labouring classes. This class prejudice is probably much more pronounced in Ireland than elsewhere in the United Kingdom.[19]

INDUSTRIAL RELATIONS AND THE LABOUR MOVEMENT

Socialist and labour organisations across Europe had condemned the slide towards militarism in the years before the war. When the war actually broke out, however, deep divisions emerged. Those who continued to oppose the conflict were in the minority, while the majority rowed in behind their respective governments. In this, the parliamentary Labour Party in Britain was typical, with the British Trade Union Congress (BTUC) committing itself to industrial peace for the duration of the war .[20]

The situation in Ireland, however, was quite different. There was a split on the war but it was based on nationalist rather than socialist lines and opponents of the conflict were very much in the majority in the labour movement. While unionist-organised labour for the most part supported the war, nationalist trade unionists viewed the confrontation as a British war against a British enemy; as James Connolly often asserted at this time, unlike Britain, Germany had never done Ireland any harm. As the banner on the front of the ITGWU headquarters at Liberty Hall put it: 'We serve neither King nor Kaiser, but Ireland'. The ITUC was an all-Ireland body, and splits on political questions were avoided when possible, with the result that while Congress's executive was clearly against the war, it was less strident in its opposition than might be expected. The desire to avoid disagreement actually led to the 1915 annual congress being cancelled. [21]

Nevertheless, while Congress wished to avoid internal discord over the war an industrial truce was out of the question given the importance of war-related issues, notably conscription and inflation. Although the government did not impose conscription on Ireland in 1916, the Irish unions identified economic conscription (meaning various controls on workers) as almost equally pernicious. When the Dublin Chamber of Commerce met in September 1914, their president, Richard K. Gamble, impressed upon those gathered the need for employers to encourage and facilitate the enlistment of their workforce. Employers should keep workers' jobs open on their return from war and explain to them that the uncertainty of trade during the conflict meant that they could not be assured that they could retain their jobs if they stayed.[22] Many companies did so, and also offered considerable allowances to the families of men who joined up, although some employers took a considerably more active approach by dismissing workers in an effort to compel enlistment.[23]

The other issue that occupied the labour movement was workers' welfare and specifically the problems caused by the continued rise in the cost of living. Congress campaigned against soaring food prices to little avail, but when the unions eventually moved on wages, they met with greater success. Before war broke out, organised labour had been, in David Fitzpatrick's description, 'abnormally docile in every sector of industry'.[24] Although the Transport Union was still struggling under the debts and low morale left by the lockout, circumstances began to swing in the workers' favour in 1916 owing to two factors.

Firstly, there was a radical change in how industrial relations operated. Under the 1915 Munitions Act, strikes in war factories were banned outright while all other industries required three weeks' strike notice with disputes being put to mandatory arbitration. Although the legislation frightened the unions at the beginning, its benefits soon became obvious. The act forced employers to the bargaining table where otherwise they might have resorted to a pre-emptive lockout or simply waited for the strike pay to run out, which it inevitably did. The Munitions Act meant that the number of strikes increased, but so too did the number of negotiations and settlements. Unsurprisingly, the act was fiercely resented by employers, who complained that bureaucrats were meddling in their businesses, while on balance the results for labour were positive.[25] For the unions, nothing succeeded like success. Compulsory arbitration created an entirely new momentum in the movement and membership snowballed. For instance, when a strike by Irish railwaymen in November 1916 resulted in the government assuming central control of the Irish railway system and the payment to workers of a war bonus, membership of the National Union of Railwaymen increased dramatically from 5,000 to 17,000.[26]

The second key war-time development was the growing scarcity of manpower which, as in other belligerent states, reinforced the bargaining power of organised labour—even in the absence (in the Irish case) of a major munitions sector. The labour market tightened further with the introduction of conscription in Britain in 1916.[27] Membership of the ITGWU expanded from 5,000 in 1916 to 120,000 in 1920, while the numbers in craft and clerical unions also grew significantly, so that by 1920 the ICTU represented 225,000 workers compared with 100,000 four years earlier.[28]

Along with membership, militancy was also on the rise as workers threatened or engaged in strikes in the face of strong war-time inflation. In a single day in October 1916, for instance, the *Irish Times* reported a threatened strike by bakers and strikes by gasworkers, grave-diggers and coal-porters in Dublin, although a strike by railwaymen on the Great Southern and Western Railway had just been resolved.[29] Members and militancy in turn fed the proliferation of trade union organisations—a development that was particularly evident in the ITGWU once the Rising had been crushed and Connolly's preoccupation with the politics of nationalist insurrection ended in his execution.

The combination of farming profits, labour shortages and state regulation also extended labour organisation into the normally quiescent sector of the landless agricultural workers. The Corn Production Act to establish guaranteed prices for wheat and oats was introduced in January 1917 and finally became law in August. Its progress through parliament had been hindered by conservative farming interests who opposed its provisions for a minimum wage for agricultural labourers, which would be looked after by an Agricultural Wages Board, as well as the capping of workers' hours and rent, so that farmers could not recoup the higher wages by increasing the cost of their workers' accommodation.[30]

Farm workers were difficult to organise,[31] but the establishment of the Agricultural Wages Board provided the ITGWU with an opportunity to make a breakthrough. In the spring of 1917 it declared the organisation of the agricultural workers to be a key objective, and by the autumn, new members flocked to the union.[32] Even if some felt that the Wages Board rates were too low, market forces caused pay rates to rise as the government instructed farmers to switch to tillage to increase the food supply, resulting in acute demand for farm labour. The wages movement in agriculture only matured in 1919 but war-time conditions had provided the spur for effective organisation of one of the largest and most exploited sectors of the Irish workforce. By 1920 60,000 agricultural workers belonged to the ITGWU.[33]

Women workers also benefited from the war, including those in historically under-organised industries, such as linen. In 1914 the Belfast-based Textile Operatives' Society of Ireland and the Flax Roughers and Yard Spinners had a combined membership of 3,000—about one tenth of its potential membership at the time—but by the end of the conflict, membership of the two unions came to some 20,000.[34] The smaller new sectors were also represented; with women working in the munitions industry being represented by the London-based National Federation of Women Workers which also included women in the food-processing industries as well as textiles in its members. Another British-based union, the Amalgamated Society of Tailors and Tailoresses, which had recently (if reluctantly) expanded into garment factories, represented thousands of women workers in Ireland by the war's end.[35] In contrast, the Irish Women Workers' Union, the sister union of the ITGWU, failed to expand its organisation or membership to any significant degree. Like the Transport Union it had been hard hit by the lockout, but it was also ravaged by personality disputes and distracted by national issues, hindering its ability to similarly recover.

Overall, the struggle to organise industrially and to raise wages was a success. Practically every section of the workforce secured wage increases, often through negotiation, even if these still trailed the cost of living .[36] Workers also dealt with the problem of profiteering on food supplies by establishing co-operatives such as the 'Workers' Bakery' formed by locked-out bakers in Tralee, Co. Kerry, which widened their sphere of activism and broadened their tactics.[37] Indeed, this period saw a significant rise in local cohesion with the formation of trades' councils in most towns across the country. Efforts to overcome the food crisis in effect broadened workers awareness, diversified trade union activity and strengthened the solidarity of the labour movement.[38]

THE POLITICS OF LABOUR

The labour movement had been tangentially involved in the crisis of nationalist politics provoked by the Rising in 1916, most notably through the leadership of Connolly and the role of the Irish Citizen Army. The following year the failed socialist peace conference at Stockholm followed by the second Russian revolution—which culminated in its socialist leader, Vladimir Lenin, taking Russia out of the war—affected the more radical Socialists. In early 1918, for example, the Socialist Party of Ireland (SPI), founded by Connolly long before the war and re-established after the first Russian Revolution in 1917, celebrated the November Revolution with a mass meeting in Dublin's Mansion House at which around 10,000 people 'hailed with delight the advent of the Russian Bolshevik Revolution'.[39] The SPI proclaimed that the revolution had 'fearlessly challenged the British people to loosen its [sic] grip upon Ireland'. But in 1918 what loosened Britain's grip was not radical socialism (a distinctly minority cause in Ireland) but a renewed crisis in nationalist politics.

Russia's withdrawal from the war and the punitive peace imposed by the German military on the Bolsheviks the following March paved the way for the Kaiser's last throw—the spring offensive on the West Front whose initial blow fell on British troops, including the 16th (Irish) and the 36th (Ulster) Divisions, provoking the collapse of the Fifth Army. The political impact of this military crisis on Ireland was acute and instantaneous as the Cabinet decided that conscription must now be imposed on Ireland in a desperate search for more soldiers to counteract an impending German victory. The British Labour members of the government warned against extending conscription to Ireland before Home Rule had been introduced; Lloyd George compromised and tied conscription to the renewed promise of Home Rule.[40]

In Ireland itself, conscription on any terms was unacceptable both to the Irish MPs and to nationalist opinion, so its eventual introduction without reference to Home Rule in April 1918 merely compounded Irish people's anger. The ITUC was at the forefront of national resistance, joining with the Irish Parliamentary Party, the All-for-Ireland League and Sinn Féin in the anti-conscription conference in the Mansion House, while the Catholic hierarchy actively supported the campaign. In a clear echo of the Ulster Solemn League and Covenant of 1913, the Mansion House conference drew up 'Ireland's solemn League and covenant—a national pledge', which vowed that conscription would be opposed 'by the most effective means at our disposal'.[41]

A united front was vitally important in this campaign, but the Congress also worked alone, using both its political contacts and industrial strength to good effect. Relations between the British and Irish labour movements had deteriorated during the 1913 lockout following Jim Larkin's failure to convince the British unions to strike in sympathy with the Dublin workers, and were never effectively rebuilt afterwards. Now the channels of communication were opened once again over the issue of conscription. On 10 April, the day after the bill had been introduced in the House of Commons, Thomas Johnson and Cathal O'Shannon travelled to London to meet members of the BTUC executive to discuss the matter. This resulted in a statement of support from the British body,[42] though it clearly had little effect on the passage of the bill and there was some resentment that only a handful of Labour MPs had voted against the measure.[43] Efforts to engage Labour's fraternal links did not end there, but the Irish unions decided a show of strength would prove more effective.

On 20 April 1,500 delegates at a special Labour convention backed a call to hold a general strike three days later on Tuesday, 23 April. One of the first general strikes to take place in western Europe, the action was 'most complete and thorough' with only banks, the law courts and government offices operating that day.[44] Because the issue was not industrial and because the politics were those of nationalism, not socialism, many employers backed their workers, although some threatened lockouts or even dismissal if employees participated.[45] The success of the strike was remarkable, not least because it was organised so rapidly and effectively despite heavy press censorship.[46] Workers protested at hundreds of meetings across the country, including 30,000 in Cork City, although fear of retaliation by the authorities inhibited gatherings in Dublin.[47] The call to strike had been heeded almost universally with one vital exception. In the north-east, it was business as usual. Belfast and its surrounding counties were committed to the war effort and the cleavage on the issue that the Congress had worked so hard to avoid opened up.

The united political and religious front, the signing of the anti-conscription pledge by hundreds of thousands, and the success of the general strike made the depth of opposition quite clear. In a misguided effort to convince workers to abandon their stance, the pro-war Labour MP and general secretary of the National Union of Railwaymen, J.H. Thomas, came to the Mansion House in Dublin to address members on conscription—he met with a predictable response.[48] When Irish Labour representatives travelled to London the following day, they fared a little better, convincing the British Labour Party to issue an appeal against conscription in Ireland 'on the grounds of principle and expediency alike' and arguing that 'the passage of the Conscription Act has done more to cement the National unity than any other act could have done'.[49] Although its appeal was unable to influence the government, its diagnosis was accurate. The strength of resistance in Ireland made it impossible to impose conscription, and while the Irish labour movement was only one component of the campaign, the power conferred on it by the war economy endowed it with vital muscle for the nationalist cause. The relationship, moreover, proved recip-rocal as the success of the strike further boosted ITGWU membership.[50]

The period following the strike represented the zenith of trade union mem-bership and confidence in Ireland, and when the annual congress of the ITUC met in Waterford that August, the atmosphere was electric. The strike seemed to have shown labour's potential and as the chairman William O'Brien told delegates, 'we shall not hurriedly neglect that lesson [...] that a solid, united and determined working class acting as one man [...] can bring to a standstill the whole industrial life of the country and all government'.[51] Bolstered by recent events, Congress decided to renew its political action, renaming itself the Irish Labour Party and Trade Union Congress, and mandated the National Executive to draft a new constitution. In early September the executive decided to field candidates in the election that would follow the war. By the time the conflict had ended, however, the country went to the polls for the first time in seven years with Labour withdrawing from the contest rather than affecting the Sinn Féin vote.

In conclusion, the Great War both transformed the situation of the Irish labour movement and delivered some harsh lessons on its margins of political manoeuvring in a society still divided more by nationalism than by class. In comparison with Britain and other major industrial societies, the war had relatively little impact on the nature of the Irish economy. Crucially, there was no break-neck expansion in engineering, chemicals and metallurgy—the industries of the post-war future—and no industrial transformation of the relatively un-industrialised bulk of the country. Nevertheless, labour's position at the end of the war was incomparably stronger to that before the conflict. The rise in prices and the unequal benefits derived from the war-time economy encouraged workers to organise and take action, while legislation, particularly the Munitions Act and the establishment of the Agricultural Wages Board, compelled employers to participate in industrial relations' processes where workers' demands which had previously been ignored with impunity could not be any more. This increased labour organisation and revived militancy in a movement that had been shattered following the Dublin lockout.

Ireland was a 'semi-detached' part of the United Kingdom, which made its society detached from the war. Although some 210,000 Irishmen fought in the conflict, the war did not have anything like the same impact on Irish society as a whole as it did in Britain. Ireland and Britain differed not only in the extent to which the war changed society but also in the nature of that change. Although it ought not be exaggerated, the war had something of a levelling impact on British society since four years of bloodletting created, as Jay Winter has noted, 'a bond of bereavement which transcended distinctions of class or caste'.[52] This is not to suggest that the war ended class distinctions—far from it. The sacrifice of war opened the way for a new era of social reform and socialist reformism—the idea of establishing a 'land fit for heroes'. This con-tributed to Labour's displacement of the Liberals as the alternative force in British politics and to the achievement of a goal unthinkable only ten years earlier—the Labour-led government of 1923–4.[53]

There were no echoes of this in Ireland. The Home Rule parliament that might have provided a framework for it never materialised. Conscription was never enforced because by 1918 it represented for most nationalists the impo-sition of a blood-sacrifice not by the Irish nation but by a foreign state. Yet without it, enlistment patterns outside Ulster tended to be divided along two lines: religion and class. In effect, it was Protestants and working-class men who joined the colours while middle-class Catholics, for the most part, abstained. Rather than a 'bond of bereavement' being established in Ireland, the war actually widened the divisions between the classes.

The Irish experience of the Great War as a war fought by certain classes and not others was also reflected in the impact of the conflict on Irish workers at home. The war boosted the agricultural economy and provided large profits in

193

certain industries, but it was working-class families who bore the brunt of food shortages and increased prices as wages failed to keep pace with war-time inflation. It was precisely this situation, and the action of workers to tackle it, that brought the Irish trade union movement back from the brink of extinction to its strongest position yet. However, in the unresolved crisis of Irish relations with Britain, this industrial power (and the distinctive 'syndicalism' to which it gave rise) could not readily be translated into an autonomous Labour politics, let alone radical socialism. As the war ended, the Congress party began to prepare once again to step onto the political stage, from an apparently far stronger position than in 1914. This time it was organised, this time it was ready. But Labour was prevailed upon to stand aside by Sinn Féin. Had it not done so, who can say how it would have fared. But unlike the false start in 1914, this was a setback from which Labour would never recover.

List of the ages of Private John Mooney's children sent to him by his wife, Roseanne, c. 1918. Mooney joined the 12th Reserve Cavalry on the 20 August 1914 in Thomas Street, Dublin, at the age of 39 (although he appears to have claimed to be 29). He was a member of the Ancient Order of Hibernians and was spurred to enlist when Germany invaded Belgium. Private collection. Courtesy of Peter Mooney

NOTHING is to be written on this side except the date and signature of the sender. Sentences not required may be erased. If anything else is added the post card will be destroyed.

I am quite well.

~~I have been admitted into hospital~~
~~{ sick)~~ ~~and am going on well.~~
~~{ wounded)~~ ~~and hope to be discharged~~ soon

~~I am being sent down to the base.~~

I have received your { letter dated *Wet 21*
~~telegram~~ ,, _____
~~parcel~~ ,, _____

Letter follows at first opportunity.

I have received no letter from you *Wet 1st or 2nd*
{ lately.
{ for a long time.

Signature } *J Mooney*
only. }

Date *6/8/15*

[Postage must be prepaid on any letter or post card addressed to the sender of this card.]

(25540) Wt.W3497-293 1,130m. 6/15 M.R.Co.,Ltd.

Field postcard from John Mooney to his wife, 6 August 1915. Cards, such as this one, were sometimes all that soldiers were allowed to send home. That which didn't apply was crossed out and very little was added apart from the date and their signature. Private collection. Courtesy of Peter Mooney.

get a pass you will send
me back the four i would
be very thankfull if you could
sent it to me if you cant ge
mony as i am very hard up
very thing is so dear all the
children is well and wishes to
be remembred to you
from Your Loven Wife Mor
X V † † †

Extract from a letter to John Mooney, from his wife, *c.* 1916. In it, she asks him to send her some money (£4) if he cannot get a pass home 'as I am very hard up everything is so dear'. Private collection. Courtesy of Peter Mooney.

13

2.9/15

WILL.

In event of my death

I give the whole of my prope

and effects to:- to My Wil

Roseanne Mooney

53 Bridgefort St

Dublin

John Mooney

Private no 3/1906

3/Leicester Re

15·8·15

Will of John Mooney, 15 August 1915. Enlisted men were required to draft a will to avoid complications upon death. By now Mooney had been transferred into the 8th Battalion Leicestershire Regiment as the generals recognised that the employment of cavalry was useless on the Western Front. Private collection. Courtesy of Peter Mooney.

(1)

next of kin and address.

mrs. Rose, anne. Mooney do.
55. Bredgefoot St. Dublin

(2)

Person to whom compulsory
allotment or stoppage is
payable to:-. Mrs. Rose—
Anne Mooney do. 55.
Bridgefoot St. Dublin

Extract from a letter to John Mooney, from his wife, c. 1917. In it she tells him that he might
'give over his wild ways' now that he has been wounded. Private collection.
Courtesy of Peter Mooney.

John Mooney's orders to return home, 18 February 1918. By now his family had moved from
Bridgefoot Street, Dublin, to Thomas Street. Private collection. Courtesy of Peter Mooney.

(9 25 40)—W372—M1960 150,000 9/17 HWV(M1351)   Forms/W3201/2   **Army Form W. 3201.**

(in pads of 50.)

FOR USE IN THE CASE OF A SOLDIER SENT TO HIS HOME

18 FEB. 1918   From a Hospital or Unit as "Medically Unfit."

8/ Leicestershire **(Regiment).**

No. *8065*, Rank *Pte*   , Name *Mooney J.*

has orders to proceed to his home:

(Address *54 Thomas Street*
Dublin

and there to await further instructions as to his discharge from the Service.

Capt Ramb   Officer Commanding.

Place *Curragh*

Date *18·2·18*   *Military Hospital*

*Here enter name of Hospital or Unit from which the Soldier proceeds.

201

IWM, Q 4694: Soldiers in a trench in the snow outside Arras, February 1917. © Imperial War Museum.

202

Certificate of discharge of No. *19065* Rank *Private*

Name: *Mooney* *John*
Surname. Christian Names in full.

Unit* and Regiment or Corps from which discharged *Depot.* *Leicestershire Regt*

* The unit of the Regiment or Corps such as Field Co. R.E., H.T., or M.T., A.S.C., etc., is invariably to be stated.

Regiment or Corps to which first posted *12ᵈ Res Cavalry Regt.*

Also previously served in..................... *Nil*

Only Regiments or Corps in which the soldier served since August 4th, 1914, are to be stated. If inapplicable this space is to be ruled through in ink and initialled.

Specialist Qualifications (Military).....................

Medals, Clasps, Decorations and Mentions in dispatches *1914-15 Star. British War Medal Victory Medal* Wound Stripes* *One* To be inserted in words.

Chevrons One Blue.

Has served Overseas on Active Service† ....

Enlisted at *Dublin* on *20/8* 19 *14.*
*Each space is to be filled in and the word "nil" inserted where necessary.
†To be struck out in ink if not applicable.

He is discharged in consequence of.....................

BEING NO LONGER PHYSICALLY
FIT FOR WAR SERVICE
PARA 392 (XVI), K.R.

after serving* *Three* years* *183* days with the Colours, and
* *Nil* years* *Nil* days in the Army Reserve or Territorial Force }
Strike out whichever inapplicable.

*Each space is to be filled in and the word "nil" inserted where necessary; number of years to be written in words.
†Service with Territorial Force to be shown only in cases of soldiers serving on a T.F. attestation.

Date of discharge *18/2/1918*

J W Hunt *Lieut* } Signature and Rank.

for Officer i/c *Infantry* Records.
Lichfield (Place).

Description of the above-named soldier when he left the Colours.

Year of Birth *1885* Marks or Scars.....................

Height *5* ft. *7⅞* in. *Nil*

Complexion *Fair*

Eyes *Brown* Hair *Dark (Grey)*

(31817.) Wt. W1912/PP1138. 760m. 5/18. S. & C. (E3267.) [P.T.O.

Left: John Mooney's Discharge Certificate, 18 February 1918. Private collection. Courtesy of Peter Mooney.

This page: John Mooney's Character Certificate, 18 February 1918. Almost like a formal reference these certificates were issued to enable ex-servicemen to find employment. Private collection. Courtesy of Peter Mooney.

Serial No. *Iuc/1208.*   Army Form B. 2067·

NOTE.—The character given on this Certificate is based on holder's conduct throughout his military career.

Character Certificate of No. *19065* Rank *Private*

Name *Mooney   John*
Surname.   Christian Names in full.

Unit and Regiment or Corps from which discharged } *Depot Leicestershire Regt*

This is to certify that the ex-soldier named above has served with the Colours for *Three* years *183* days.
To be inserted in words.

and his character during this period *has been*

Good

B Wray Lt Col
} Signature and Rank.

Officer i/c *Infantry* Records.

Date of discharge *18·2·1918* *Lichfield* Place.

To safeguard the holder of this Certificate from impersonation it should be noted that, in the event of any doubt arising as to the *bona fides* of the bearer, reference should be made to the description, when he left the Colours, of the soldier to whom this Certificate was given, which is recorded on his Discharge Certificate (Army Form B. 2079, Serial No. *Iuc/1222*.), and should be in his possession.

(A14377-P453) Wt. W3302/P2741 150,000 10/19 Sch. 41 D. D. & L.
Forms/B2067/8   (P.T.O.

WARNING.—If this Certificate is lost a duplicate cannot be issued. You should therefore on no account part with it or forward it by post when applying for a situation, but should use a copy attested by a responsible person for the purpose.

NOTE.—This Certificate is to be issued without any alteration in the manuscript.

205

DISABLED SAILORS AND SOLDIERS

WHAT EVERY MAN SHOULD KNOW

THAT he can get the fullest information as to what can be done for him from his War Pensions Local Committee.

THAT the address of the Committee can be obtained at the Post Office nearest his home.

THAT the War Pensions Local Committees are not distributing charitable funds, but funds provided by the State.

THAT every man disabled by War Service has a right to a pension or gratuity.

THAT he has a right to the most careful and effective treatment obtainable FREE.

THAT if he requires an artificial limb, it will be supplied and maintained in good order FREE of charge.

THAT if his disability prevents him from returning to his old trade he will receive FREE training for a new one.

THAT unless a man claims a pension based on his former earnings, no account is tak[en] of his earnings or earni[ng] capacity, or of the extent [to] which this may be improv[ed] by any training that may [be] given to him.

THAT no permanent pension w[ill] be reduced because a man h[as] accepted training.

THAT while he is being trained [he] will receive additions to [his] pension for the support [of] himself and his family.

THAT neither treatment nor tra[in]ing will cost him a penny.

THAT his Local Committee [will] help him to find employme[nt].

THAT his Local Committee w[ill] look after him if he suffe[rs] from illness at any time as [a] result of his service.

THAT if he is in any doubt [or] difficulty, or thinks he has [not] got his proper pension, [his] Local Committee will take [up] his case and help him.

THAT HE MUST TELL HIS [LOCAL COMMITTEE WH]AT HE WANTS.

[Ministry of Pensions : Official.

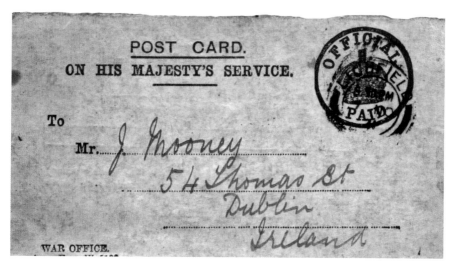

POST CARD.

ON HIS MAJESTY'S SERVICE.

OFFICIAL PAID

To

Mr. *J. Mooney*

54 Thomas St

Dublin

Ireland

WAR OFFICE.

Army Form W. 5132.

You are informed that the { 1914-15 Star. British War Medal. Victory Medal. } awarded

to you in respect of your service as No. *19065* Rank *J. Mooney*

(Unit and Corps) LEICESTERSHIRE REGT

is now available for issue.

Please report on attached Reply Postcard (which needs no further stamp) your correct address and return it. The decoration will then be forwarded to you under Registered Cover.

Record Office Stamp and Date.

INFANTRY RECORD — LICHFIELD

•

Left: 'Disabled sailors and soldiers, what every man should know', 1918. This sheet was given to wounded ex-servicemen when they were discharged from the forces. Private collection. Courtesy of Peter Mooney.

This page: Medal Notification, for the British War Medal and the Victory Medal, sent to John Mooney, 7 November 1921. During his 3 years and 183 days of service, he was awarded the 1914-15 Star, the British War Medal and the Victory Medal. Private collection. Courtesy of Peter Mooney.

•

NMI, HA/2006/51: Irish nurses from the 'Good Samaritan hospital' keep up the spirits of their charges by playing chess and reading, 1914–18. Courtesy of the National Museum of Ireland.

CHAPTER 8

Survivors

JANE LEONARD

WOUNDED!
MISSING!
PRISONERS OF WAR!

INFORMATION

obtained and searches made

FREE OF CHARGE

on application to

BRITISH RED CROSS SOCIETY
AND ST. JOHN AMBULANCE ASSN.

Apply, HON. SECRETARY,
ENQUIRY DEPARTMENT,
51 DAWSON STREET, DUBLIN.

'Wounded! Missing! Prisoners of war!', 1914–18. Courtesy of John Horne.

More than 100,000 veterans of the Great War returned as civilians to Ireland between the armistice and the early summer of 1920. That figure represents less than half of those Irishmen who had served in the war, excluding those who had enlisted outside Ireland. We know that some 30,000 died. The remainder re-enlisted in the new armies, stayed on in Britain after demobilisation, emigrated or were invalided out of the forces prior to the war's end.[1]

Coming home was in many respects the same for Irishmen as for millions of other combatants of the Great War. They brought with them the scars of the war experience, whether physical or psychological. They attempted to restore family life and to find work. But in important respects, the Irish home-coming was different from that in Britain and had more in common with other parts of Europe where borders were being redrawn and political identities re-moulded. For Irish veterans returned to a country not at peace, but where a different war was raging. Did they take part in this new conflict? On which side did they fight? Did the establishment of the Irish Free State and Northern Ireland materially affect veterans? Were there major differences in the veteran experience on either side of the Irish border created in 1921? Let us explore some of these issues through the lens of individual experience.[2]

DISABLED VETERANS

Long before the armistice, survivors had been returning to Ireland. Official estimates suggest that the number of disabled veterans in Ireland that were discharged before the armistice did not exceed 5,000. Naturally, a far greater number of ill or wounded men had convalesced or died in Ireland in the course of the war. In war-time Dublin alone, two ambulance trains transported over 12,000 service patients from the docks to hospitals.[3] Convalescents in their distinctive 'hospital blues' became familiar figures on Irish streets. Sam Hutchinson, a Belfast soldier who spent 1918 in the Ministry of Pensions Hospital on Carysfort Avenue in Blackrock, Co. Dublin, told me, in 1993, how 'the finger of scorn was pointed at us' as he and his comrades limped around a Dublin changed utterly by the Rising in 1916.

In the spring of 1917 the first Irish hospital specialising in the treatment of shell-shocked soldiers and sailors opened in the grounds of the Hermitage Golf Club in Lucan. Its patients (described as suffering from neurasthenia) slept in open-air huts, learned how to make baskets and hats, and looked after pigs and rabbits. They were encouraged to use the golf links and were allowed to play hockey if their health improved. Two further centres for neurasthenics were opened, the UVF Hospital at Craigavon House in Belfast (formerly the home of James Craig) and the Ministry of Pensions Hospital at Leopardstown Park in south Co. Dublin. Alone among more than 50 military hospitals and nursing homes established in Ireland during the war, these last two retain a vestigial existence to this day.[4]

The presence of thousands of afflicted or mutilated men, though potentially demoralising, inspired widespread curiosity about the victims and their prospects of leading a normal life. At a summer fête in Dublin in 1919, limbless men demonstrated two new gadgets. Which was better: the P.K. Mechanical Hand and Arm, invented in Belfast, or the Bray Arm, the brainchild of a surgeon at the Duke of Connaught Limbless Hospital? Though perfect for chopping wood and digging potatoes, the Bray Arm was not so flexible as its Belfast rival, which allowed one to make boots, write, cycle, fish and cut food properly. Observers cheerily agreed that the two were not strictly comparable as the Belfast wearers had longer stumps, making it easier to hook on the attachment.

The public idolised veterans who triumphed over their disability. The first British officer to be blinded was from Belfast—Captain Gerald Lowry, wounded at Neuve Chapelle in October 1914. After recuperating at St Dunstan's Hostel for the Blind in London, Lowry retrained as a masseur and became an osteopath there. He also became a sporting legend. When Lowry boxed at the Sporting

Club of Paris in 1927, the spectators included Colonel Charles Lindbergh (who had just flown across the Atlantic) and General John Pershing. In a film released that year, *Victory over Blindness*, our hero effortlessly boxed, sprinted, swam, skated, sailed, beagled, waltzed and played bridge after his day's bone-setting. Weekends were spent travelling to Belfast to hold an osteopathic clinic. Lowry maintained that those who watched his matches could not tell which fighter was the blind man, an approach that clearly infused his entire life after the war.

Yet the medical records of disabled veterans reveal less uplifting stories. Many had recurring nightmares in which the moment of injury returned. Inquests on suicides often testified to the profound depression that followed mutilation or shell shock. In 1917 an Irish international rugby player who had served with the 7th Royal Dublin Fusiliers at Gallipoli and Salonika was invalided out of the army with shell shock and insanity. A month later, he placed himself on the railway track at Dalkey tunnel and was decapitated by a train bound for Bray. His depression had intensified on leaving hospital when patrons in a London café jeered him for being in mufti. The jury at the inquest sharply criticised the military and medical authorities for discharging him from hospital.

For many survivors, uninterrupted sleep remained elusive for years. When an unemployed Lurgan weaver killed himself two weeks after his mother's death in 1921, the inquest noted that grief, alcohol and lack of sleep had contributed to this Mesopotamian veteran's death. Troubled by wounds and drinking heavily since his demobilisation, he left a farewell note that was both despairing and businesslike: 'Broken hearted and weary and long to find oblivion. Good Night. Good Night. P.S. Insurance cheque to be paid to my sister as I will not be here'.[5] The family of an ex-Munster Fusilier in Cobh still recall how he would sleep-walk and curl up on a stairway window-sill, a recess uncannily like the trench fire-step he had crouched on before going over the top. To this day, neighbours in East Belfast relate how the blitz in 1941 reignited the horrors of the Western Front for one shell-shocked veteran. He disappeared when the bombing started and was found next morning, trembling, in a hole he had dug during the night in his allotment.

HOMECOMINGS

To prevent a flow of weapons, uniforms and recruits to the Irish Volunteers, most Irish servicemen were demobilised at dispersal centres in Britain such as the Crystal Palace in London. Armed with their discharge papers and one month's furlough pay, wearing ordinary clothes at last (though army greatcoats

213

could be retained or exchanged at railway stations for £1), they straggled home one by one.

Welcome-home functions were held for veterans who returned to unionist communities throughout Ireland. Those from nationalist backgrounds received a more muted reception, though there were exceptions. Joe Devlin, MP, hosted a function for men of the 16th (Irish) Division at Celtic Park in West Belfast but political divisions marred the Peace Day parades held in the summer of 1919. Whereas unionist veterans marched alongside serving troops and members of the Royal Irish Constabulary (RIC), nationalist veterans in Dublin and elsewhere boycotted the event in protest at the failure to deliver on the promises of 1914. In Derry, nationalist veterans made their boycott even more pointed by marching with Sinn Féin, the Ancient Order of Hibernians and the trade unions in the Lady Day parade on 15 August.

The first challenge for the demobilised man was to rebuild relationships with his family, friends and workmates (if his old job had been kept open for him). The pre-war male environment of the bank teller or the government clerk had vanished as rivalries between 'flappers' and veterans enlivened office life. Within the home, domestic harmony following long separation was often elusive, disrupted all too often by violence, marital breakdown or suicide.

Returning servicemen imported some exotic tastes. Cheering crowds in Dublin had 'jazz-danced' down Grafton Street on Armistice Night 1918. Soon afterwards, the Elysée Hall on Dawson Street was opened by two ex-officers who promised patrons the chance to practise all the dances learnt in France. Musicians such as the Philadelphia Coon Band kept the Elysée crowds dancing until 3a.m. American soldiers and sailors studying at UCD and Trinity College, while waiting to be shipped home, showed Dubliners how to play baseball in exhibition matches. The more sedentary veteran could indulge a taste acquired in the trenches for French newspapers, novels and music when the Parisian publisher, Bloud et Gay, opened a bookshop in South Anne Street in 1919.

Within months of the armistice, Irish travel agents were offering commercial tours to the battlefields. Thomas Cook on Grafton Street charged £11 9s for a week in France and Flanders, departing Dublin. Independent travel was also possible using guides such as John McDonald. A pre-war emigrant from the Ards Peninsula in Co. Down who served with the Canadians in France, he stayed on in Boulogne as a chauffeur taking Irish families to visit graves. Inter-war pilgrimages from Ireland to the Western Front were organised by the British Legion and by groups as diverse as the Belfast Unionist Labour Association, Dundalk Methodist Church and the Catholic Travel Association in Dublin. The mood of such trips was not exclusively solemn. A party of over 500 Irish veterans visiting the Somme in 1928 abandoned their char-à-bancs in order to march once more towards familiar points, singing songs learned in the trenches. 'Place greatly changed since July 1916', as one survivor of the Ulster Division chirpily recorded a year later in the visitors' book at Thiepval.[6] When the novelist St John Ervine, who served with the Royal Dublin Fusiliers in France and lost a leg, visited Gallipoli in 1936, he lamented 'the waste of our gallantry on that rock', but also recalled the phrase used when dysentery struck: 'I'm between the Devil and the W.C'.[7]

FINDING WORK

Though reconstruction plans had been drawn up by the British government long before the war ended, their implementation in Ireland was chaotic. Numerous government departments looked after different aspects of the veteran's transition into civil life, with negligible co-ordination. In 1920 none of the responsible authorities could estimate the number of disabled men in Ireland. A civil servant from London, visiting Cork that year, was horrified to find that nothing had been done with thousands of applications for financial assistance from Munster veterans.

While Irish veterans received the same basic benefits as their counterparts in Britain in terms of pensions, unemployment assistance, training opportunities and medical care, the political climate after 1916 made certain measures difficult to implement. In local authorities controlled by Sinn Féin, ex-soldiers were refused admission to technical colleges, hospitals and asylums. The staff and premises of local War Pensions Committees frequently came under attack, as did the officials and clubrooms of the two main organisations competing for veterans, the Comrades of the Great War and the Federation of Discharged and Demobilised Soldiers and Sailors.[8]

Training courses at universities and technical colleges and placements on farms and in workshops were provided for veterans, including a handful of ex-servicewomen. There were campus romances between veterans. Florine Irwin entered Trinity in 1916 she left to become a VAD, and returned to study medicine. Back at Trinity, she met and married Nigel Ball, an ex-officer of the 16th (Irish) Division and now a botany instructor. While an ex-service student at University College Cork (UCC) in 1919, Patrick Hennessy had a placement at the new Ford tractor factory in Cork. A job offer followed and he eventually retired as company chairman. Ex-Captain Emmet Dalton of the Royal Dublin Fusiliers took a course at the Royal College of Science in Dublin but dropped out to join the IRA. Dalton had retained his greatcoat on demobilisation and it came in handy in jail-breaks.

Unemployment was far higher among veterans in Ireland than in Britain, where only 10% were out of work by the autumn of 1919. In Ireland, where 76,000 veterans had returned by that stage, 46% were receiving the out-of-work donation of 29s per week (ex-servicewomen only qualified if disabled).[9] One in two Irish veterans remained unemployed a year later. The crisis looming once the donation period expired was somewhat alleviated by the resumption of emigration in late 1920, as ex-servicemen took advantage of subsidised settlement schemes in the colonies.

The situation in Ulster was less severe than in the west and south. Yet northern veterans, especially in Belfast, were less likely to find work if they had not also been in the UVF. Whether employed or incapacitated, nationalist veterans there were particularly vulnerable as the revolution intensified. The hostility they faced was not exclusively republican. Former members of the 16th (Irish) Division were among the Catholic workers expelled from the shipyards by loyalists in 1920. Those condemning this action included their former commander, Major-General Sir William Hickie, who sent a few pounds to help them. When loyalists threatened Catholics receiving treatment for shell shock at the UVF Hospital in 1922, the Ministry of Pensions moved the twenty veterans to another medical institution until the intimidation abated.

About one in five unemployed Irish veterans was disabled. The King's National Roll, adopted in Britain in 1919, whereby private employers pledged to hire disabled veterans, was not extended to Ireland. It was feared that trade union opposition and support for Sinn Féin would make the scheme unworkable. After 1922, when it was eventually introduced in Northern Ireland, employers were lacklustre in their support. Though veterans did receive preferential employment in the Northern Ireland civil service, many remained out of work indefinitely.

Even so, many contrived to scrape a living, if only as organ-grinders or door-to-door salesmen. Ex-soldiers wishing to set up as porters or jarveys could get a small grant to buy a donkey and cart or pony and trap. Vigorous lobbying by the parish priest at Claddagh, Co. Galway, yielded loans for fishermen, who had served in the Royal Navy, to buy their own boats. As unemployment persisted throughout the 1920s, the British Legion also initiated several employment schemes. These included the IREX furniture factory in Mespil Road, Dublin, and the car-park attendant service provided by disabled veterans in Belfast.

'HOMES FIT FOR HEROES'

Fears that unemployed veterans in rural areas would be drawn into the IRA prompted the British government's legislation in 1919 that provided rented landholdings and cottages. Republicans seized on the historical connotations of planting ex-soldiers on the land, despite the efforts of veterans to assert their credentials as Irish countrymen. At a rally of Mullingar ex-servicemen in 1919, their leader declared that it was far preferable to have 'discharged soldiers living on the land than bullocks'.[10] Only a few of the thousands who applied had moved to the land by 1920 and many found it hard to make a living. Homes and allotments were frequently attacked while sales of produce and livestock were boycotted.

From 1920 onwards, the focus switched to larger urban developments. Within fifteen years, over 3,600 homes had been constructed, sometimes with street-names recalling the war, such as Flanders Villas in Nenagh, Mons Terrace in Castlebar and Givenchy Terrace in Andersonstown, West Belfast. The homes for heroes were built by heroes. At Killester, on Dublin's north side, some 800 veterans laboured on the largest scheme. When completed, it contained nearly 300 homes. Another extensive suburb was laid out at Cregagh in East Belfast where almost 150 houses were built on six criss-crossing streets commemorating Ulster's greatest battle—Albert Drive, Bapaume Avenue, Picardy Avenue, Hamel Drive, Thiepval Avenue and Somme Drive.

Tenants of the Irish Sailors' and Soldiers' Land Trust in both states had to fight bitter and lengthy battles to have high rents reduced and to have shops, schools, churches and recreational facilities provided on their estates. Yet, in this respect, Irish veterans fared better than their counterparts in Britain, for whom no such model garden suburbs were built.[11]

VETERANS IN A DIVIDED IRELAND

Since nearly 63,000 Irish servicemen had previously belonged to the Irish National Volunteers or the UVF, it is striking that so few joined paramilitary movements on returning home.[12] Ireland thus differed from many other combatant countries where returning veterans dominated post-war revolutionary organisations. Many thousands, however, re-enlisted in the new armies and armed police forces. Over 300 policemen who had served with the Irish Guards and other units rejoined the RIC after the war, while recruits to both the regular RIC and to the new police forces raised during the revolutionary period included a couple of thousand Irish veterans. Though the Black and Tans and Auxiliaries, in the popular mind and numerous cinematic treatments, have Cockney, Glaswegian or Welsh accents, in reality they included many Irishmen.

The British government's fear that a vast army of unemployed veterans in Ireland would swell the IRA was not realised. Only a tiny proportion of ex-servicemen were actively involved in the movement. Of the hundreds who joined most served as drill and ammunition instructors or as flying columnists. A handful of ex-officers worked in intelligence and publicity, among them Erskine Childers and his cousin Robert Barton. While those who joined the IRA were predominantly veterans of the British forces, it also recruited a few men from the American, Australian, Canadian, Indian and French armies.

On the other hand, numerous ex-servicemen fell foul of the IRA. Between 1919 and 1924 more than 120 civilian veterans of the Great War were killed by the IRA or by the anti-Treaty republican forces.[13] Although some veterans were acting as intelligence agents for the RIC and British Army or were employed in military barracks, the vast majority appear to have been killed simply as retribution for their part in the war. A fretwork plaque that commemorates ex-Sapper William Patterson vividly conveys the bewilderment of the bereaved. In May 1922 the IRA entered a Belfast cooperage, asked workers their religion and killed Patterson and five others who identified themselves as Protestants. The plaque contains his war medals and photograph, the embroidered cards he had sent home from the trenches to his six children, and a succinct inscription: 'Survived Armageddon. Was Murdered in Belfast'.[14]

In the uneasy no man's land of post-war Ireland, individual veterans were ambivalent about both the IRA and the British forces. Disabled men resented the taunts they attracted from both sides and especially the indignity of body searches, when the iron of a surgical boot might be mistaken for a concealed weapon. Sarcasm was put to good effect by one man who was angered when troops searching the Sinn Féin hall in Kingstown (now Dún Laoghaire) burst into the adjoining ex-soldiers' club. Ordered to put his hands up, he retorted that he had never done that for the Germans.

Even though the leaders of the government-funded Comrades of the Great War endorsed British policy in Ireland, some local branches were highly critical of reprisals by British troops and on occasion sent representatives to IRA funerals. When an ex-soldier was killed by troops in Miltown Malbay, Co. Clare, local ex-servicemen recited a rosary for the victim and bitterly recalled that he had fought 'for what we were assured was the liberty of small nations'.[15]

Though the Federation (closed to ex-officers) had more radical social policies than these men, and its stance on Irish politics approximated those of the British Labour and Home Rule parties, its clashes with Sinn Féin were no less bitter than its disputes with government.

The outbreak of the Civil War was a catalyst for rallying ex-servicemen behind the Irish Free State. It was officially estimated that approximately half of the 55,000 who enrolled in the National Army were ex-servicemen.[16] Its officer corps between 1922 and 1924 included more than 600 veterans of the Great War.[17] Most of these had been rankers or subalterns but commissions were willingly issued to five who had commanded brigades on the Western Front and to one officer (a former Tipperary GAA star) who, in the crude language of one Dublin newspaper, had commanded 'a battalion of Southern darkies at the front'.[18] This was Major Jack Prout, a pre-war regular officer of the famous New York 'Fighting 69th', who ended the war in command of black troops from Illinois.[19]

One of the early fatalities in the Civil War was George Adamson, who had won the Distinguished Conduct Medal in Egypt with the Machine Gun Corps. Returning to Westmeath, he led an IRA flying column before the Treaty. As a Brigadier in the National Army, he was killed near Athlone Barracks in April 1922. The overlap between his two wars was evident at his funeral, when hundreds of the Athlone ex-servicemen turned out to pay their respects. The most famous veteran to die on the anti-Treaty side in the Civil War was the brilliant propagandist and novelist Erskine Childers, executed in November 1922. The National Army officer who presided at his court martial was a former Captain of the Royal Dublin Fusiliers and the son of a Redmondite MP.

In the same way that many Redmondite veterans joined the National Army, so unionist ex-servicemen stiffened the Ulster Special Constabulary. Many of these 'Specials' had also served in the revived UVF or in other vigilante units patrolling the province after the war, including the rather Prussian-sounding Ulster Imperial Guards. How the commemoration of the war was overtaken by the conflict at home became painfully apparent in Armagh in April 1921. Special Constable John Fluke, an ex-corporal of the Royal Irish Fusiliers, was to have attended the unveiling of his church's roll of honour for those who had returned safely from the war. When his name was read out during the dedication by the rector, there was 'a hush as of death in the crowded church'.[20] Fluke had been killed in an IRA ambush outside Crossmaglen a week earlier.

If veterans played a significant role in defending and policing the new states, how prominently did they participate in the new political structures? All war veterans elected for Irish constituencies in the 1918 general election were unionists, except for Sinn Féin's Robert Barton and Captain William Archer Redmond (son of the late Home Rule leader). As in Britain, Irish ex-service organisations were divided over whether to support existing political parties or to put forward their own members. In the 1920 municipal elections, the ex-servicemen had some success, particularly in garrison towns. The Ulster Ex-servicemen's Association achieved a sensational victory at the West Belfast by-election in 1923, when one of its leaders, Colonel Philip Woods, was elected to the Northern Ireland parliament as an independent unionist. Scores of ex-service patients at the UVF Hospital turned up at the count to cheer his defeat of the official unionist candidate, Joseph Davison, a future Grand Master of the Orange Order.

Many of the unionist MPs elected to the inter-war Northern Ireland and Westminster parliaments were veterans. In the Irish Free State, a scattering of veterans was elected to the Dáil. Most were independents or members of Cumann na nGaedhael (later absorbed into Fine Gael), though TDs with war service also included members of Fianna Fáil, the Farmers' Party and the National League. The League, established in 1926 by Captain Redmond, won eight seats in the following year and briefly attracted strong support from veterans. Its sister organisation in Northern Ireland likewise attracted Catholic ex-service voters before it too faded away in the early 1930s.

It is noteworthy that the main veterans' organisation, the British Legion, never became a political force in either Northern Ireland or in the Irish Free State. Although most existing veterans' bodies in Britain merged as the British Legion in 1921, moves towards unity in Ireland took longer. It was not until 1925 that the southern veterans adopted the name British Legion and affiliated, like their northern counterpart, with the legion in Britain. But membership of the British Legion throughout the island between 1925 and 1939 never exceeded 9,000, less than 10% of the veteran population.[21] This was partly because several rival organisations remained active for some years after the legion was established, among them the Irish Nationalist Veterans' Association (whose founders included Tom Kettle's widow, Mary) and the Ulster Ex-Servicemen's Association.

Another explanation for why the legion failed to attract more members was the competition it faced from existing fraternities, including freemasonry, the Orange Order and the Ancient Order of Hibernians. Orange lodges composed exclusively of veterans were formed from the armistice onwards, sometimes acquiring the warrants of those established by the Ulster Division on the

Western Front. Orange and green flute bands also recruited from the ranks of demobilised musicians. A flute band performing in an Orange parade from Portadown to Armagh in 1919 carried a banner emblazoned 'Fragments from France' (a tribute not to King Billy but to 'Old Bill', the character immortalised in Bruce Bairnsfather's trench cartoons).[22] In Enniskillen, Catholic veterans formed the Grattan Flute Band and on occasion led the Armistice Day parade.

Rather than joining the legion, Catholic veterans in Northern Ireland often preferred to enrol in groups such as the 16th (Irish) Division Association or to rejoin local Ancient Order of Hibernian divisions. In some Ulster towns, the legion met in Orange halls, thus inhibiting Catholics from joining. Many Irishmen found their regimental old comrades' association more congenial than the legion. In the 1970s while the worsening conflict in Northern Ireland and the ageing veteran population hastened the closure of many British Legion clubs in the Republic, branches of the old comrades' associations of the Connaught Rangers, the Royal Dublin Fusiliers and other disbanded Irish infantry regiments were still attracting new recruits.[23]

221

REMEMBRANCE

Though paid-up members of the British Legion in Ireland were relatively few, survivors, their families and the relatives of the war dead demonstrated their solidarity by turning out in huge numbers on Armistice Day, as press photographs and newsreels attest. In 1924 press reports estimated that 20,000 veterans assembled in College Green, Dublin, in front of 50,000 people. In 1927, 18,000 veterans were said to have paraded in the Phoenix Park before a crowd of 80,000. While such statistics need to be treated with caution, the visual evidence, police reports and records of poppy sales all suggest that Armistice Day in Dublin of the 1920s was even more widely observed than in Belfast.[24]

Interviewed in the 1980s and 1990s, veterans and their children recalled the darker sides of such gatherings, when razor blades were placed inside poppies to dissuade snatchers and when the dances, smoking concerts and screening of war films that marked Armistice Week were interrupted by bomb and arson attacks. In 1993 the daughter of a veteran remembered her childhood in Seafort Gardens, Dublin, built for the disabled:

Poppies weren't then a forbidden thing in Sandymount. Maybe I'm wrong but it's like a dream to me that I remember going to Mass as a child in the Star of the Sea Church in Sandymount and seeing people selling poppies ... I suppose, maybe with the Troubles and the IRA, you wouldn't be that keen to be wearing a poppy nowadays. You'd be aggravating the situation.

Her comments are a useful reminder of how the conflict in Northern Ireland muffled remembrance of the Great War during the 1970s and 1980s so effectively that personal experiences jarred with the accepted version of the Irish past.

In recent years, renewed public and political acknowledgement of Irish losses in the war, spurred by moves towards peace in Northern Ireland, has to some extent rectified the marginalisation of this important episode in Irish history.[25] On the day he resigned as Taoiseach in April 2008, Bertie Ahern explained that his government had 'dusted down the monuments and cut the grass' at the Irish National War Memorial in order to convince unionists that the Republic respected how central the war was to their identity. In June 2008 the former First Minister of Northern Ireland, Ian Paisley, delivered a sermon at a memorial service for the 16th (Irish) Division in Flanders before laying a wreath at the grave of Major Willie Redmond, MP, a nationalist he saluted as 'a man well before his time'. His newspaper column, 'Paisley's Porridge', appearing on the eve of the 12 July celebrations, reiterated that the war dead came 'from every part of Ireland'.[26] The clock had finally turned back to the 1920s when similar acknowledgements had been made by W.T. Cosgrave and James Craig.

Those who survived the war, and were still living as this political retrenchment began in the 1990s, were too frail and elderly to appreciate it.[27] One of the last Great War veterans to live at Leopardstown Park was Sam Hutchinson. Over his evening Guinness (a perk that Uncle Arthur supplied gratis to the patients), Sam often returned to his main regret concerning the war. It bothered him that the text-books his grandchildren studied made little mention of the extent of his generation's involvement. 'We backed the wrong horse', he liked to say.

What patterns emerge from this brief survey of the veteran experience, North and South? Irish veterans, like ex-combatants elsewhere in Europe, were vulnerable but far from passive during the years of revolution and civil war. Once the border was consolidated, their day-to-day experiences were broadly similar to those of veterans in Britain. If unemployment levels in the South remained high throughout the 1920s, this was also the case in Northern Ireland

and throughout industrialised Britain. Southerners and northerners alike resented the high rents charged in ex-service estates and the long queues for local-authority housing. Unlike veterans in Northern Ireland, southern veterans did not get preference when applying for government clerkships (unless they had served in the National Army as many had). No distinction was made between British provision for veterans North and South, with one important exception: those living in the Irish Free State did not qualify for assisted imperial emigration schemes after 1922.

Did Irish veterans back the wrong horse? Though southern veterans lived in a state that was both embarrassed and ambivalent about its citizens' contribution to the war, survivors and the bereaved none the less kept faith with each other and with the dead. While the northern state officially venerated the 36th (Ulster) Division, many unionist veterans felt that they lost out in terms of status and job opportunities to UVF members who had not joined up. The racing analogy possibly applied most to nationalist veterans in Ulster, for whom reintegration into their community or finding commonality with unionist society often proved impossible.

223

Yet amid the diversity of survivors' experiences, perhaps the most pervasive themes are restlessness and discontent. When refused time off by the northern Ministry of Labour to observe the two minutes' silence on Armistice Day 1938, an Enniskillen veteran angrily protested that 'we are Britain's broken dolls'.[28] This phrase, echoing a famous chorus of the war, highlights the predicament of Irish veterans, disabled and able-bodied, North and South:

> For I gladly took my chance
> Now my right arm's out in France
> I'm one of England's Broken Dolls.

Dülmen (Westf.), 25/5/16

I am prisoner of war and stationed at **Dülmen**, Westf.

My address is:

Name and christian name: *John Byrne 3511*

Rank: *Rfn*

Regiment: *8th City of London Rfn*

Gefangenenlager **Dülmen** i. W.

Germany

NAI, 1096/10/20: Postcard to Michael Byrne from John at Dulme, POW camp. Also shown (next page) Territorial Forces Records Office POW report, 5 June 1916. Report sent to Michael Byrne, Leighlinbridge, Co. Carlow, of Rifleman John Byrne's (presumably his son) capture on 21 May 1916. Courtesy of the National Archives of Ireland.

Army Form B. 104—83.

No.

(If replying, please quote above No.)

TERRITORIAL FORCE

4, LONDON WALL BLDGS. E.C.

Record Office,

_____ Station.

5 JUN 1916 191 .

SIR,

I regret to have to inform you that a report has this day been received from the War Office to the effect that (No.) *3511*

(Rank) *Rfn.* (Name) *Byrne J*

(Regiment) **8th Bn. The London Regt.**
(Post Office Rifles). was

Strike out part which does not apply.

{*posted as "missing" after
*taken prisoner during} the engagement at *not stated*

225

_____ on the *21st May 1916*

Should he subsequently rejoin, or any other information be received concerning him, such information will be at once communicated to you.

I am,

SIR,

Your obedient Servant,

G. F. Bartelot Major for COL

I/C TERRITORIAL FORCE RECORD OFFICE,

LONDON.

Officer in charge of Records.

(4 27 1) W 12909—2398 200,000 3/15 H W V (P) Forms/B. 104—80/2

A chaplain writing letters home for wounded troops during the campaign at Cambrai, France, 1 January 1917. © Popperfoto/Getty Images.

Capt.   25 St Jos. Nha. Dublin
                                                21.11.16.

H. Cooney ~~Esq~~ ~~Capt.~~
for O. I/C. Infantry Records Office ~~Dublin~~
            Island Bridge
                        Dublin

Sir
        I am in rect of yours 27 Oct.
Ref "Cas.—102" — reporting the death
                    Private 8738 C
of my son, ̩Edmond Fras Hogan, 8th
Battⁿ R D Fus. ^while serving with the Exp Force France
                    ~~which in action~~
~~on 6th f̶e̶l̶d̶~~

    ~~✗✗✗~~ I held a Field Post Card from
my son dated 9th Sep — but thinking
    he made a
he ~~was~~ mistake ̶s̶ in dating same —
I wrote his Commanding Off in
France ~~to~~ see if he could ~~~~~ say
when he actually last saw my
son & have had a reply from
                    last
him stating he ^saw him on the
morning of the ^9th. Sep — Also
I have been Speaking to a ret
Soldier who says he ~~was ta~~ spoke to him

- - - - - - - - - -

NMI, HA/2004/205: Draft of a letter from John Hogan regarding his son, Private E.F. Hogan to Island
Bridge Infantry Records, 21 November 1916. Hogan's son was reported dead on 6 September 1916 but the
last field postcard received from Private Hogan was dated 9 September. The soldier was sighted twice on the
morning of 9 September and his father suggests that he might not be dead but could be a 'prisoner—or in
hospital badly wounded'. Courtesy of the National Museum of Ireland.

~~& my son~~ on the morning of the
9th —— If therefore you will in view of the this crepancy in date
kindly make
~~please~~ further investigations ~~his~~
~~call~~ in case he may be a
prisoner — or in hospital badly
wounded, I shall be extremely
grateful —
            Yrs truly
            John F Hogan —

Also wrote
The Secretary
          War office Ldn Sh.
Sir. I have had a report of
the death of my Son Pte 8728
Ed.F. Hogan 8th Batt.n R D Fus.
in action in France on 6th Sep.
last —— I will be glad to receive
any personal effects of his
which may have been found. Yrs truly
NMIHA 2004.205(1)   John F Hogan

229

E/360786/1   (Accounts 4.)

The following is a true copy of a Will executed by the late No.18798, Private Patrick O'Donnell, 9th (Service) Battalion, Scottish Rifles, while in actual Military Service within the meaning of the Wills Act, 1837, which is recognised as valid by the War Department.

War Office records of the contested will of Private Patrick O'Donnell (9th Scottish Rifles). On 23 April 1917 O'Donnell, from Limerick, is claimed to have promised to leave all his possessions to his aunt, Sarah Brown. The previous September, however, he had willed his property and effects to Bridget Lynch, his sweetheart. Mrs Brown contested the will and appears to have been unsuccessful. In general the army adhered to a soldier's will rather than any testamentary statements made in letters. Courtesy of the National Archives of Ireland.

230

13

WILL.

In the event of my Death

I give the whole of my

property and Effects to

my Sweetheart

Miss Bridget Lynch

Kelmallock Infirmary

Kelmallock
———

C/o Limerick

Ireland.
———

Signature   pte P O Donnell

Rank and Regt   9th Scottish Rifles

Words underlined are in print.)

Date   24/9/16

Certified that the above is a true copy of the copy of the Will retained in this Department.

for the Assistant Financial Secretary.

ar Office, S.W. 7.

16th March, 1918.

April 28/4/17

Write soon.

Pte.P O Donnell
18793 B. Company
8 Platoon
9th Scottish Rifles
B E F
France

Dear Auntie

    I am writing these few lines Hoping that you are in the Best of Health as it leaves Me at present. Dear Sarah I have just been ask by My sergeant Major who was my next to kin so I told Him that you were My auntie so if you thing Happen Me you will get all My Money and other property so I hope you stick to what I have said If they send and ask you Dont for get to tell them that you are my aunt. you Might Just as well have the Money as the Goverment Give My love to our Danny & Tommy and tell them I am doing well Hoping to hear that Danny as go over his wounds. will you send Me some fags & papers as I never Got the last lot you send me.

    I think I have said all for present

I remain your
truly your loving
nephew patsy.

XXXXXXXX
XXXXXXXX
XXXXXXXX
XXXXXXXX

Francis Ledwidge, *c.* 1915. Lance-corporal in the Royal Inniskilling Fusiliers, Ledwidge was a staunch nationalist and was described in his obituary in the *Irish Independent* as a 'peasant poet'. He was killed by a shell in Flanders on 31 July 1917.
© 2007 Getty Images.

CHAPTER 9

Writing the war

TERENCE BROWN

STAND NOT UPON THE ORDER OF YOUR GOING, BUT GO AT ONCE

Shakespeare. Macbeth 3-4

ENLIST NOW

In 1979, ten years after the modern Irish 'Troubles' broke out, Seamus Heaney included in his volume *Field work* a poem entitled 'In memoriam Francis Ledwidge'. In so doing he was invoking an iconic figure, one of a few Irish poets who might be included among the soldier poets who died in the Great War and who made that conflict seem, in cultural memory, a poet's war. In his poem, Heaney ponders in the late twentieth century, in the midst of a conflict between loyalism and Irish republicanism, the enigma that a nationalist Irishman should have been among the British soldiery who perished in the Great War. Among those who lost their lives, we remember, were such renowned war poets as Julian Grenfell, Isaac Rosenberg and Wilfred Owen. Heaney designates Ledwidge 'our dead enigma' and recalls his Co. Meath origins and the tender Georgian pastoralism of his verses, and quotes from a letter written by Ledwidge shortly before he was killed at the Battle of Passchendaele on 30 July 1917.

In that letter, the poet, serving in the king's uniform in the Royal Inniskilling Fusiliers, had regretted that 'party politics should ever divide our tents' and hoped for a time when a new Ireland would 'arise from her ashes in the ruins of Dublin, like the Phoenix, with one purpose, one aim and one ambition. I tell you this in order that you may know what it is to me to be called a British soldier while my own country has no place

'Stand not upon the order of your going, but go at once', 1915.
© Royal Irish Academy.

amongst the nations but the place of Cinderella'.[1] In so writing, Ledwidge was responding to the events of April–May 1916 when the Easter Rising had been crushed by other soldiers wearing the king's uniform, an outcome that had affected him profoundly. Indeed, the figure of the soldier poet that shadows Ledwidge's war-time verses is no victim of the Dardanelles or the Western Front. Rather it is Thomas McDonagh, Pádraig Pearse and Joseph Plunkett—whom Ledwidge views as martyrs for Ireland when they paid the ultimate sacrifice upon their execution in Dublin—who preoccupy him. It is they who are honoured in his poem 'The blackbirds', written in July 1916, with its nationalist iconography and tones of lament:

> I heard the Poor Old Woman say:
> 'At break of day the fowler came,
> And took my blackbirds from their songs
> Who loved me well thro' shame and blame.
>
> And when the first surprise of flight
> Sweet songs excite, from that far dawn
> Shall there come blackbirds loud with love,
> Sweet echoes of the singers gone.
>
> But in the lonely hush of ever
> Weeping I grieve the silent bills'.
> I heard the Poor Old Woman say
> In Derry of the little hills.[2]

And perhaps Ledwidge's best-known poem is 'Thomas McDonagh' with its plangent, sorrowing cadences:

> He shall not hear the bittern cry
> In the wild sky, where he is lain,
> Nor voices of the sweeter birds
> Above the wailing of the rain.

The actual experience of war is not directly represented in Ledwidge's poetry (although he does make graphic reference to it in some of the letters which he sent back from the war zone). However, the intensifying homesickness it registers may be taken as a symptom of the increasing alienation he felt both as an Irishman in British uniform after 1916 and as a 'unit in the Great War, doing and suffering' while facing the prospect of a likely violent death. That homesickness expressed itself in poems like 'In France' where: 'Whatever way I turn …/The hills of home are in my mind/And there I wander as I will'. In poem after poem, rural Co. Meath is evoked in idyllic terms, as a pastoral place of fairy lore and sweet birdsong.

One senses that Ledwidge the poet, in so concentrating on the pastoral antithesis to his life as a soldier, unwittingly aligns his work with other war poets who did admit the conditions of industrial warfare to their verses. (Where Ledwidge does refer to the war itself it is in rather conventionally poetic terms, without the realism that was to mark some of the most compelling of Great War poetry.) A good deal of the poetry of the Great War did in fact highlight the gulf between the pastoral landscapes close to the front, the horrors of trench life and the desolate, shell-ruined zone of no man's land. One thinks of Rosenberg's 'Returning, We hear the Larks', with its 'heights of night ringing with unseen larks,/Music showering on our upturned list'ning faces' of soldiers returning to camp and 'a little safe sleep'. It is as if Ledwidge, sick with longing for his native place, fixed his being on the pastoral mode that fellow poets of the Great War set in apposition to the realities of trench warfare in Picardy and Flanders.

In Heaney's Ledwidge poem, the pastoral quality of the Meathman's verse is sensitively acknowledged in its invocation of 'the leafy road from Slane/Where you belonged'; but it is the enigma of Ledwidge that most engages the Derry poet. Heaney is stimulated to his reflections by a war memorial in the northern sea-side resort of Portstewart, with its 'loyal fallen names on the embossed plaque', which he remembers first encountering as an uncomprehending child. Not that adulthood has brought much greater understanding, for the poem concludes by reckoning that Ledwidge followed 'a sure confusing drum' and that he was not 'keyed or pitched like these true-blue ones', commemorated in Portstewart, who perhaps knew what they were dying for. It is as if the varying motives that took men to their deaths earlier in the century epitomise for Heaney an island still riven by divided loyalties—party politics continue to 'divide the tents'. The only certainty in the muffled pain of this memorial is that 'all of you consort now underground'.

Heaney's invocation of an 'underground' at the conclusion of this poem mysteriously confirms it as a Great War poem in more than its subject matter. It reminds us, of course, of Wilfred Owen's great poem 'Strange meeting', in which mortal enemies encounter one another after death in a 'sullen hall' that is accessed 'down some profound dull tunnel, long since scooped/Through granites which titanic wars had groined'. In that poem, the soldier's experience of the trenches, in which life became a matter of subterranean survival, is made the basis of a mythic perspective. And the imagery of mining encapsulated by Owen's lines also reminds us that much of the war was fought underground by the sappers who sought to undermine the enemy's front-line defences. Sebastian Faulks' well-known novel of 1993, *Birdsong*, was powerfully alert to this aspect of Great War combat and the mole-like burrowing it involved. He was accurately reflecting the fact that, as the historian Eric J. Leed has observed, the Great War was 'in general ... a war of engineers' or, as Paul Fussell termed it, 'a troglodyte world'.[3] Leed comments: 'the silence, darkness, disorientation, and almost unbelievable tension suffered by the mining solders was [*sic*] an intensification of the experience of trench warfare'.[4] So powerful indeed was the sense of the war as a conflict being fought beneath the surface of the earth that, as Leed argues, the concept of 'underground' achieved a near-mythic explanatory force in the minds of many soldiers, who felt themselves trapped in a terrible cave. In Owen's poem, the only escape from the trenches is through death and the ultimate sleep with which that poem concludes.

Two prose works by the Donegal writer Patrick McGill (known as 'the navvy poet'), who served with the London Irish Regiment and was injured in France, powerfully evoke the subterranean world of the common soldier. *The red horizon* (1916) describes, for example, a shell-bombardment in the following terms:

> The suspense wore us down; we breathed the suffocating fumes of one explosion and waited, our senses tensely strung for the coming of the next shell. The sang-froid which carried us through many a tight corner with credit utterly deserted us, we were washed-out things; with noses to the cold earth, like rats in a trap, we waited for the next moment which might land us in eternity. The excitement of a bayonet charge, the mad tussle with death on the blood-stained field, which for some reason is called the field of honour was denied us; we had to wait and lie in the trench, which looked so like a grave, and sink slowly into the depths of depression.[5]

One notes here the suggestion of entrapment and underground death-in-life. In *The great push: an episode of the Great War* (an account of the Battle of Loos in September 1915, also published in 1916) McGill captured once again the periods of awful anxiety involved in such warfare, in which the earth itself was no protection:

> The shells were loosened again; there was no escape from their frightful vitality, they crushed, burrowed, exterminated; obstacles were broken down, and men's lives were flicked out like flies off a window-pane. A dug-out flew skywards, and the roof-beams fell in the trench at our feet. We crouched under the bomb-shelter, mute, pale, hesitating.[6]

There was a more general sense in which the experience of fighting men in the Great War was open to metaphoric representation as an underground world. It was underground in the sense that many on the home front did not wish to be told of its true nature. There is, accordingly, a powerful sense of taboos being broken in the English war poetry of the period, of the suppressed being provocatively exhumed. One thinks of Owen's 'Dulce et Decorum Est' with its emphatic images of intolerable suffering, that give the lie to conventional patriotic pieties, and of his admonitory preface to his poems, which restricts the poet to the role of one who must issue warning, eschewing poetry. If a poet, such as Owen, felt driven to such aesthetic asceticism, the Irishmen who might have wished to register in literature the experience of combat in the Great War would have laboured under a double disadvantage. For not only were those at home disinclined to have their noses rubbed in the mud and blood of Flanders or elsewhere, but after 1916 and the events that led to partition and the establishment of the Irish Free State there were obvious ideological and political reasons that made literary treatment of the war highly problematic. A poem by the nationalist intellectual and university teacher Thomas Kettle anticipated how such as he could be disavowed 'in time to be' (this phrase is from Yeats's poem 'Easter 1916', completed in its first form in the same month as Kettle met his death). Kettle had enlisted in the 16th (Irish) Division in passionate support of Home Rule and 'gallant little Belgium' and lost his life at the Somme in September 1916. In 'The gift of love', Kettle addresses a daughter whom he imagines asking 'in wiser' days why he abandoned her for the dangers of the soldier's calling ('to dice with death'). His answer, movingly if unconvincingly, makes his action seem an anti-imperialist Christian solidarity with the wretched of the earth, as if he knows his sacrifice will be misunderstood:

> So here, while the mad guns curse overhead,
> And tired men sigh, with mud for couch and floor,

Know that we fools, now with the foolish dead,
Died not for Flag, nor King, nor Emperor,
But for a dream, born in a herdsman's shed,
And for the Secret Scripture of the poor.

The attitude of the poet W.B. Yeats to the Great War was that as an artistic
and poetic subject it should be buried and stay buried, especially in the case of
non-combatants. In February 1916 he composed a poem which on its first publication was entitled 'A reason for keeping silent', and subsequently 'On being
asked for a war poem'. In this he wrote:

I think it better that in times like these
A poet's mouth be silent, for in truth
We have no gift to set a statesman right;
He has had enough of meddling who can please
A young girl in the indolence of her youth,
Or an old man upon a winter's night.

It might have been remarked when this poem first appeared in 1916 that
Yeats had not hitherto felt inhibited about commenting on political matters, as
the first edition of his volume *Responsibilities* strenuously indicated. Published
in 1914 that volume did not hide his elitist disdain for Irish political mediocrity.
And those familiar with the Yeats's circle might have been tempted to read in
the poem's invocations of an indolent young girl and an old man some hint of
the amatory confusions that were in fact assailing the poet in 1916. For upon
the execution of John MacBride following the Easter Rising, he would feel
obliged once again to propose marriage to MacBride's estranged widow, his
own great love of youthful years, Maud Gonne. When she once more refused
him, he would turn his attention to her daughter, the fitful and often indolent
Iseult Gonne.

Yeats would have known of Iseult's moody laziness from concerned letters
he had been receiving from Maud during the war, which also told him how
terrible battles were unfolding in France. In this context, Yeats, in his poem, can
be seen as repressing this knowledge, preferring to cultivate amatory feeling
within a circle of intimates as a poetic subject. Gonne's letters, however, would
have alerted him to the personal costs of the war. For she had reported the
deaths-in-action of a nephew and of her first lover's son; mourned the loss of
Hugh Lane, Lady Gregory's nephew, in the sinking of the *Lusitania*; and
worried for Lady Gregory when her son Robert chose to enlist in the British

forces. And she wrote passionately of the suffering of the French Army, whose wounded she and Iseult helped to nurse:

> *I am nursing the wounded from 6 in the morning till 8 at night and trying in my material work to drown the sorrow and disappointment of it all—and my heart is growing up in wild hatred of the war machine which is grinding the life out of these great nations and reducing their population to helpless slavery and ruin, among all the wounded I have nursed only one man who spoke with real enthusiasm of returning to the front.[7]*

Gonne's experience as a nurse brought her, as she wrote, 'in contact with awful suffering and heroic courage and a great deal of the waste and squalor of war'.[8] One death amid all that waste Yeats could not suppress or disregard for it involved his own immediate circle in the most brutal way. On 23 January 1918 Major Robert Gregory was killed on the Italian Front when, returning from a mission, his plane was brought down by 'friendly fire' in a dreadful accident. So Yeats's patron, close friend and collaborator lost her only son, father of her three grandchildren, the man upon whom her hopes for the future of a family, house and estate at Coole, Co. Galway, rested. It was a most terrible blow that Yeats as a poet could not ignore. Silence was not an option. Yeats wrote four poems in Gregory's memory all of which involved complex negotiations of a central, unpalatable fact about the major: he was an unabashed imperialist who had enlisted as Roy Foster terms it 'with alacrity early in the war' in the Royal Flying Corps.[9] The best-known of the four poems, 'An Irish airman foresees his death', exhibits the poet engaged in the avoidance, if not quite suppression, of this uncomfortable facet of Gregory's character, which was at odds with his mother's and Yeats's Irish nationalism.

Yeats's ploy in the poem is to disregard Gregory's known imperialism and to attribute his participation in the conflict to parochial loyalties and affections ('My country is Kiltartan Cross/My countrymen Kiltartan's poor') and to a 'A lonely impulse of delight' which 'drove' him to a 'tumult in the clouds'. In other words, the Irish airman risked the death of which he had prescience, in loyalty to his home ground and in an act of radical self-definition. And in so doing, it was as if he had not died in the war at all, but in some private, chivalric wager of his own, bred of regard for a native place and of high adventure. Yet in writing in this way, as Roy Foster has commented, Yeats had composed the 'war poem' that he had earlier claimed he would not provide.

'An Irish airman foresees his death' is a 'war poem' in two special senses, beyond the fact that it immediately addresses the death of a combatant. Firstly, in imagining Gregory at a great height 'somewhere among the clouds above', Yeats, whether he knew it or not, was giving expression to a general mode of consciousness that had emerged in the terrible conditions of trench warfare. To quote Eric J. Leed once more:

> The aerial perspective—assumed to belong to the flyer—was one of the most significant myths of the war. The necessity for this myth lay precisely in those constrictions that so fragmented the perceptions and purpose of the frontsoldier. The myth of the flyer, of adventure in the air as the last home of chivalric endeavor, is clearly a compensatory notion. It serves to keep open the realm of purpose and meaning with which many entered the war. [10]

So Yeats's airman was able to assess and welcome his own version of fate far above the random slaughter of earth-bound engagements. And in imagining this zone of near metaphysical elevation, Yeats, as a poet, was occupying the same almost mythic dimension that is envisaged in what are indisputably war poems by an Irish survivor of the Great War, Thomas MacGreevy. In his 'Nocturne', dedicated to a soldier who 'died of wounds', MacGreevy sets earth and starry universe in absolute apposition: 'I labour in a barren place/Alone, self-conscious, frightened, blundering;/Far away stars wheeling in space'. In 'De Civitate Hominum' an 'airman' 'high over' the battlefield, is shot down, 'a stroke of orange in the morning's dress' to the awestruck horror of an observer: 'My sergeant says, very low, "Holy God!/'Tis a fearful death"'. [11]

Secondly, as a historian of Irish aviation observed to me, the final lines of Yeats's poem, in their carefully managed rhythmic equilibrium, suggest the actual experience of piloted flight in a small plane, its controlled exhilaration:

> I balanced all, brought all to mind,
> The years to come seemed waste of breath,
> A waste of breath the years behind
> In balance with this life, this death.

The poem floats on its fixed, phrasal wings in one of the very few moments in Yeats's poetic oeuvre when the technology of modernity impacts on the poet's imagination.

The Great War was of course a conflict marked by the deployment of innovative technology and it saw the machine triumph at the expense of the human. This was something the dramatist Seán O'Casey fully understood as is evidenced not only by his Great War play, *The silver tassie* (1928), but also by his drama of the 1916 Rising, *The plough and the stars* (1926). The latter makes compelling reference in its dialogue to the Great War as the context in which the Easter Rising took place. But as a theatrical spectacle, it does so even more significantly, since one of its most striking effects is to dramatise how the Irish Volunteers and the Irish Citizen Army with their showy uniforms and flags are overcome and decimated by the devastating force of modern firepower. There is, too, an awareness of how, in the twentieth-century, war had become 'total', with civilians being caught up and even targeted in generalised assaults on towns and cities. The final, ironic image of British Tommies brewing tea and singing 'Keep the Home Fires Burning' (a popular Great War song) in a Dublin tenement amid the flames of destruction, is a powerful symbol of the domestic invaded by the violence of modern warfare.

The insight shown by O'Casey into Great War realities in *The plough and the stars*, a play Yeats admired, makes Yeats's notorious decision to reject *The silver tassie* when the dramatist sought to have it produced at the Abbey Theatre, all the more troubling. And in light of *The plough and the stars'* sense of how the Easter Rising, like the Great War, saw romantic chivalry pitted against ruthless dehumanising force, Yeats's assertion in a letter to the dramatist that O'Casey was 'not interested in the great war' because he had 'never stood on its battlefields or walked its hospitals', seems uncharacteristically obtuse.

The silver tassie takes Dublin football hero, Harry Heegan, from sporting success by way of the collective slaughter of the Western Front to injury and a convalescence that does nothing for his permanent disablement. The horror of industrial warfare is powerfully represented in its experimental, expressionist second act. In central position on stage is a howitzer gun, which points directly at the audience as if to threaten them with the fate that awaits the cannonfodder in the cast. As Nuala Johnson has remarked of this *coup de theatre*, 'this piece of military hardware is one of the most enduring symbols of the machinery of the war'. And in the play it demands that audiences become fully aware of the terrible attrition wrought by mechanised carnage and of the suffering it left in its wake, knowledge, the play insists, that must not be suppressed or kept 'underground'.[12]

O'Casey's *The silver tassie* probably found some of its inspiration in Wilfred Owen's poem, 'Disabled'. Indeed the play's final images of a former athlete in a wheel-chair at a dance as flirtation and courtship go on without him, seem clearly to derive from Owen's lines (also about a cruelly wounded former football star and soldier): 'To-night he noticed how the women's eyes/Passed from him to the strong men that were whole'. *The silver tassie* also caught some of the poem's bitterness about the home front as a world of women who would offer pity to the war's surviving sacrificial victims, but little more, as the vital possibilities of peace beckoned. Perhaps Yeats, in damning O'Casey's play in 1928, detected something in it of the slightly maudlin atmospherics of its likely source. Certainly, in his letter in which he gave his views on the play he seemed to regret that O'Casey had not struck the appropriate tragic note, in a play governed by 'opinions' worthy only of a newspaper.

Be that as it may, by 1936, when his own view of the necessity for tragedy in art had hardened into the near-doctrine encompassed in his phrase 'tragic joy', it would be Owen himself who would bear the brunt of Yeats's denigra-tion. In what seemed to many an act of wilful suppression, Yeats, as editor, excluded Owen from the *Oxford book of modern verse*, published that year. In the 'Introduction' he justified his decision by stating that 'passive suffering is not a theme for poetry' and he extolled the masculinity of John Synge's verse as if in exemplary contrast. In a letter, he was unabashedly dismissive of Owen: 'When I excluded Wilfred Owen, whom I consider unworthy of the poet's corner of a country newspaper, I did not know I was excluding a revered sandwich-board man of the revolution … He is all blood, dirt and sucked sugar-stick … There is every excuse for him, but none for those who like him'.[13]

By that act of exclusion Yeats appeared to compound the impression given in 1928 that somehow the Great War should be off-limits as an artistic subject, especially for the Irish writer (though *The silver tassie* did get an Abbey pro-duction in 1935). For the Oxford book not only dispatched Owen to oblivion and excluded other English war poets but it also included swathes of verse by Irish poets who did not advert to the Great War at all. It was as if that catas-trophe had only tangentially registered in the aesthetic sphere and had com-pletely passed the Irish poetic imagination by (apart from Yeats's own poem 'An Irish airman foresees his death' and a cursory reference to 'bombs and mud and gas' in a poem by Louis MacNeice).

In this way, Yeats could be seen as giving a kind of *imprimatur* to what the historian Keith Jeffery has identified as the 'amnesiac tendency of southern Ireland to the war'.[14] Indeed, the works by Irish writers who have directly broached the war seem to infringe a Yeatsian interdiction and to reject a set of allied cultural and social conventions by their unearthing of the experience of the Great War. In Jennifer Johnston's novel of 1974, *How many miles to Babylon*, for example, recovering the buried front-line experience reveals how the war for Irish combatants could be a site of unexpected sexual and class alliances that cement mysterious male solidarities.[15] Frank McGuinness's play *Observe the sons of Ulster marching towards the Somme* (1985), takes up, as it were, where O'Casey left off in *The silver tassie* by exploring the homoerotic implications of military comradeship—explicit in O'Casey's probable poetic source and implied at moments in his play.[16] But this time, a 'southern' playwright observes the 'other' Ireland where the myth of the Somme had retained a powerful, public meaning, since the men the play follows are loyalist soldiers of the 36th (Ulster) Division.

Sebastian Barry's novel, *A long long way* (2005), combines a gruesome realism of blood and mud with a sensuous lyricism as if to endorse and extend Wilfred Owen's aesthetic that Yeats had so excoriated, even as it revives the subject of conflicting loyalties in the nationalist tradition of the kind that Ledwidge embodied.[17] And the poet, Michael Longley, who has made the Great War and the image of the 'war poet' a central preoccupation, introduced this theme in his poem 'In Memoriam' (composed for a soldier father who survived the war). Exploring the theme he employs tones that suggested he was deliberately resurrecting familial memories which must be given their full due if his poetry is to avoid mere poeticism:

> My father, let no similes eclipse
> Where crosses like some forest simplified
> Sink into my mind, the slow sands
> Of your history delay till through your eyes
> I read you like a book.[18]

The irony of all this *vis-à-vis* Yeats was that, despite his words and actions, his own poetry was certainly affected by the Great War. Notably, after 1918 his work takes on a marked internationalist aspect. Where formerly Yeats's verse had its eye fixed on the personal life of the poet, on Ireland and on eternity, after the Great War it is the current condition of the world that begins to alarm him. In his protracted spiritualist experiments with his wife, George, which began in the autumn of 1917, history and the meaning of the historical moment in the scheme of things become a dominant concern of that strange activity. So much was this the case that when Yeats reacted in verse to Black-and-Tan atrocities in Lady Gregory's district (the events took place in 1920), he did so in a poem that on its first publication bore the title 'Thoughts upon the present state of the world'. And that poem with its historical perspectives on how a long Victorian and Edwardian peace had given way to 'dragon-ridden' days, can be read as a Yeatsian commentary on the break-up of empire that the Great War set in motion. In this poem, epochal historical changes come home to roost in the local world with a particular viciousness, revealing 'the weasel's twist, the weasel's tooth'.

Furthermore, a poem that was to acquire some of its imagery from George's automatic writing seems to have had its inception in the poet's alarm in the summer of 1918 at events in distant Russia. For Jon Stallworthy has shown how an early draft of Yeats's famous poem of world historical crisis and apoc-alypse, 'The second coming' (begun in the late summer of 1918), contains the phrase 'the Germans are (——) now to Russia come', and he argues that the poem went through a process of composition whereby what were probably allusions to revolutionary events in Russia and to the peace settlement imposed by the German military on the Bolsheviks at Brest-Litovsk in March 1918— became buried in a panoramic vision of violent transformation. Accordingly, Stallworthy asserts that this poem stems 'from a mood of depression brought on by the First World War'.[19]

The internationalism of mind that found expression in Yeats's great post-war poetry was of course something that he shared with his fellow-writer, James Joyce, who had spent some of the war years at work on his experimental, encyclopedic novel *Ulysses*, published in 1922. Set in Dublin in 1904 it could of course make no direct reference to the events of 1914–18, which had compelled Joyce to take refuge in neutral Switzerland. Arguably, however, in its various references to battles ancient and modern and in its profound sense of history as a nightmare from which it is necessary to awake, it too can be read as a work upon which the Great War had significant literary impact. Joyce's ultimate response to the spectacle of human history that so appalled Yeats even as it excited him in 'The second coming' can perhaps be discerned in Leopold Bloom's pacifism, making *Ulysses* a salutary point at which to conclude this survey. 'But it's no use, says he. Force, hatred, history, all that. That's not life for men and women, insult and hatred.'[20]

REMEMBERING

TCD, EPB: *Our Heroes*, 30 July 1915. 1. Lieutenant H.B. Hodges, 2. Captain H.L. Crofton, 3. Lieutenant M.K. Anderson, 4. Captain D. Gaussen, 5. Major St John Adcock, 6. Captain Claude A. French, 7. Lieutenant R.A. Finlay, 8. Lieutenant Maurice C. Rogers, 9. Lieutenant C.D. Considine. This supplement to *Irish Life* published photographs and brief biographies of officers of Irish regiments and Irish officers in British regiments who either died in action or were mentioned in despatches. Reproduced by permission of the Board, Trinity College Dublin.

War memorial at Island Bridge, Dublin, designed by Edwin Lutyens. Courtesy of Keith Jeffery.

•

Stained-glass window of St Philip's Church of Ireland, Dartry, Dublin. It depicts an angel with her arm around a soldier pointing heavenwards and is titled 'Sacrifice'. The theme of a 'blood sacrifice' for the greater good was not uncommon with those dying in the war being beckoned to a better life in heaven. Courtesy of Reverend Sonia Gyles.

•

View of College Green, Dublin, 11 November 1924. Crowds still showed up in great numbers to remember the dead of the Great War despite the fact that the Free State had recently been founded and that the Civil War had just ended. © English Collection.

250

IRISH FREE STATE.

No. 391

DOWNING STREET,

23 November, 1926.

Sir,

I have the honour by command of His Majesty the King, to transmit to Your Excellency, to be laid before your Ministers, the accompanying letter addressed to His Majesty by Miss Emily K.Harris of Ashgrove Cottage, Glenageary Road, Kingstown, County Dublin.

2. I should be glad if, in any reply sent to Miss Harris, it may be made clear that her letter was, by His Majesty's command, referred to the Government of the Irish Free State.

I have the honour to be,

Sir,

Your most obedient,

humble servant,

J.S. Amery

th Nov.

252

Received from C.O.
24 NOV. 1926

GOVERNOR GENERAL,
    HIS EXCELLENCY,
        T.M.HEALY, ESQ., K.C.,
            etc., etc., etc.,

NAI, Department of the Taoiseach 5215: Dispatch from J.S. Amery, Secretary of State for the Dominions, to T.M. Healy, Governor General, 23 November 1926. Courtesy of the National Archives of Ireland.

Following pages: NAI, Department of the Taoiseach 5215: Miss Emily K. Harris to the king of the United Kingdom, 10 November 1926. Miss Harris describes the case of nurses who had served in the Great War and are now in dire circumstances. Courtesy of the National Archives of Ireland.

COPY.

BRITISH RED CROSS HOSPITAL,

Equipped by E.K.Harris,   CORRIG   CASTLE,

For wounded and sick   KINGSTOWN, Co. DUBLIN.
 Sailors and Soldiers
 Officers and Men.

With fully equipped Theatre
& X Ray Room.

Opened March 15, 1915:   42 Beds
Closed Feb. 5, 1919.   14 extra available.

Officers treated,Naval & Military, ..   56
Sailors 356
Soldiers 1128

Deaths 0

10. 11. 26.

TO
    His Most Excellent Majesty
         THE KING,

    May it please your gracious Majesty,

          It was your Majesty's loyal subject's delight and
privilege as a daughter of The British Empire during the late
Great War, to serve as an officer in Your Majesty's Army in my
woman's sphere being specially trained for that purpose in that
my profession of Nursing, to make good the ravages of warfare,
by building anew the wornout, maimed tissues and bodies of the
sons of Your Majesty's vast Empire, fighting for the glory of
their King. For the honour of the Regiment, as a soldier's
daughter, I did my duty, without pay, serving my King for Love.
Thus one of they who needs must, serve best.

          Sunrise and sunset saw Your Majesty's devoted
subject at her post holding Florence Nightingale's lamp, without
weariness, continuing without a falter during the subsequent
civil strife and all the bitter antagonism which fell upon the
faithfull's head.

          And for the reason, Your Majesty's loyal subject
was not a hired servant, I do dutifully, respectfully and humbly
beg Your Gracious Majesty's protection from the stigma now

vouchsafed those loyal women who served also.

That they may not be demoralized by been thrown by the Sheriff's men on the roadside, or they that were injured physically during their ministrations on duty, may not be dragged from their beds and be conveyed to the Union Infirmary, such which has taken place in Kingstown just recently to Miss de Cadiz,

And furthermore an eviction order having been obtained against this, Your Majesty's loyal subject, now awaits her turn for the same indignity,

Your Majesty's loyal subjects do not make appeals to Your Majesty's Bounty of the Private Purse.

It is to Your Majesty's gracious influence on our behalf.

In grief and sorrow, my lovely Home, the trophies of my profession, has been sold by public auction. The presents from grateful patients, each household god fraught with fragrant memories of triumph and success.

And Your Majesty's loyal subject's heart is broken, having returned the Royal Red Cross bestowed by Your Gracious Majesty, in order to obtain justice by been relieved of the onus of my service to my beloved King in Ireland. The Courts are for my justice. Your Majesty, this loyal subject craves only for her Sovereign's protection against been thrown by the Sheriff's men on the roadside.

While Your Majesty's humble petitioner will ever pray to continue Your Majesty's most devoted loyal subject

                              (SGD.) EMILY K. HARRIS.

                              Ashgrove Cottage,
                                Glenageary Road,
                              Kingstown, Co. Dublin.

From

    Miss Emily K. Harris, A.R.R.C.,

        (late) Commandant and Matron

            British Red Cross Hospital, Corrig Castle.

Bagenalstown Branch of the British Legion of Ex-Service Men

We the undersigned respectfully ask that you would consider the following applications re Ex-Soldiers.

In Co. Kilkenny we learn that the rent of the cottages and plots are 3/- per week, and we in Bagenalstown are paying 5/- per week and taxes.   The general run of houses in this town are rented from 1/- to 1/6 per week.

There has been no employment here for Ex-Service men for the past 2 or 3 years, and there is no scheme whatever around here to provide work for them   In fact 90% of them are out of work, and no prospect of getting any in the near future.

James Mara
John Culleton
George Darcy
John Monaghan
Michael Cunningham
Martin Hanlon
Francis Cosgrove
Laurence Lakes
Peter Hayes
Ben. Ryan
James Dudley
Joseph Dorgan
Jeremiah Clarke
Thomas Foy
William Stevenson
Thomas Walsh

NAI, f 42: Petition from the Bagenalstown (Co. Carlow) Branch of the British Legion of Ex-Servicemen, 28 May 1928. In it the veterans list their difficulties in surviving without work and with high rents. Courtesy of the National Archives of Ireland.

55 Shandon Park,
Phibsboro
15. 7. 1957.

Mr De Valera
Government Buildings

Dear Sir.

    ✗ My husband John Freeman late of Ordnance Survey Office, Phoenix Park, has retired on £3 5 weekly pension. This leaves us in very poor circumstances, and his gratuity has almost dwindled away trying to support, and keep us in our home.

    He fought in the 1914 – 1918 war, and returned, was reinstated in his job, but receives no military pension. In view of this fact, may I request you very ardently to have his case looked into with a view to granting him a pension, as we are in very poor circumstances. In fact leaving our home is the spectre looking into our faces, if some attention is not paid to our case.

        Yours faithfully,
        Mrs. Margaret Freeman.

17 Iúil, 1957.

A chara,

     I am to acknowledge the receipt
of your letter of the 15th instant addressed
to the Taoiseach and to state that the
question of an award of pension in respect
of service in the World War of 1914-1918
would not be a matter for the Government of
Ireland.

     Mise, le meas,

Rúnaí Príobháideach

Mrs. Margaret Freeman,
55, Shandon Park,
Phibsboro,
Dublin.

·

NAI, Department of the Taoiseach, 14097/b2: Margaret Freeman to Eamon de
Valera, 15 July 1957. She explains how her husband, a veteran of the Great War, and
herself are in dismal circumstances. 'In fact leaving our home is the spectre looking into
our faces'. The reply from de Valera's private secretary is terse 'an award of pension in
respect of service in the World War of 1914–1918 would not be a matter for the
Government of Ireland' reflecting the unwillingness of newly independent Ireland to
acknowledge the contribution of veterans of the Great War. Courtesy of the National
Archives of Ireland.

·

Victory parade in Dublin, 19 July 1919. Scene from rooftops of Trinity College looking up Westmoreland Street towards O'Connell Bridge. The Union Jack flies over College Green and Trinity College. Despite large crowds, thousands of veterans refused to march and salute Lord French as Lord–Lieutenant of Ireland. © RTÉ Stills Library.

IWM, ART 3013: *Just come from the Chemical Works, Roeux*: 21st May 1917 by William Orpen. A Royal Irish Fusilier takes a rest after experiencing the horrors of a chemical works. © Imperial War Museum.

CHAPTER 10

Echoes of war

KEITH JEFFERY

262

The King commands me

to assure you of the true sympathy

of His Majesty and The Queen

in your sorrow.

Kitchener

No part of Irish life—its politics, society, economy or culture—was unaffected by the Great War of 1914–18, the impact of which and its resonances echo down through the years in some, perhaps, unexpected places.[1] Two anecdotes illustrate the ubiquity of what we might call the 'cultural legacy' of the war—and show, too, that 'culture' is not just a matter of so-called 'high' art, literature or music, but also concerns the popular end of the spectrum including the apparently trivial.

The first anecdote is about the naming of biscuits. Shopping for bread one day in a Belfast home bakery, I noticed among the displays at the counter some jam-sandwich-type biscuits with icing on top.

> 'What do you call those?' I asked the assistant.
> 'German biscuits', she said.
> 'In New Zealand', I said, parading my international expertise, 'they call them "Belgian biscuits"'.
> 'Yes', replied the assistant, 'some people call them that as well'.

'German' or 'Belgian', does it make a difference? The biscuits are the same, but the naming of them certainly 'made a difference' in New Zealand in the autumn of

NMI, HA/2004/132: Standard note from king and queen offering sympathy, signed by Kitchener on their behalf. Sent to Mrs Laura Boland, from Cork City, on the event of her son, Sidney's, death. Sidney had followed his elder brother, William, to Canada in hopes of enlisting in the same regiment. Four of Mrs Boland's sons served in the armed forces during the Great War: William, Sidney, Harry and Wilfred, only Wilfred survived. Courtesy of the National Museum of Ireland.

1914, when it, a small country, was mobilising on behalf of another small country, Belgium, in the face of invasion by an aggressive, militarist neighbour. And the change of name survives—rather in the same way that 'German shepherd' dogs became 'Alsatians' at that time—as a cultural legacy of the war, even if the reason for the change, or the change itself, has been long forgotten.

The second story concerns the naming of streets. When I was a child, living in the Belfast inner suburb of Cregagh, we had our newspapers delivered by the 'Hamel Newsagency', an unusual spelling which means nothing until you look at the street-names around the shop: Picardy, Bapaume and Thiepval avenues; Hamel, Albert and Somme drives; all names from the Battle of the Somme in 1916. 'Hamel' derives its name from Beaumont Hamel where in just 40 minutes on the first day of the battle, the Newfoundland Regiment (men from another island who had come a long way to fight) suffered over 90% casualties.[2] In Cregagh, there is a 'colony' of houses—homes fit for heroes—built for ex-servicemen by the Irish Sailors' and Soldiers' Land Trust in the 1920s. There are clusters of Land Trust houses across the whole island and you can sometimes spot them from the street-names. There is a Jellicoe Avenue in North Belfast, named after the British admiral; a Messines Park in Derry, named after the Belgian battlefield where the 16th (Irish) and 36th (Ulster) divisions fought alongside each other in 1917; and a Haig Gardens in Cork City, named after Sir Douglas Haig, the commander-in-chief of the BEF in France from 1915 to the end of the war.

What is remarkable about these battlefield place names is the way in which terrible sites of death and destruction are commemorated in what have become prosaic home addresses. The French have a word for it: *banalisation*.[3] It is difficult to translate this precisely, but it conveys the sense of rendering something banal or ordinary, and in this particular case it is making something frightful and extraordinary quite mundane and commonplace. But, all the same, one wonders how it was for those veterans returning from the horrors of the war to be thus reminded of the trenches and the slaughter every day; with places where comrades had died becoming a mere address where people live. Perhaps that is as it should be. Yet there remains, to turn a phrase, a little corner (or two) of an Irish field (an Ulster one in this case) which is forever France. There are other ways in which Western Front place names have been embedded into the lives of Irish people. A recent study of the war memorial in Portadown, Co. Armagh, draws our attention to Edward Jones, a 38-year old stretcher-bearer serving with the Royal Irish Fusiliers who was killed in action in Belgium on 16 August 1917. His widow Maria named their yet-to-be-born son Edward *Ypres* Jones after his dead father and the place where he was killed.[4]

The names of the war dead are commemorated on war memorials all over Ireland: statues, obelisks, Celtic crosses and the like, which we may pass by without a second thought about their history or the stories of those they commemorate. Yet each memorial and every name has a tale to tell; every individual commemorated who failed to return left a family to mourn, for whom that very monument may have been the only gravestone for a beloved husband, father, brother or sweetheart. Some of the war memorials themselves are works of art. There are two extraordinary larger-than-life figures on the Derry memorial: one a soldier with rifle and fixed bayonet apparently about to disembowel some unfortunate German; the other an amazing, muscular barefoot sailor, perhaps the greatest, and certainly the most powerful, figurative public sculpture on the island. In Cobh, Co. Cork, there is a fine memorial to those who were lost on the *Lusitania*, torpedoed by a German U-boat in May 1915, with two weary and grieving fishermen, representatives of those who went out to rescue the victims of the attack. In other places, the sculpture was more modest, such as in Downpatrick, where the soldier, carved by a local man, was reportedly so awful 'that when it was unveiled an old soldier in the crowd dropped down dead'.[5]

The grandest Irish war memorial is the national one at Islandbridge on the River Liffey, just opposite Phoenix Park in Dublin. It is a landscaped park with a 30-ft high cross, a 'Stone of Remembrance', rose-gardens, fountains and four stone pavilions linked by pergolas. Designed in the 1930s by Edwin Lutyens, one of the greatest British imperial architects (though he had an Irish mother), it was partially completed by 1939, but was left to deteriorate and be vandalised for 50 years. Recently magnificently restored, it is a place both of tranquil beauty where one can contemplate the loss of tens of thousands of Irish lives in both world wars and, now also, full of life, it is a well-used public park where folk can take a Sunday constitutional and children play.[6]

Edwin Lutyens did very little work in Ireland, but in St Patrick's Catholic Church in Donegall Street, Belfast, there is a picture frame he designed for a painting by John Lavery, entitled *The Madonna of the lakes*. The picture shows Lavery's wife Hazel—who was a celebrated beauty (and later appeared symbolising an Irish colleen on the first banknotes of the Free State)—as the Madonna, a role she had taken in London society *tableaux vivants* ('living pictures') to raise funds for Great War charities. Lavery was baptised in the church and he gave the painting as a memento of his family's connection with it. In 1917 John Buchan, the head of the new British Department of Information—a sort of high-class propaganda outfit—appointed Lavery as an official 'war artist', and he spent the rest of the war, mostly in Britain, painting scenes far from the battle front, of hospitals, barrage balloons and distant naval manoeuvres. Only when the war was over did he go to France to paint the battlefields themselves. The single major war painting of his that hangs in a gallery in Ireland is one of some two dozen pictures he donated to the Belfast Municipal Museum and Art Gallery in 1929. It is called *Daylight raid from my studio window, 7 July 1917*, and shows Hazel Lavery looking up out of a tall west London window at a distant squadron of German Gotha bombers. Hazel is a helpless civilian, a potential victim, and the painting reminds us that in this war, for virtually the first time, civilians too could be in the front line, that in this new, industrialised and mechanised 'total war', the fighting and the killing were by no means confined to the battle-zone itself.

Along with Lavery, Dublin-born William Orpen was also a British official war artist. Unlike Lavery, Orpen spent a lot of time in 1917 and 1918 in France and Flanders itself, just behind the front line, painting an extraordinary range of beautiful and disturbing pictures. During 1917 he worked on the Somme battlefield where the previous year the 36th (Ulster) Division had suffered terribly on the battle's opening day, 1 July, and where the 16th (Irish) Division— 'John Redmond's pets'—had fought two months later. Orpen's pale, pastel-coloured paintings show a dream-like landscape, occasionally scarred by shell craters and rusting barbed wire, and almost entirely without any people, or at least living people. But Orpen also painted formal portraits of generals and politicians (portraiture was one of his great strengths), as well as marvellous images of 'ordinary' soldiers, such as his charcoal drawing of an exhausted Irish Fusilier *Just come from the chemical works, Rœux: 21st May, 1917*: an Irish everyman in British uniform (see p. 260). Another painting from 1917, *Changing billets, Picardy*, is altogether darker: a bleak landscape with modernistic searchlights cutting through the night sky, with two decidedly unheroic soldiers, one clearly too tired to care about anything and the other roughly embracing a reluctant female companion.[7]

After the war, Orpen was sent to the peace conference in Paris and was commissioned by the recently founded Imperial War Museum (IWM) to paint three grand, composite pictures of the political and military leaders involved. He completed two of these, featuring the politicians: David Lloyd George, Woodrow Wilson, Georges Clemenceau and the rest. He began work on the third painting, which was to feature generals and admirals, but changed his mind half-way through, painted out the servicemen and replaced them with a solitary flag-draped coffin flanked by two spectral figures, half-naked British 'Tommies', with rifles and bayonets fixed. When asked what this meant, Orpen replied that, 'after all the negotiations and discussions, the Armistice and the

Peace, the only tangible result' was 'the ragged unemployed soldier and the Dead'. The IWM was not impressed and refused to take the painting, but it was a great success with the public, who voted it 'Picture of the Year' at the London Royal Academy's 1923 summer exhibition. Five years later, Orpen painted out the ghostly soldiers and presented the picture to the museum as a memorial to Earl Haig, who had recently died.[8] It hangs in the museum to this day, a moving and contemplative image indeed, but by no means as subversive and disturbing as the first version.

The Ulster Division's experience of the Somme, which became for Ulster unionists a sacred sacrifice where the union was sealed with the blood of Ulstermen, spawned its own crop of cultural resonances. As previously mentioned, a famous painting by James P. Beadle, depicting men from the division going over the top at the start of the battle now hangs in Belfast City Hall. The painting itself was much reproduced in popular prints, banners of Orange lodges and sometimes in those murals that are such a distinctive feature of contemporary Belfast. Many loyalist murals commemorate and celebrate the service and sacrifice of Ulstermen—invariably assumed to be *unionist* Ulstermen, as if there could be no other—in the Ulster Division during the war. Cementing the memory of this stupendous battle, and the tragic losses which accompanied it, is a Presbyterian and Biblical sense of pilgrimage, personal commitment and noble, self-sacrificial endeavour: 'Greater love', indeed, 'hath no man than this, that a man lay down his life for his friends'.[9]

In the loyalist lexicon this sacrifice was not just for the comrades who served together at the battlefront, but for political friends too, unionist friends, wherever they may have been. Joined with that other resonant river, the Boyne, the Somme has become embedded in the liturgy of loyalism to such an extent that the very battle itself and the actual, appalling events of 1 July 1916, have often become divorced from what we might call the 'cultural memory' of the event. Some years ago in a loyalist souvenir shop in East Belfast I purchased a greeting card with Beadle's painting on the front. It was, in fact, a birthday card; on the outside was 1 July 1916—when the British Army suffered its greatest ever casualties on a single day—and inside it read: 'Many happy returns of the day'. Here, again, we have *banalisation*. The image of the war, its representation on this piece of ephemera, remains important—otherwise it would not have been used in the first place—but what that picture represents in terms of history and what happened on that terrible day have become detached, divorced perhaps, from thier modern meaning as a kind of loyalist icon. In a paradoxical way the Somme and the 'memory' of the Somme have taken on a life of their own and become so overwhelmingly important that they have come to suffuse all sorts of everyday things, even such an unlikely artefact (though important in its own way) as a birthday card.

Over the past twenty years or so, several bodies have been formed to ensure that Ireland's engagement with the Great War has become better understood. For example, the Somme Association was founded in 1990 with the intention that 'the efforts of Irishmen to preserve world peace between 1914 and 1919 are remembered and understood', and the Royal Dublin Fusiliers Association was founded in 1997 with the purpose of remembering 'those who have been forgotten for a long time, particularly the tens of thousands of Irishmen and indeed many women, who fell in the First World War'. With a magnificent effort and hard work, the Somme Association established the Somme Heritage Centre near Newtownards, Co. Down, with displays and exhibits, a 'multi-media recreation of the battle', a 'hands-on' activity area aimed especially at school groups, and a souvenir shop. While the centre is valuable in bringing knowledge of the battle and the Great War to new generations of people, the categorisation of the Somme as 'heritage' inevitably entails 'merchandising' and a certain 'commodification' of the war and its experience. With the souvenir shop come Somme pencils, Somme erasers, Somme mugs, ties and plastic carrier-bags, all items as banal, if not more so, than any birthday card.

I suppose these artefacts might themselves be conceived as types of war memorial. Perhaps 'war memento' would be a better way of putting it. But many of them are quite practical things, and this itself is an old story. There was a debate in the 1920s among those who wanted to create war memorials as to what form they should take. In effect this boiled down to two alternatives: either you build a memorial or a monument, which is essentially symbolic and commemorative in nature, or you create some practical thing of tangible benefit for the bereaved, the damaged survivors or the community in general. An example of a symbolic memorial is the small obelisk displaying a figure of a Munster Fusilier which stands on the South Mall in Cork, though this particular monument also carries a very definite political message about what the soldiers who served, and those who died, were actually doing in the war. It was, says the inscription, erected by the nationalist-leaning Cork Independent Ex-Servicemen's Club, 'in memory of their comrades who fell in the Great War fighting for the freedom of small nations': Belgium, Serbia, and, for them, Ireland.

On the practical side, some suggestions were more ambitious than the funds allowed. In Lurgan, Co. Armagh, a technical school, a cottage hospital and a public swimming baths were all suggested, before the plans were scaled down and a symbolic 'modest temple' surmounted by a bronze figure representing 'the spirit of Victorious Peace' was erected in 1928. Memorial stained glass windows, common in Protestant churches, and a few Catholic ones too, perhaps combine utility with a symbolic quality. War memorial halls were quite a popular option, and there are many dotted around the country, including one on Eden Quay, Dublin, remembering the 500 dead from the mail-boat, *Leinster*, torpedoed by a German U-boat on its way to Holyhead from Dún Laoghaire (or Kingstown as it was then called) just a month before the end of the war. A new operating theatre was built for the county hospital in Cavan. Trinity College Dublin combined symbolic function with utility by erecting a Hall of Honour, bearing the names of the TCD men who served in the war, which acted as the entrance to a new reading room for its library, the ensemble constituting the College War Memorial. The case for a practical memorial was firmly expressed by H.M. Pollock, Minister of Finance in the Northern Ireland government, in 1926, at the dedication of the Presbyterian War Memorial Hostel in Belfast, which provided accommodation for 200 young people, protecting them from the terrors and temptations of the big city. 'Much', he declared, 'was said of memorials in marble and stone and of statues, but the object of the hostel memorial was to carry out a noble purpose, the combating of evil influences and the attacks of the microbes of evil.'[10]

There were also Irish musical responses to the Great War, both at the time and since, and they provide a useful focus on the broader patterns of war remembrance in Ireland. The Dublin-born Charles Villiers Stanford, who had long been resident in England and a pillar of the 'British' musical establishment, wrote some patriotic 'war music' during the conflict itself, including 'The Aviator's Hymn' of 1917, and the same year he dedicated his Irish Rhapsody No. 5 to the Irish Guards, the senior regiment of Irish infantry in the British Army. In 1924 (the year he died) a song entitled 'With the Dublin Fusiliers' was published. In it, Stanford's arrangement of an old Irish air was paired with words by another Irishman, Alfred Perceval Graves (brother of the poet, writer, Great War officer and sometime Irishman, Robert Graves). With an echo of 'gallant little Belgium' and the impulses that apparently propelled Corkmen to the front, the verses celebrate the time:

> When Irishmen together band
> In arms to aid a Sister Land
> And free her from a tyrant's hand

The song ends on a upbeat note, even though by the time it was published Ireland had experienced the violence and bitterness of war and civil war, and the Dublin Fusiliers themselves, as an Irish regiment of the British Army, had been disbanded:

> Then Peace returned and from the war
> By land and sea we homeward bore
> Till all along old Dublin's shore
> Rang out a shout of welcome.[11]

The comforting vision purveyed by this song of Irishmen, nationalists and unionists, marching off to help sister nations in their time of peril, and returning to some sort of triumphant welcome, was not so very far from what actually happened. Many people in the Free State appreciated the part played by Irish soldiers in the Great War, and their sacrifice, although it had not led directly to the creation of the new state. Ten years after the war began, 20,000 veterans paraded at the 1924 Armistice Day commemoration in front of an estimated 50,000 spectators in College Green, Dublin (see pp. *250–1*). Thousands upon thousands of men and women participated in the annual Remembrance ceremonies throughout the interwar period in the Free State as well as in Northern Ireland. In the 1920s the new Cumann na nGaedheal government was represented every year in the wreath-laying at the Cenotaph in London, and even de Valera's Fianna Fáil government granted a public subsidy after 1932 for the construction of the national memorial at Islandbridge.

Yet it would be surprising if the seismic political changes in Ireland resulting from the war had not provoked a different, republican response that contested the retrospective legitimisation of the war, and which found expression in commemorations of the Easter Rising during the same period. This, too, was put into verse and music. Writing during the conflict, Dora Sigerson Shorter, a passionate Irish republican, slipped into a poem, 'Loud shout the flaming tongues of war', a reference to the disastrous campaign at Gallipoli, where the 10th (Irish) Division was blooded in August 1915. In the poem, she excoriates those who had fallen under the spell of 'the Lion'—England—and had misguidedly gone to fight in the Great War, while the martyrs of the 1916 Rising are mourned by 'Grannia Wael' (Granauaile)—Grace O'Malley, the legendary late sixteenth-century woman captain and prototype Irish patriot.

> Ah, Grannia Wael, thy stricken head
> Is bowed o'er thy dead,
> Thy dead who died for love of thee,
> Not for some foreign liberty.

Shall we betray when hope is near,
Our Motherland whom we hold dear,
To go to fight on foreign strand,
For foreign rights and foreign land?[12]

Thus the beaches of Gallipoli, Suvla Bay and the rest, are dismissed as no more than a 'foreign strand', while the 'rights of small nations', 'gallant little Belgium' and so on are merely 'foreign rights and foreign land'.

After the war, this tradition and the special place reserved for the Gallipoli campaign was encapsulated in one of the most famous and enduring Irish 'rebel' songs of modern times, 'The Foggy Dew', whose words were written by a parish priest from Ulster, Father (later Canon) Charles O'Neill. He wrote the lyrics some time shortly after he witnessed the first meeting of the Irish republican parliament, the Dáil, in Dublin in 1919. The music was not original and comes from an old love song, recorded by the celebrated Irish tenor John McCormack in 1913 (McCormack, incidentally, played his part in the allied war effort, recording war-time songs such as 'It's a long way to tipperary', and 'Keep the home fires burning'). O'Neill's song reflects on the contrast between those Irish who fought with the rebels in 1916, and those who served with the British Army in the Great War (though he did *not* remark on the fewness of the former, and the many of the latter):

Right proudly high over Dublin town they hung out the flag
    of war.
'Twas better to die 'neath an Irish sky than at Suvla or Sed el
    bar.
[...]
'Twas England bade our Wild Geese go that small nations
    might be free.
But their lonely graves are by Suvla's waves and the fringe of
    the grey North Sea.[13]

This view of Gallipoli stands in sharp contrast to the 'heroic-romantic' version that prevailed in Australia during the same period, which drew on the epic of the ANZACs (Australian and New Zealand Army Corps) as narrated in the official history of the war by the journalist, C.E.W. Bean, to provide a founding myth of nationhood.[14] Australia was created, as a federal state, only in 1901 and Gallipoli, while a calamitous failure, was the first time that young men from the island continent went to war, and died, *as* Australians. In this respect, it was equivalent to the Easter Rising since both events demonstrated that, quite apart from the immediate military outcome, defeat in war can consecrate other identities—with the 'flag of war over Dublin town' serving this function in independent Ireland, especially in the republican view of history.

Subsequently, the notion that the Great War had been an essentially pointless power conflict in which Irish lives (among many others) were needlessly wasted came to hold wider sway in independent Ireland. The real turning-point was the Second World War, when the Free State remained neutral and any commemoration of the Great War could become identified with support for the British war effort, so much so that Armistice Day parades in Dublin were banned. Official silence was compounded by a growing public reticence to commemorate the Great War openly, especially with the onset of the civil conflict in Northern Ireland in 1969. A stark reminder of just how emotive the symbolism of the Great War could still be was provided by the IRA's bombing at the Enniskillen Remembrance Sunday ceremony in 1987.

This view, though politicised by the particular antagonisms of the Irish conflict, found parallels in a wider perception from the 1960s, at least in the English-speaking world, that the Great War had been a particularly futile confrontation whose only real message was the soldiers' suffering. This was the lesson taken by the British public from the 1964 BBC TV series on *The Great War*.[15] It was reinforced in the case of Australia by that country's controversial participation in Vietnam for which, unlike the Great War, soldiers were conscripted, and was captured perfectly by the 1972 song written by Eric Bogle at the height of the anti-Vietnam agitation, 'And the band played Waltzing Matilda'. In it, a keen young man from Sydney goes off to war, but returns home, broken and disillusioned by the bloody experience of battle. In the final verse, now among the few old surviving veterans, he watches an Anzac Day parade and sees the ex-servicemen marching past as 'tired old heroes from a forgotten war', and 'the young people ask, what are they marching for?'

The song was a worldwide hit, and was much played in Ireland with The Dubliners recording a memorable version. There were Irish imitations too, though in contrast to Bogle's consistent anti-war sentiment, they emphasised the 'Foggy Dew' notion that republican insurrection redeemed the pointlessness of the Great War. The latter is epitomised by 'Gallipoli', sung by The Irish Brigade, in which a brave young Irish boy is 'blown to Kingdom Come on the shores of Gallipoli':

You fought for the wrong country, you died for the wrong
   cause
And your Ma often said, it was Ireland's great loss,
All those fine young men who marched off to war on foreign
   shores,
When the greatest war of all was at home.[16]

Given the prevalence of an unfavourable nationalist perspective on the war, it is scarcely surprising that, during the fiftieth anniversary celebrations for the Easter Rising in 1966, the events in Dublin predominated to the exclusion of almost everything else. The Great War, if mentioned at all, was no more than a tragic backdrop to the 'main action'—the 'greatest war of all'—at home. But in one largely forgotten instance the cultural resonance of the Great War, and Ireland's engagement with it, was incorporated in a work commissioned by RTÉ to mark the occasion. This was the cantata, 'A Terrible Beauty is Born' by the Irish composer, Brian Boydell. In a recent study of how the Easter Rising was commemorated in 1966, this work is virtually ignored, perpetuating the view of the war as an irrelevance to any study of the topic.[17]

But what Boydell and his librettist Tomás Ó Súilleabháin did, in a remarkably pioneering way, was to recognise the essentially 'seamless robe' of the Rising and the war, and incorporate it into their work. The text naturally drew on Yeats's famous poem 'Easter 1916', and also the work of Thomas MacDonagh, one of the 1916 leaders executed after the Rising. But it also quoted poems by Francis Ledwidge and Tom Kettle, who were both killed on the Western Front. The climax of the piece, indeed, is a setting of Kettle's poem 'Cancel the Past', which envisioned reconciliation in some future free Ireland between Irishmen who had fought on different sides during the war: 'Bound, from the toil of hate we may not cease/Free, we are free to be your friend'.[18]

Since the end of armed conflict in Northern Ireland in the 1990s, and with the process of North–South reconciliation set in train by the Belfast Agreement of 1998, it has become much easier to conflate the 1916 Rising with the Great War and to recognise the powerful connections between the two, even if this is still not universally accepted. The clearest example in commemorative terms is the inauguration on 11 November 1998 of the Island of Ireland Peace Tower at Mesen/Messines in Belgium, near the spot where the 16th (Irish) and 36th (Ulster) divisions fought alongside each other in 1917. Equally noteworthy in the Republic was the government's decision in 2006 to commemorate the ninetieth anniversaries of both the Rising and the Battle of the Somme. A recent

273

musical manifestation of the same trend was the English National Opera's production in 2000 of an opera based on Seán O'Casey's play *The Silver Tassie*, by the English composer, Mark Anthony Turnage, which was staged in Dublin the following year.

In the opera, as in the play (see Chapter 9), the action travels from Dublin to the Western Front and back, during which the footballer hero, Harry Heegan, is reduced to a helpless and embittered cripple. Amanda Holden, Turnage's librettist, in fact, originally specified that the operatic version should be set in 'a town somewhere in Britain'. But Turnage insisted on retaining the Irish locations of the original, remarking that 'to ignore the Irishness of it' was 'almost obscene'.[19] Bearing in mind the apparent resolution of the Northern Irish 'Troubles' and the growing understanding that at the end of the twentieth century as much as in its early years Irish and British allegiances on the island both had legitimacy, Turnage felt that O'Casey's play and his opera had something to say regarding Ireland's contemporary situation.

We are perhaps a little too ready (albeit for the best of motives) to make facile generalisations about motivations, commitments and the 'equality of sacrifice' of Irish Catholics and Protestants, nationalists and unionists, in the Great War. The Irish dead of the conflict have today been conscripted (as the living Irish of the war years never were) to serve in a very political, if well-meaning, project of mutual communal understanding and reconciliation. Although a number of people at the time hoped that common service in the trenches might actually bring Irishmen together and help heal the divisions between different political and religious groups, it may well be that most Irish soldiers could not have cared one way or the other. We will never finally know exactly what the 'historical reality' of 1914–18 was beyond the grim fact that many of those who went to the war never returned. Indeed, while we shall never know precisely how many died, the dead are the *only* certainty.

Of all the places where Irishmen lie forever in foreign fields and foreign soil, perhaps the most poignant and evocative are those unmatched and moving Commonwealth War Graves Commission cemeteries at Suvla Bay on the peninsula of Gallipoli. It is a wild, distant, beautiful place. Dubliners in the Irish Division who landed there in August 1915 found a 'pebbly white strand like the beach at Portmarnock', and low clay cliffs 'rather like the shore at Killiney Bay'. For these men, *banalisation* worked the other way. Seeking to assert some control over their strange and foreign new situation, they found familiar places to compare with the Mediterranean countryside. And thus they endeavoured to tame that battlefield and find some homely comfort in their predicament.

In 1921 G.C. Duggan, a civil servant by profession, published a slim
volume of lyrical verse, *The watchers on Gallipoli*. He dedicated the book 'To
my brothers George and Jack [see pp. *108–29*], 10th (Irish) Division, killed at
Suvla, 16th August, 1915—this memorial'. In his final poem, 'The rearguard'
Duggan draws together brothers from across Great Britain and Ireland and
beyond, from 'the wide plains of Southland', from the Sussex hills and Scottish
highlands, and also 'brothers from the West', scented with the gorse from 'soft
Irish hills' and who 'loved your Island's honour best'.

> March away, my brothers; softly march away;
> The waves are hissing round us, the East is turning grey.
> The coast, the cliffs are silent. Gone are we all, but they
> Watch ever in the stillness that falls o'er Suvla Bay.[20]

Those losses, those individual lives lost, multiplied 10,000-fold, remain the
central reference-point for any 'memory', cultural or otherwise, of the Great
War. And that is why, no matter how inconsequential or distant any Irish
resonance of the war (or any resonance anywhere) may seem to be, it can never,
ever, be 'banal'.

275

Derry memorial: a muscular sailor and a soldier about to bayonet the enemy. Symbols of war's violence live on in post-war Northern Ireland. Courtesy of Keith Jeffery.

Endnotes

Chapter 1

[1] The prominent place of the war in Northern Irish life means that Ulster soldiers were for a long time more visible, including in the official history of the 36th Division by Cyril Falls, published as early as 1922 and recently reissued (*The history of the 36th (Ulster) Division* (London, 1998)) and the important work based on oral testimonies by Philip Orr, *The road to the Somme: men of the Ulster Division tell their story* (Belfast, 1987). Pioneering work has been done on soldiers from the rest of Ireland and from Catholic and nationalist backgrounds by (among others) Terence Denman, *Ireland's unknown soldiers: the 16th (Irish) Division in the Great War* (Dublin, 1992), Myles Dungan with *Irish voices from the Great War* (Dublin, 1995) and *They shall grow not old. Irish soldiers and the Great War* (Dublin, 1997) and Philip Orr in his latest book, *Field of bones. An Irish division at Gallipoli* (Dublin, 2006); Timothy Bowman, *The Irish regiments in the Great War—discipline and morale* (Manchester, 2003). For a full list, see Selected Reading at the end of this volume. However, many topics that have been opened up by work on combat and soldiers' experiences in other countries, remain to be tackled. They include soldiers' faith and the role of chaplains, relations with the home front, shell shock, discipline and executions, life behind the lines (sport and music-hall entertainment), the changing nature of combat, prisoners-of-war, demobilisation and returning home, veterans' organisations and family memories.

[2] The exceptions include David Fitzpatrick's pioneering *Politics and Irish life 1913–1921: provincial experience of war and revolution* (Dublin, 1977; new edn., Cork, 1998); an influential volume of student essays, David Fitzpatrick (ed.), *Ireland and the First World War* (Dublin, 1986); Thomas Hennessy, *Dividing Ireland. World War I and partition* (London and New York, 1998); Keith Jeffery's stimulating cultural history, *Ireland and the Great War* (Cambridge, 2000); a set of essays that focuses firmly on the war, Adrian Gregory and Senia Pašeta (eds), *Ireland and the Great War: 'A war to unite us all?'* (Manchester, 2002); Jérôme aan de Wiel, *The Catholic Church in Ireland, 1914–1918: war and politics* (Dublin, 2003), which is informed by international scholarship on the war; and Nuala C. Johnson, *Ireland, the Great War and the geography of remembrance* (Cambridge, 2003).

[3] Antoine Prost and Jay Winter, *The Great War in history. Debates and controversies, 1914 to the present* (Cambridge, 2005), 6–33.

[4] Stéphane Audoin-Rouzeau and Annette Becker, *14–18. Understanding the Great War* (Paris, 2000; trans. Catherine Temerson, New York, 2002), 114–16.

[5] Sigmund Freud, *Thoughts for the times on war and death* (1915) reproduced in The Penguin Freud Library, *Group psychology, civilization and its discontents and other works* (London, 1991), vol. 12, 65.

[6] John Horne, *State, society and mobilization in Europe during the First World War* (Cambridge, 1997), 1–17.

[7] John Horne, '"Propagande" et "vérité" dans la Grande Guerre', in Christophe Prochasson and Anne Rasmussen (eds), *Vrai et faux dans la Grande Guerre* (Paris, 2004), 76–95.

[8] Ben Novick, *Conceiving revolution. Irish nationalist propaganda during the First World War* (Dublin, 2001), 246–7.

[9] For an influential example, see Jean-Jacques Becker and Stéphane Audoin-Rouzeau (eds), *Guerre et cultures, 1914–1918* (Paris, 1994).

[10] David Fitzpatrick, 'Militarism in Ireland, 1900–1922', in Thomas Bartlett and Keith Jeffery (eds), *A military history of Ireland* (Cambridge, 1996), 379–406 (here 388).

[11] Freud, *Group psychology*, 79–80.

[12] Jeffery, *Ireland and the Great War*, 33–5. The 49,000 recorded on the National War Memorial at Islandbridge, Dublin, include Irishmen recruited in Britain and the empire and non-Irishmen serving in Irish regiments. Thirty thousand is a better approximation of those who died having enlisted from Ireland.

[13] The exception, and precursor, is the American Civil War; see Drew Gilpin Faust, *This republic of suffering. Death and the American Civil War* (New York, 2008).

[14] Avner Ben Amos, *Funerals, politics and memory in modern France, 1789–1996* (Oxford, 2000), 216–19; Alex King, *Memorials of the Great War in Britain: the symbolism and politics of remembrance* (Oxford, 1998).

[15] Jane Leonard, 'The twinge of memory: Armistice Day and Remembrance Sunday in Dublin since 1919', in Richard English and Graham Walker (eds), *Unionism in modern Ireland. New perspectives on politics and culture* (Basingstoke, 1996), 99–114.

[16] George Mosse, *Fallen soldiers. Reshaping the memory of the world wars* (Ithaca, NY, 1990), 96–8.

[17] Adrian Gregory, *The silence of memory. Armistice Day 1919–1946* (Oxford, 1994), 149–83; Antoine Prost, *In the wake of war. 'Les Anciens Combattants' and French society* (Providence and Oxford, 1992), 51–78.

[18] Jay Winter, *Sites of memory, sites of mourning. The Great War in European cultural history* (Cambridge, 1995), 78–116.

[19] Hennessy, *Dividing Ireland*, 80–5.

[20] John Horne and Alan Kramer, *German atrocities, 1914. A history of denial* (New Haven and London, 2001), 9–86.

[21] In this volume, *Irish National Volunteers* refers to the nationalist Volunteer movement of 1913–14, prior to its split in September 1914. At this point the organisation fractured in two becoming the *National Volunteers* who remained loyal to John Redmond and the *Irish Volunteers* who supported Eoin MacNeill, opposing Redmond's war policy.

[22] T.M. Kettle, 'The Last Crusade', in T.M. Kettle, *The ways of war* (London, 1917), 47.

[23] Wiel, *Catholic Church in Ireland*, 41.

[24] Orr, *Field of bones*.

[25] Arrigo Serpieri, *La Guerra e le classi rurali italiani* (Rome and Bari, 1930), 83–91.

[26] Philip Bull, *Land, politics and nationalism: a study of the Irish land question* (Dublin, 1996), 176–92.

[27] John Horne, 'Labor and labor movements in World War I', in Jay Winter, Geoffrey Parker and Mary Habeck (eds), *The Great War and the twentieth century* (New Haven and London, 2000), 187–227.

[28] Daniel Moran and Arthur Waldron (eds), *The people in arms. Military myth and national mobilization since the French Revolution* (Cambridge, 2003).

[29] David Fitzpatrick, 'The logic of collective sacrifice: Ireland and the British Army, 1914–1918', *Historical Journal* 38 (1995), 1017–30.

[30] On Irish identity and the war, see Hennessy, *Dividing Ireland*, 80–124.

[31] J.M. Winter, *The Great War and the British people* (London, 1985), 94–5. Of those who served (3,015), 15.1% were killed as opposed to 18% at Cambridge and 19.2% at Oxford.

[32] Paul Bew, *John Redmond* (Dundalk, 1996), 32–9.

[33] Kettle, *Ways of war*, 10.

[34] James Connolly, 'In Praise of the empire', *Workers' Republic*, 9 October 1915.

[35] Trinity College Dublin Library, Papyrus 53–5.

[36] Michael Laffan, *The resurrection of Ireland. The Sinn Féin Party, 1916–1923* (Cambridge, 1999), 128–42.

[37] Winter, *Great War and the British people*, 75.

[38] Robin Prior and Trevor Wilson, *The Somme* (New Haven and London, 2005), 300–1.

[39] Kettle, *Ways of war*, 8.

[40] Liam O'Flaherty, *Return of the brute* (1929; new edn., Dublin, 1998).

[41] Deirdre McMahon (ed.), *The Moynihan brothers in peace and war, 1909–1918* (Dublin, 2004), 168 (letter of 12 March 1918).

[42] Jeffery, *Ireland and the Great War*, 107–43.

[43] Ken S. Inglis, *Sacred places. War memorials in the Australian landscape* (Melbourne, 1998); on Canada see Jonathan Vance, *Death so noble. Memory, meaning and the First World War* (Vancouver, 1997).

[44] Johnson, *The geography of remembrance*, 141–66; Mary E. Daly, 'Less a commemoration of the actual achievements and more a commemoration of the hopes of the men of 1916', in Mary E. Daly and Margaret O'Callaghan (eds), *1916 in 1966. Commemorating the Easter Rising* (Dublin, 2007), 21–3.

[45] Mark Cornwall, 'Mémoires de la Grande Guerre dans les pays tchèques, 1918–1928', in John Horne (ed.), *Démobilisations culturelles après la Grande Guerre, 14–18 Aujourd'hui, 5* (Paris, 2002), 88–101.

CHAPTER 2

[1] Royal Archives, Windsor Castle (RA), George V's diary, 21 July 1914.

[2] Quoted in Jean-Jacques Becker and Stéphane Audoin-Rouzeau (eds), *Les Sociétés européennes et la guerre de 1914–1918* (Paris, 1990), 40.

[3] Thomas P. Dooley. 'Politics, bands and marketing: army recruitment in Waterford City, 1914–15', *The Irish Sword* 18 (1991), 206.

[4] Hansard, House of Commons (HC), vol. 65, col. 1030, 27 July 1914.

[5] *Manchester Evening News,* 27 July 1914, 3, and *Devon and Exeter Gazette,* 27 July 1914, 6.

[6] National Archives of Ireland (NAI), Bureau of Military History (BMH), Witness Statement (WS) 1, Kevin O'Sheil, 770 (n.d.).

[7] *Cork Constitution,* 13 August 1914.

[8] National Library of Ireland (NLI), MS 10923, George Berkeley's diary, 4 August 1914.

[9] NLI, MS 9620, A Dubliner's diary, 15 August 1914.

[10] NAI, BMH, WS 695, Thomas McCrave, 1956.

[11] NAI, BMH, WS 1770, Kevin O'Sheil, n.d.

[12] NLI, MS 9620, A Dubliner's diary, 6 August 1914.

[13] Stephen Royle (ed.), *From Mons to Messines and beyond: the Great War experiences of Sergeant Charles Arnold* (Studley, 1985), 15.

[14] Imperial War Museum (IWM), 04/37/1, Docs: Whitehouse, Percy, 1966.

[15] *Cork Free Press,* 6 August 1914.

[16] Claire Carroll, Helen Crowley, Ruth Donaldson, Clodagh Kelleher *et al.,* 'The approach of war, July and August 1914', *Times Past* 7 (1990–1), 5.

[17] NLI, MS 9620, A Dubliner's diary, 6 August 1914.

[18] *Western Nationalist,* 15 August 1914.

[19] Theresa Moriarty, 'Work, warfare and wages: industrial controls and Irish trade unionism in the First World War', in Adrian Gregory and Senia Pašeta (eds), *Ireland and the Great War: 'A war to unite us all?'* (Manchester, 2002), 75.

[20] *Church of Ireland Gazette,* 21 August 1914.

[21] The National Archives, London (TNA), CO 904/94, R.I.C. County Inspector report, Cavan, September 1914. See also Margaret Downes, 'The civilian voluntary aid effort', in David Fitzpatrick (ed.), *Ireland and the First World War* (Dublin, 1986), 27.

[22] Public Record Office of Northern Ireland (PRONI), D/2109/9/1 (Duffin family papers), 26 August 1914.

[23] *Cork Constitution,* 23 September 1914.

[24] *Cork Examiner,* 28 September 1914 and *Cork Examiner,* 25 September 1914.

[25] *Cork Constitution,* 10 October 1914.

[26] *Church of Ireland Gazette,* 27 November 1914.

[27] *Irish Times,* 20 November 1914.

[28] University College Dublin Archives (UCDA), School of History and Archives, LA11 (papers of William Patrick Ryan)/E/190/29, 11 September 1914.

[29] Horne and Kramer, *German atrocities, 1914.*

[30] NLI, MS 9620, A Dubliner's diary, 8 October 1914.

[31] Manus O'Riordan, 'The justification of James Connolly', in Francis Devine and Manus O'Riordan (eds), *James Connolly, Liberty Hall and the 1916 Rising* (Dublin, 2006), 25.

[32] *Freeman's Journal,* 17 August 1914, 6.

[33] TNA, CO 903/18, Intelligence notes, 1914.

[34] *Cork Weekly News,* 22 August 1914. My thanks to Tim Harding for this reference.

[35] Timothy Michael Healy, *Letters and leaders of my day* (2 vols, London, 1928), vol. 2, 546.

[36] *Sligo Champion,* 15 August 1914.

[37] TNA, CO 903/18, Intelligence notes, 1914.

[38] NLI, MS 9620, A Dubliner's diary, 26 August 1914.

[39] PRONI, D/2109/9/1, 28 August 1914.

[40] *Roscommon Messenger,* 8 August 1914.

[41] *Leitrim Advertiser,* 3 September 1914.

[42] *Cork Constitution,* 27 October 1914.

[43] Frank Callanan, *T.M. Healy* (Cork, 1996), 511.

[44] NLI, MS 9620, A Dubliner's diary, 7 August 1914.

[45] Oonagh Walsh (ed.), *An Englishwoman in Belfast: Rosamond Stephen's record of the Great War* (Cork, 2000), 20.

[46] NLI, MS 13266/1, George Berkeley letters, 2 September 1914.

[47] NLI, MS 22863, Shane Leslie, 12 November 1914.

[48] HC, vol. 65, col. 1809, 3 August 1914.

[49] This statement was originally issued on 17 September 1914. See *The Times,* 17 September 1914, 10.

[50] Eunan O'Halpin, *The decline of the union: British government in Ireland 1892–1920* (Dublin, 1987), 107.

[51] Fergus Campbell, *Land and revolution: nationalist politics in the west of Ireland, 1891-1921* (Oxford, 2005), 196.

[52] F.X. Martin, *The Irish Volunteers, 1913–1915: recollections and documents* (Dublin, 1963), 154.

[53] Patrick Callan, 'British recruitment in Ireland, 1914–1918', *Revue Internationale d'Histoire Militaire* 63 (1985), 49.

[54] See Patrick Callan, 'Recruiting for the British Army in Ireland during the First World War', *The Irish Sword* 17 (1987) 42–56; Fitzpatrick, 'The logic of collective sacrifice', 1017–30; Martin Staunton, 'Kilrush, Co. Clare and the Royal Munster Fusiliers: the experience of an Irish town in the First World War', *The Irish Sword* 16 (1986) 268–72.

[55] Timothy Bowman, 'The Irish recruiting campaign and anti-recruiting campaigns, 1914–1918', in Bertrand Taithe and Tim Thornton (eds), *Propaganda: political rhetoric and identity 1300–2000* (Stroud, 1999), 234.

[56] NLI, MS 22667/1, Sheehy-Skeffington papers, 27 September 1914.

[57] *Freeman's Journal,* 26 September 1914.

[58] Séamas Ó Buachalla (ed.), *The letters of P.H. Pearse* (Gerrards Cross, Bucks., 1980), 330.

[59] NAI, BMH, WS 714, Thomas Hynes, 1952.

[60] NAI, CSO CR 297-298, Index of Chief Secretary's Office registered papers, 1914.

[61] F.S.L. Lyons, *John Dillon: a biography* (London, 1968), 361.

[62] NLI, MS 26159, Joseph Brennan papers, 22 January 1915.

CHAPTER 3

[1] T. Bartlett and K. Jeffery (eds), *A military history of Ireland* (Cambridge, 1996), 337.

[2] James W. Taylor, *The 1st Royal Irish Rifles in the Great War* (Dublin, 2002), 1–25; James W. Taylor, *The 2nd Royal Irish Rifles in the Great War* (Dublin, 2005), 1–19; www.greatwar.ie/mb-hel.html (last accessed 16 July 2008).

[3] Orr, *Field of bones,* 10–11.

[4] Orr, *Field of bones,* 10–26.

[5] Orr, *Road to the Somme,* 37–60.

[6] Denman, *Unknown soldiers,* 43–4.

[7] Denman, *Unknown soldiers,* 43–60; Bowman, *Irish regiments,* 82–3.

[8] T.M. Kettle, *The day's burden and other essays* (Dublin, 1916), 138–9.

[9] Denman, *Unknown soldiers,* 62–5.

[10] Orr, *Road to the Somme,* 85–139.

[11] www.greatwar.ie/mb-hel.html (16 July 2008).

[12] Casualty figures from the authoritative Australian governmental site—http://blog.awm.gov.au/Gallipoli 2007/?page_id=23 (16 July 2008).

[13] Orr, *Field of bones,* 66–174.

[14] Orr, *Field of bones,* 180–238.

[15] IWM, Journal of J.H.M. Staniforth, 6th Connaught Rangers and 7th Leinster Regiment, April 1915 and IWM, W.A. Lyon papers, 60; TNA, CAB 45/289, Papers of J.K.D. Conyngham, 20 May 1929, and TNA, CAB 45/289, papers of unknown origin, 30 April 1929, both in a folder entitled 'Gas attacks near Hulluch'.

¹⁶ Denman, *Unknown soldiers*, 68–75; Bowman, *Irish regiments*, 127.

¹⁷ Martin Middlebrook estimates approximately 5,000 casualties and 2,000 deaths—Martin Middlebrook, *The Somme battlefields* (London, 1994), 109—but these figures may be based on the losses on 1 July, which were supplemented by further casualties on 2 and 3 July—see Orr, *Road to the Somme*, 200.

¹⁸ Orr, *Road to the Somme*, 140–229 and Bowman, *Irish regiments*, 147.

¹⁹ For contrasting discussions of the battle from the British perspective, see Gary Sheffield, *The Somme* (London, 2003), which is more appreciative of the British High Command, and Prior and Wilson, *The Somme*, which is less so.

²⁰ The Kettle correspondence is quoted in Laurence Housman, *War letters of fallen Englishmen* (London, 1930), 168.

²¹ Denman, *Unknown soldiers*, 78–104.

²² Rudyard Kipling, *The Irish Guards in the Great War—the 1ˢᵗ battalion* (new edn., Staplehurst, 1997), 138–9.

²³ Robin Prior and Trevor Wilson, *Passchendaele. The untold story* (London and New Haven, 1996).

²⁴ IWM, Journal of F.H.T. Tatham, 77ᵗʰ and 177ᵗʰ Brigades, Royal Artillery, 4 August 1917.

²⁵ IWM, Staniforth journal, 31 July–7 August 1917; Michael Moynihan (ed.), *God on our side—the British padre in World War One* (London, 1983), 198–207.

²⁶ Orr, *Road to the Somme*, 202–09; Denman, *Unknown soldiers*, 104–23; Nicholas Perry, *Major General Nugent and the Ulster Division 1915-1918* (Stroud, 2007), 99.

²⁷ Bowman, *Irish regiments*, 153.

²⁸ Denman, *Unknown soldiers*, 148–170.

²⁹ National Army Museum, 7607-69-4, Noel Drury's journal, November 1918; TNA, PRO 30/71/3, Guy Nightingale's papers, letter dated 18 November 1918; Francis Clere Hitchcock, *Stand to—a diary of the trenches, 1915-1918* (new edn., London, 1988), 314.

³⁰ Felix Lavery (ed.), *Great Irishmen in war and politics* (London, 1920), 176.

³¹ Kipling, *Irish Guards*, 286–328.

³² Gardiner S. Mitchell, *Three cheers for the Derrys!* (Derry, 1991), 209.

³³ Taylor, *The 2ⁿᵈ Royal Irish Rifles*, 132.

CHAPTER 4

¹ On this point, see Patrick Maume's edition of John Mitchel's *The last conquest of Ireland (perhaps)* (Dublin, 2005).

² Quoted in Eric Hobsbawm, *On history* (London, 1997), 317–18.

³ *Northern Whig*, 17 April 1915.

⁴ Michael Wheatley, *Nationalism and the Irish Party: provincial Ireland 1910–1916* (Oxford, 2005).

⁵ *Northern Whig*, 11 June 1915.

⁶ *Weekly Freeman's Journal*, 10 July 1915.

⁷ *Northern Whig*, 20 May 1915.

⁸ *Weekly Freeman's Journal*, 12 May 1912.

⁹ Warre B. Wells, *John Redmond: a biography* (London, 1919), 172.

¹⁰ *Daily Chronicle*, 11 June 1915.

¹¹ *Northern Whig*, 29 June 1915.

¹² Alvin Jackson, 'Modern unionism and the cult of 1912–14', in Maurice J. Bric and John Coakley (eds), *From political violence to negotiated settlement: the winding path to peace in twentieth-century Ireland* (Dublin, 2004), 112.

¹³ *Northern Whig*, 19 October 1915.

¹⁴ *Weekly Freeman's Journal*, 6 November 1915.

¹⁵ *Northern Whig*, 29 November 1915.

¹⁶ *Northern Whig*, 13 December 1915.

¹⁷ Patrick Maume, *The long gestation: Irish nationalist life 1891–1918* (Dublin, 1999), 174–5.

¹⁸ *Northern Whig*, 14 January 1916. For Redmond's personal unease—correctly detected by 'Old Fogey'—see Patrick Walsh, *The rise and fall of imperial Ireland. Redmondism in the context of*

Britain's conquest of South Africa and its Great War on Germany (Belfast, Cork and London, 2003), 558–9. I owe to Patrick Maume the information that 'Old Fogey' was E.G. Robinson, a veteran Belfast journalist.

[19] *Saturday Review*, 5 February 1916.

[20] *Northern Whig*, 4 January 1916.

[21] *Northern Whig*, 17 March 1916.

[22] *Northern Whig*, 18 March 1916.

[23] *Northern Whig*, 10 April 1916; Roger Sawyer, *Casement: the flawed hero* (London, 1984), 117.

[24] Emily Lawless and Michael MacDonagh, *Ireland* (3rd edn., London, 1923), 446.

[25] Stephen Gwynn, *John Redmond's last years* (London, 1919), 223.

[26] *The Irishman*, 4 January 1820.

[27] *Northern Whig*, 28 April 1916.

[28] Terence Denman, *A lonely grave: the life and death of William Redmond* (Dublin, 1995).

[29] Reverend John Redmond, *Church, state, industry 1827–1929 in east Belfast: vivid records of social and political upheavals in the 1920s* (Belfast, 1961).

CHAPTER 5

[1] Cartoon signed 'Geo Monks', *Shamrock* n.s., 1 (1919).

[2] This figure incorporates about 58,000 men mobilised at the outbreak of hostilities (21,000 regulars, 18,000 reservists, 12,000 special reservists, 5,000 naval ratings and some 2,000 officers). War-time enlistments included about 134,000 soldiers, 3,700 officers with direct commissions, 6,000 members of the Royal Navy and the Naval Reserve, and 4,000 air force personnel. For the basis of these and other statistics cited in this chapter, see Fitzpatrick, 'The logic of collective sacrifice', 1017–30.

[3] NAI, 1916/21680, Chief Secretary's Office, Registered papers, G.P. Kurten to Sir Matthew Nathan, 19 January 1916.

[4] A.G. Butler, *The Australian Army medical services in the War of 1914–1918* (3 vols, Canberra, 1943), vol. 3, 882, 889, 891; Bill Gammage, *The broken years: Australian soldiers in the Great War* (Ringwood, Victoria, 1990; 1st edn., 1974), app. 1, 2.

[5] 'Address by Frederick John MacNeice, 11 April 1916', *Carrickfergus Advertiser*, 14 April 1916.

[6] University of Leeds, Liddle Collection (ULLC), Olive Armstrong's diary, 2 August 1915.

[7] Returns in the *Labour Gazette* and *Abstract of Labour Statistics* give the estimated number of insured workers in July or October, and the number of unemployment books lodged compulsorily at labour exchanges or unemployed fund offices at the end of each quarter. Between 30 June 1914 and 30 June 1918, the proportion unemployed in Ireland declined from 7.0% to 4.0% in building and construction, 4.9% to 2.5% in engineering, and 4.5% to 1.1% in shipbuilding.

[8] Fitzpatrick, *Politics and Irish life*, 251.

[9] PRONI, D 3889/1, Charlie Pearson to Mrs Isaac Pearson, 4 January 1918.

[10] 'Address by Frederick John MacNeice, 10 November 1929', *Carrickfergus Advertiser*, 15 November 1929.

[11] ULLC, Olive Armstrong's diary, 28 September 1915.

[12] *Clare Champion*, 8 May 1915.

[13] 'Letter to editor from A.E. Lett (Enniscorthy), 26 April 1915', *Irish Times*, 27 April 1915.

[14] *Veritas* 3 (1918), 343, 358. I am grateful to Jane Leonard for this reference.

[15] Major Robert Gregory, MC, 4th Battalion Connaught Rangers and Royal Flying Corps, was accidentally shot down on 23 January 1918 during a practice flight in Italy. See Chapter 9 below.

CHAPTER 6

[1] Letter from E. Myles in *The Lady of the House*, 15 March 1915. On women and the war, Gail Braybon, 'Winners or losers. Women's symbolic role in the war story', in Gail Braybon (ed.), *Evidence, history and the Great War. Historians and the impact of 1914–1918* (New York and Oxford, 2003), 86–112; Ute Daniel, *The war from within. German working class women in the First World War*, 1989; English translation (Oxford, 1996); Margaret H. Darrow, *French women and the First World*

War. Stories of the home front (Oxford, 2000); Susan R. Grayzel, *Women's identities at war. Gender, motherhood and politics in Britain and France during the First World War* (London, 1999); and Françoise Thébaud, 'The Great War and the triumph of sexual division', in Françoise Thébaud (ed.), *A history of women in the west, vol. 5, toward a cultural identity in the twentieth century* (English translation, Cambridge, MA, 1994).

[2] Caitriona Clear, *Social change and everyday life in Ireland 1850–1922* (Manchester, 2007), 4–56; Fintan Lane, 'Music and violence in working-class Cork; the band nuisance 1879–82', *Saothar: Journal of the Irish Labour History Society* 24 (1999), 24–31, and John McGrath, 'Sociability and socio-economic conditions in St Mary's Parish, Limerick 1890–1950', unpublished MA thesis, University of Limerick, 2006; Margaret Ward, *Unmanageable revolutionaries: women and Irish nationalism* (Dingle, 1983), 40–87.

[3] Mary Clancy, 'On the western outpost: local government and women's suffrage in Co. Galway 1898–1918', in R. Gillespie and G. Moran (eds), *Galway: history and society* (Dublin, 1996), 557–87.

[4] Michael O'Kane, *Woman's place in the world* (Dublin, 1913), 1–2.

[5] R.M. Fox, *Rebel Irishwomen* (Dublin, 1935); Rosemary Cullen Owens, *Smashing times: a history of the Irish women's suffrage movement 1889–1922* (Dublin, 1984); Cliona Murphy, *The women's suffrage movement and Irish society in the early twentieth century* (Hemel Hempstead, 1989); Charlotte Fallon, *Soul of fire: a biography of Mary McSwiney* (Cork, 1986); J. Holmes and D. Urquhart (eds), *Coming into the light: the work, politics and religion of women in Ulster 1840–1940* (Belfast, 1994); Mary Jones, *These obstreperous lassies: a history of the Irish Women Workers Union* (Dublin, 1988); Diane Urquhart, *Women in Ulster politics 1890–1940* (Dublin, 2000); Maedhbh McNamara and Paschal Mooney, *Women in parliament: Ireland 1918–2000* (Dublin, 2000); Louise Ryan and Margaret Ward (eds), *Irish women and the vote: becoming citizens* (Dublin, 2007).

[6] The most complete research on Irish women and the Great War is by Eileen Reilly, 'Women and voluntary war work' in Adrian Gregory and Senia Pašeta (eds), *Ireland and the Great War: 'a war to unite us all?'* (Manchester, 2002), 49–72. On VADs, 'Ypres on the Liffey' in *The Lady of the House*, 15 May 1916; Margaret Ward, *Maud Gonne: Ireland's Joan of Arc* (London, 1990), 106–08.

[7] Cullen Owens, *Smashing times*, 128.

[8] Yvonne McEwen, *It's a long way to Tipperary: British and Irish nurses in the First World War* (Dunfermline, 2006).

[9] Photograph in *Irish Independent*, 19 August 1914.

[10] Eugene Nolan, *A history of the school of nursing and of developments at the Mater Misericordiae Hospital 1891–1991* (Dublin, 1991).

[11] *Annual report of the local government board for Ireland 1914–16* (Dublin, 1916), xxi; Jeffery, *Ireland and the Great War*; Myrtle Hill, *Women in Ireland: a century of change* (Belfast, 2003), 68. Thanks also to Mrs Sarah Paterson at the Imperial War Museum.

[12] McEwen, *Tipperary*, 158.

[13] All the information about Catherine Black is taken from her autobiography, *King's nurse beggar's nurse*, (London, 1939).

[14] For Marie Martin, see Mary Purcell, *To Africa with love: the biography of Mother Mary Martin* (Dublin, 1987).

[15] Peter Downham (ed.), *Diary of an old contemptible: from Mons to Baghdad 1914–1919 by Pte Edward Roe, East Lancashire Regiment* (Barnsley, 2004), 173–5. Thanks to Manus Lenihan for drawing my attention to this book.

[16] Hill, *Century of change*, 67–8.

[17] 'The women of Ireland's part in the war', *The Lady of the House* (15 January 1915).

[18] Reilly suggests, albeit cautiously, that Catholic women were not as active as Protestant in voluntary war work, but the *Catholic Bulletin*, which she uses as one of her main sources for this assertion, was a very nationalist/separatist publication whose price put it beyond the reach of most Irish Catholics at the time. See Reilly, 'Women and voluntary war work', 67. For list, see for example, 'Irish ladies honoured', *Irish Independent* (20 October 1917), and on subsequent days.

[19] For example, Red Cross meeting at the R.D.S., *Irish Times* 11 August 1914; Irish Volunteer Aid Association meeting reported in the *Irish Independent*, 10 August 1914; and the Women's National Health Association of Ireland: Women's Employment Section, *Irish Times,* 7 January 1915.

[20] 'Comment', *Galway Express,* 8 January 1916. Thanks to John Cunningham for this reference and for other information about Professor Donovan O'Sullivan.

[21] Purcell, *Africa with love,* 18–35; 'The women of Ireland's part in the war', *The Lady of the House,* 15 January 1915.

[22] 'Castle throat' in 'Through Erin's isle', *The Lady of the House,* 15 January 1915; suffrage organisations, Cullen Owens, *Smashing times,* 95–8.

[23] 'A doctor's good work in the west', photograph and short caption, *Irish Independent,* 23 April 1915.

[24] Cork City and Co. Limerick, 'The women of Ireland's part in the war, Part II', *The Lady of the House,* 15 February 1915; Trinity VADs, 'Through Erin's isle', *The Lady of the House,* 15 June 1915; gifts acknowledged, Princess Patricia Hospital Bray, *Irish Independent,* 6 October 1915.

[25] 'How to help the war fund', Advertisement, *Irish Independent,* 5 October 1914.

[26] 'Irish distressed ladies fund work depot, 20 Dawson Street, Dublin', *Irish Times,* 22 August 1914.

[27] Letter signed 'All Hands', *Irish Independent,* 12 April 1915, and response the following day headed 'Shop Workers and Recruiting'.

[28] Emmet O'Connor, *A labour history of Ireland 1824–1960* (Dublin, 1992), 91–101.

[29] Hill, *Century of change,* 70–1; W. Black, 'Industrial change in the 20th century', in J.C. Beckett and R.E. Glasscock (eds) *Belfast: origins and growth of an industrial city* (London, 1967), 157–68.

[30] *Annual report of local government board for Ireland 1914–15* (Dublin, 1915), see the War Relief section, xxx; *Annual report of local government board Ireland 1917–18 for year ended 31 March 1918* (Dublin, 1919), see the War Relief section, xx; toy-making, 'The women of Ireland's part in the war', *The Lady of the House,* 15 January 1915; WNHA work-rooms, *Irish Times,* 7 January 1915.

[31] 'Catholic women: Dublin conference', contribution by Agnes O'Farrelly, *Irish Independent,* 16 October 1915.

[32] *Irish Independent,* 9 April 1915.

[33] I am indebted to Mary Clancy for this information; also William Henry, *Galway and the Great War* (Cork, 2006), 104–08.

[34] 'Through Erin's isle', *The Lady of the House,* 15 October 1916.

[35] Nora Tynan O'Mahony, 'Need for economy: some signs of the times', *Irish Independent,* 12 October 1915.

[36] *Annual report of the local government board for Ireland for the year 1917–18* (Dublin, 1919), see Section II, Poor Relief: statistics of pauperism, xxvii.

[37] 'Army separation allowances: increases recommended. Report of the select committee,' *Irish Times,* 3 February 1915.

[38] Tynan O'Mahony, 'Need for economy'.

[39] 'Milk scandal: growing revolt in Dublin', *Irish Independent,* 14 October 1915, and 'Jail for waterers of milk: defending the poor', *Irish Independent,* 17 October 1917.

[40] See, e.g., *Fifty-third detailed annual report of the Registrar-General (Ireland) for 1916* (Dublin, 1917–18), see Tables Xa , Xb and Xc, xxv–xxvii (maternal mortality) and Table Xe on xxix (infantile mortality); *Fifty-fifth detailed annual report of the Registrar-General (Ireland) for 1918* (1919) see Table XIIc, xxvi (maternal mortality), and Table XIII, xxix (infantile mortality); Irvine Loudon, *Death in childbirth: an international study of maternal care and maternal mortality* (Oxford, 1992), 14.

[41] Joanna Bourke, *Husbandry to housewifery: women, housework and economic change 1890–1914* (Oxford, 1993), 236–62.

[42] Hill, *Century of change,* 66.

[43] Cullen Owens, *Smashing times,* 97; Margaret Ward, 'Rolling up the map of suffrage: Irish suffrage and the First World War', in L. Ryan and M. Ward (eds), *Irish women and the vote,* 136–53, specifically 145–6; Carmel Quinlan, *Genteel revolutionaries: Anna and Thomas Haslam* (Cork, 2002); and 'Women patrols' a letter from Edith Sanderson to the *Irish Times,* 2 January 1915.

[44] 'City street scenes. Woman patrol's experience', letter to the editor from C.M., *Irish Independent* , 18 October 1915.

[45] E. Sylvia Pankhurst, *The home front: a mirror to life in England during the First World War* (London, 1932; this edn. Cressett Library, 1987), 100–01.

[46] John Springhall, '"Corrupting the young?" Popular entertainment and "moral panics" in Britain and America since 1830', in V. Alan McClelland (ed.), *Children at risk* (Hull, 1994), 95–110; *Criminal*

and judicial statistics of Ireland 1915–18 (Dublin, 1919): Table 1: Assizes: number of persons for trial, nature of offences and result of proceedings.

[47] Sidney Gifford Czira, *The years flew by: recollections of Madame Sidney Gifford Czira* (Dublin, 1974; new edn., Galway, 2000), 2–3, for a personal experience of the cumbersome clothes of the Edwardian era.

[48] James Laver, *Costume and fashion: a concise history* (London, 1969; new edn., London, 1982), 227–30.

[49] The love debate, 'Should a man fill a woman's life?', *The Lady of the House,* 15 October 1916; Miss White's letter, 'What are women's post war prospects?', *The Lady of the House,* 14 August 1915.

[50] S.S. Holton, *Feminism and democracy: women's suffrage and reform politics in Britain 1900–1918* (Cambridge, 1986); Arthur Marwick, *Women at war 1914–1918* (London, 1977), 157; Martin Pugh, *Electoral reform in war and peace, 1906–1918* (London, 1978).

[51] Caitriona Clear, *Women of the house: women's household work in Ireland 1921–61* (Dublin, 2000), 14–15, 1–45, 211–13; Virginia Nicholson, *Singled out: how two million women survived without men after the First World War* (London, 2007).

[52] Siân Reynolds, *France between the wars: gender and politics* (London, 1996); G. Bock and P. Thane (eds), *Maternity and gender policies: women and the rise of European welfare states 1880s–1950s* (London, 1994), and specifically on Ireland, Clear, *Women of the house,* 14–15, 1–45, 211–13 ; Maryann Valiulis, 'Neither feminist nor flapper: the ecclesiastical construction of the ideal Irish woman', in M. O'Dowd and S. Wichert (eds), *Chattel, servant or citizen: women's status in church, state and society* (Belfast, 1995), 168–78; Louise Ryan, *Gender, identity and the Irish press 1922–1937: embodying the nation* (Lewiston, NY, 2001).

CHAPTER 7

[1] The Irish Trades' Union Congress (ITUC) suffered tension following partition and the Congress of Irish Unions (CIU), largely based in the South, eventually split from the ITUC in 1945. However, fourteen years later, in 1959, the CIU and ITUC merged to form the Irish Congress of Trade Unions (ICTU).

[2] H.D. Gribbon, 'Economic and social history,' in W.E. Vaughan (ed.), *New history of Ireland, Ireland under the Union, II, 1870-1921* (7 vols, Oxford, 1996), vol. 6, 343.

[3] *Irish Worker,* 22 August 1914.

[4] Gribbon, 'Economic and social history', 346.

[5] *Irish Times,* 28 July and 2 August 1915. For Arthur Griffith's caustic response to the Home Rulers' complaints on the issue, see *Nationality,* 31 July 1915 (quoted in G.D. Kelleher, *Gunpowder to guided missiles. Ireland's war industries* (Cork, 1993), 135).

[6] Emmet O'Connor, *A labour history of Ireland* (Dublin, 1992), 96.

[7] Gribbon, 'Economic and social history', 347.

[8] Gribbon, 'Economic and social history', 347.

[9] Peter Murray, 'The First World War and a Dublin distillery workforce: recruitment and redundancy at John Power and Sons, 1915–1917', *Saothar* 15 (1990), 48–56: 55.

[10] By September 1914, for instance, employees in several industries had been put on short time, while half the skilled and unskilled workers in the painting and decorating trade were out of work, and unemployment among women was high with dress-making particularly hard hit. See *Irish Times,* 8 and 12 September 1914.

[11] *Irish Times,* 30 April and 15 May 1915.

[12] Cormac Ó Gráda, *Ireland: a new economic history* (Oxford, 1994), 312.

[13] *Irish Times,* 15 May 1915.

[14] Murray, 'A Dublin distillery workforce', 53.

[15] E.J. Riordan, *Modern Irish trade and industry* (London, 1920), 156.

[16] *Irish Times,* 28 July 1917.

[17] *Irish Times,* 13 April 1917.

[18] Quoted in Thomas P. Dooley, *Irishmen or English soldiers? The times and world of a southern Catholic Irish man (1876–1916) enlisting in the British Army* (Liverpool, 1995), 126.

[19] Circular letter from the Central Council for the Organisation of Recruiting in Ireland, 11 August 1915, in A.C. Hepburn, *Conflict of nationality in modern Ireland* (London, 1980), 92. Emphasis added.

[20] Horne, 'Labor and labor movements in World War I', 187–227; John Turner, 'British politics and the Great War', in J. Turner (ed.), *Britain and the First World War* (London, 1988), 127.

[21] Arthur Mitchell, **Labour in Irish politics, 1890-1913: the Irish Labour movement in an age of revolution** (Dublin, 1974), 60.

[22] *Irish Times,* 8 September 1914.

[23] Companies and sectors which offered allowances and promised to hold jobs included Michelin and railway and insurance companies (*Irish Times,* 8 and 12 September 1914). See J. Anthony Gaughan, **Thomas Johnson, 1872-1963: first leader of the Labour Party in Dáil Éireann** (Dublin, 1980), 86; Séamus Cody, John O'Dowd and Peter Rigney, **The parliament of labour : 100 years of the Dublin Council of Trade Unions** (Dublin, 1986), 107; *Workers Republic,* 13 November 1915, cited in Moriarty, 'Industrial controls', 76; C.D. Greaves, *The Irish Transport and General Workers' Union: the formative years* **1909-1923** (Dublin, 1982), 149, on compulsion.

[24] David Fitzpatrick, 'Strikes in Ireland, 1914–1921', *Saothar* 6 (1980), 26–39.

[25] G.R. Rubin, 'Law, war and economy: the Munitions Acts 1915–17 and corporatism in context', *Journal of Law and Society* 11 (1984), 319.

[26] Moriarty, 'Industrial controls', 79–81; Gribbon, 'Economic and social history', 350; O'Connor, *Labour history of Ireland,* 96.

[27] O'Connor, *Labour history of Ireland,* 92–4.

[28] O'Connor, *Labour history of Ireland,* 98; Emmet O'Connor, *Syndicalism in Ireland, 1917-23* (Cork, 1988), 23.

[29] *Irish Times,* 21 October 1916.

[30] Kathleen Burk, 'Wheat and the state in the First World War', in Michael L. Dockrill and David French (eds), *Strategy and intelligence: British policy during the First World War* (London, 2003), 137.

[31] O'Connor, *Syndicalism,* 34. Although land and labour leagues had operated in Munster, especially since the late nineteenth century, they were geared towards politics rather than industrial action and had been weakened by splits in the movement. Dan Bradley, *Farm labourers: Irish struggle 1900-1976* (Belfast, 1988), 26–31.

[32] Bradley, *Farm labourers,* 33; Greaves, *ITGWU,* 180, 188.

[33] O'Connor, *Syndicalism,* 22, 26; Emmet O'Connor, 'War and syndicalism 1914–1923', in Donal Nevin (ed.), *Trade union century* (Cork, 1994), 56.

[34] Moriarty, 'Industrial controls', 83–9.

[35] Moriarty, 'Industrial controls', 85.

[36] Greaves, *ITGWU,* 189.

[37] Thomas N. Crean, 'Labour and politics in Kerry during the First World War', *Saothar* 19 (1994), 34.

[38] O'Connor, *Syndicalism,* 22; O'Connor, *Labour history of Ireland,* 97.

[39] Emmet O'Connor, *Reds and the green. Ireland, Russia and the communist internationals 1919-43* (Dublin, 2004), 15.

[40] A.J. Ward, 'Lloyd George and the Irish conscription crisis', *The Historical Journal* 17 (1974), 110.

[41] J.A. Gaughan, *Thomas Johnson,* 91.

[42] J.A. Gaughan, *Thomas Johnson,* 88.

[43] With 85 nationalist or Liberal Irish MPs, this meant that at least 18 British MPs voted against the bill. According to one report, 7 Labour MPs were among them (*Irish Independent,* 22 April 1918). However, many Labour (and Liberal) MPs had only voted in favour of conscription because they believed it would herald new Home Rule legislation. See Ward, 'Lloyd George', 123.

[44] *Irish Independent,* 25 April 1918; *Irish Times,* 27 April 1918.

[45] *Irish Independent,* 25 April 1918.

[46] *Irish Independent,* 22 April 1918.

[47] *Irish Independent,* 25 April 1918.

[48] *Irish Independent,* 29 April 1918; Thomas J. Morrissey, *William O'Brien, 1881–1968. Socialist, republican, Dáil Deputy, editor and trade union leader* (Dublin, 2007), 150.

[49] G. Bell, *Troublesome business. The Labour Party and the Irish question* (London, 1982), 37.

[50] O'Connor, *Labour history of Ireland,* 98.

[51] Morrissey, *William O'Brien*, 150.

[52] Winter, *Great War and the British people*, 305.

[53] J.M. Winter, *Socialism and the challenge of war. Ideas and politics in Britain, 1912-18* (London, 1974), 270–88.

CHAPTER 8

[1] Calculated from a variety of official returns. The combined Irish membership claimed in this period by veterans' organisations often exceeded 250,000. Such claims were wildly exaggerated.

[2] This chapter is derived from interviews conducted since 1987 with veterans, their families and the descendants of men killed in the war; diaries and correspondence of veterans; newspaper reports; records of ex-service organisations; official archives and publications; and published and unpublished memoirs.

[3] John Plumridge, *Hospital ships and ambulance trains* (London, 1975), 126–7.

[4] Both hospitals expanded in the 1920s to provide general and surgical treatment for veterans. While the Somme Nursing Home (formerly the UVF Hospital) and Leopardstown Park Hospital still care for veterans of the United Kingdom forces, civilians are also admitted.

[5] *Lurgan Mail*, 9 April 1921.

[6] PRONI, WGC/1/3, Ulster Tower Visitors' Book, 1929–31.

[7] St John Ervine, *A journey to Jerusalem* (London, 1936), 150, 161.

[8] Unemployed veterans in rural areas fared better than their British counterparts during the period they received the out-of-work donation, as it exceeded the average Irish agricultural wage. On the obstacles faced by veterans, see Jane Leonard, '"Facing the finger of scorn": veterans' memories of Ireland after the Great War', in Martin Edwards and Ken Lunn (eds), *War and memory in the twentieth century* (Oxford, 1997), 59–72, and Jane Leonard, 'Getting them at last: the IRA and ex-servicemen', in David Fitzpatrick (ed.), *Revolution? Ireland, 1917–1923* (Dublin, 1990), 118–29.

[9] HC, vol. 121, col. 77, 10 November 1919. The total number of unemployed Irish veterans at that period was almost 40,000. See also Fitzpatrick, 'Militarism in Ireland', 399.

[10] *Irish Times*, 5 April 1919.

[11] Murray Fraser, *John Bull's other homes. State housing and British policy in Ireland, 1883–1922* (Liverpool, 1996), 240–71.

[12] The Irish National Volunteers contributed 32,000 while the UVF sent almost 31,000. See David Fitzpatrick, *The two Irelands* (Oxford, 1998), 52–4.

[13] Estimate calculated from a range of official sources, press reports and obituaries, hospital and cemetery registers and war memorials. See Leonard, 'Getting them at last', for an analysis of 82 killings occurring before the July 1921 truce and Leonard, '"Facing the finger of scorn"', for other forms of intimidation.

[14] Now deposited in the Linen Hall Library, Belfast.

[15] *Clare Champion*, 1 May 1920; *Irish Independent*, 28 April 1920.

[16] Department of Defence Archives, Dublin, Chief of Staff's Office Memorandum on the Development of the Defence Forces, 1923–27.

[17] Based on my analysis of National Army personnel files in the Department of Defence Archives, Dublin; *Iris Oifigiúil*, 14 October 1924; and profiles of individual officers in contemporary press reports.

[18] *Weekly Freeman*, 13 May 1922.

[19] Prout's unit, the 370th Regiment, was part of the 93rd Division, one of two black American divisions seconded for service under the French Army. See Arthur E. Barbeau and Florette Henri, *The unknown soldiers. African-American troops in World War I* (New York, 1996), 81, 127.

[20] *Armagh Guardian*, 22 April 1921.

[21] Derived from the returns of area affiliation fees for Northern Ireland and the Irish Free State, printed in the annual reports and accounts of the British Legion, 1925–39, and from charts recording the membership, by area, including Northern Ireland and the Irish Free State, in Niall Barr, *The lion and the poppy: British veterans, politics and society, 1921–1939* (Westport, CT, 2005), 59–60.

[22] *Armagh Guardian*, 25 April 1919.

[23] Over 40 British Legion branches in the Republic closed between 1971 and 1976. I wish to thank Ray Duke, the late Robin Hill, the late Michael and Louisa Kenny and the late Terence Poulter for access to records of regimental associations.

[24] Leonard, '"The twinge of memory"', 99–114.

[25] On the publications and cross-community dialogue that have resulted, see my reviews in *Familia* 18 (2002), 104–6; *Fortnight*, June 2003, and *Seanchas Ard Mhacha* 21 (2006), 371–5.

[26] Interviewed on *Evening Extra*, BBC Radio Ulster, 2 April 2008; *Newsletter*, 30 June, 11 July 2008.

[27] Unlike Australia a decade earlier where renewed public interest in the war was keenly grasped by veterans: Alastair Thomson, *Anzac memories. Living with the legend* (Melbourne, 1994).

[28] *Fermanagh Times,* 17 November 1938.

CHAPTER 9

[1] Quoted in Herbert Dunn, *Francis Ledwidge and the literature of his time, Ireland* [sic] (Dublin, 2006). I am indebted to this work and to Alice Curtayne's *Francis Ledwidge: a life of the poet* (London, 1972).

[2] Quotations from Ledwidge's poetry are taken from the *Complete poems of Francis Ledwidge* (New York, 1919).

[3] Eric J. Leed, *No man's land: combat & identity in World War I* (Cambridge, 1979), 138; Paul Fussell, *The Great War and modern memory* (Oxford, 1975), 36–74.

[4] Leed, *No man's land*, 138.

[5] Patrick McGill, *The red horizon* (1916; new edn., Dingle, 1984), 196.

[6] Patrick McGill, *The great push. An episode of the Great War* (1916; new edn., Edinburgh, 2000), 13.

[7] Anna MacBride White and A. Norman Jeffares (eds), *The Gonne–Yeats letters 1893–1938: always your friend* (London, 1992), 351.

[8] MacBride White and Jeffares, *The Gonne–Yeats letters*, 358.

[9] Roy Foster, *W. B. Yeats: a life* (2 vols, Oxford, 1997–2003), vol. 2, 118.

[10] Leed, *No man's land*, 13.

[11] Quotations from MacGreevy's poetry are taken from Thomas Dillon Redshaw (ed.), *Thomas McGreevy, collected poems* (Dublin, 1971). MacGreevy, born Tarbert, Co. Kerry, was twice wounded in the war. He became Director of the National Gallery of Ireland in 1950.

[12] Johnson, *The geography of remembrance*, 120.

[13] Allan Wade (ed.), *The letters of W.B. Yeats* (London, 1954), 874. Saros Cowasjee first linked O'Casey with Owen when he suggested the latter's poem 'Disabled' as a source for *The Silver Tassie*. See Saros Cowasjee, *Sean O'Casey: the man behind the plays* (Edinburgh and London, 1965), 114–15.

[14] Jeffery, *Ireland and the Great War*, 73.

[15] Jennifer Johnston, *How many miles to Babylon* (London, 1974).

[16] Frank McGuinness, *Observe the sons of Ulster marching towards the Somme* (Dublin, 1985; new edn., London, 2004).

[17] Sebastian Barry, *A long long way* (London, 2005).

[18] Michael Longley, 'In Memoriam', in *Collected poems* (London, 2006).

[19] Jon Stallworthy, *Between the lines: Yeats's poetry in the making* (Oxford, 1963), 24.

[20] James Joyce, *Ulysses* (World Classic edn., Oxford, 1993), 319. James Fairhall considers *Ulysses* as a text of the Great War in *James Joyce and the question of history* (Cambridge, 1993), 161–213.

CHAPTER 10

[1] Some of the themes explored in this essay, and the examples used, are covered at greater length in my book *Ireland and the Great War*.

[2] Of the 752 men who went over the top, only 68 returned unscathed (Martin Middlebrook, *The first day on the Somme* (Penguin edn., London, 2001), 189.

[3] Jean-Jacques Becker, *The Great War and the French people*, trans. Arnold Pomerans (Leamington Spa, 1986), 105–24.

[4] James S. Kane, *Portadown heroes* (Portadown, 2007), 149–50.

[5] Maurice Hayes, *Black puddings with slim: a Downpatrick boyhood* (Belfast, 1996), 166.

[6] The history of the Irish National War Memorial is well narrated in Fergus A. Darcy, *Remembering the war dead: British Commonwealth and international war graves in Ireland since 1914* (Dublin, 2007).

[7] The best single work on Orpen is Bruce Arnold, *Orpen: mirror to an age* (London, 1981).

[8] Jeffery, *Ireland and the Great War*, 86–9.

[9] John, 15:13.

[10] *Belfast Telegraph*, 10 June 1926.

[11] Jeffery, *Ireland and the Great War*, 92–3.

[12] Dora Sigerson Shorter, *The tricolour* (Cork, 1976), 22.

[13] I am grateful to Miss Kathleen Dallat of Ballycastle, Co. Antrim, and her brother Dr Cathal Dallat, for allowing me access to the manuscript of this song. For a note about its composition and the full text of the lyric, see Cathal O'Boyle, *Songs of the County Down* (Skerries, Co. Dublin, 1979), 56–7. The song was popularised by the Clancy Brothers and Tommy Makem, originally on an album entitled *Rising of the Moon* (1956).

[14] Jenny Macleod, *Reconsidering Gallipoli* (Manchester, 2004), 5–6.

[15] Dan Todman, *The Great War. Myth and memory* (London, 2005), 29–36.

[16] The Irish Brigade, *About Time*, vol. 6 (*c.*1990). I am most grateful to Dr Patrick Maume for drawing my attention to this song.

[17] Daly and O'Callaghan, *1916 in 1966*.

[18] Jeffery, *Ireland and the Great War*, 136.

[19] This, and other 'theatrical' cultural products, are discussed in my essay, '"Writing out of opinions": Irish experience and the theatre of the Great War', in Santanu Das (ed.), *Race, empire and First World War writing* (Cambridge, forthcoming).

[20] G.C. Duggan, *The watchers on Gallipoli* (Dublin, 1921), 36–8.

AN APPEAL TO YOU

NLI, Ephemera Collection, WAR/1914-18/3: 'An appeal to you: "Give us a hand old man"', 1914–18. Poster issued by the CCORI. Courtesy of the National Library of Ireland.

"Give us a hand old man!"

PRESERVATION OF EGGS.

4.—New-laid eggs will be plentiful until July, and we strongly recommend the Irish people to store quantities for household use during the autumn and winter by preserving the required quantity now.

As pointed out in a previous circular, water-glass (sodium silicate or potassium silicate) can be purchased from chemists and grocers. Full particulars of the quantities of waterglass required and the amount of water to be added are given on the tins in which the water-glass is sold, and the purchaser has only to follow these instructions exactly. The following simple precautions are required :—

1. No egg for preservation must be more than two or three days old.

2. Infertile eggs are best if they can be obtained, but eggs may be used if not over two days old. The shells must be clean and uncracked, but washing is undesirable as it removes a protective covering.

3. One cracked egg will spoil a whole crock full of sound eggs.

4. When the preserving jar is full it should be sealed and put in a cool place where it need not be moved till the time comes for opening it.

5. The waterglass should cover the eggs by at least inches, and the jar should be inspected from time to time to see that no evaporation has taken place. A little cold boiled water may be added to make up the loss if any is required.

6. If when the eggs are removed they are to be used for boiling, a small hole should be pricked before putting them in the boiling water.

5.—Butter-making and cheese-making should be carried on extensively in the home. Cheese as a milk product and an economical food is more valuable than butter. Cheese-making utensils are manufactured by **The Dublin Metal and Galvanising Co., Ltd., 60 New Street, Dublin.**

6.—Rabbits, salmon, etc., are useful additions to the larder. Most people will know how to get them and what to do with them.

7.—Lay in supplies of tinned goods, such as beef, mutton, fish, condensed milk; also dried foods—beans, peas, lentils, rice and tapioca, etc. Do not keep large supplies of food in any one place.

FUEL.

It should be obvious to everyone that owing to the greatly reduced supplies of coal available for Ireland from now on, that unless turf-cutting is carried on extensively, great hardships will be inflicted on the people this coming autumn and winter. Our supplies of fuel should be maintained at all costs.

PHILIP J. MacMAHON,
Sinn Fein Food Director.

Notes on contributors

PAUL BEW is Professor of Political Science at Queen's University Belfast and a historian of Ireland. He is particularly a specialist on Parnell, Redmond and the political history of later nineteenth and early twentieth century Ireland, and has just published *Ireland, the politics of enmity, 1790-2006* (Oxford, 2007).

TERENCE BROWN is Professor of Anglo–Irish literature at Trinity College Dublin and a leading cultural and literary historian of Ireland, known among other things for his *Ireland. A social and cultural history, 1922–2002* (1ˢᵗ edn., London, 1985). He has published articles on the subject of Irish literature and the Great War.

CAITRIONA CLEAR is a lecturer in the Department of History, National University of Ireland, Galway. She specialises in Irish social history and the history of women. She has published *Women of the house. Women's household work in Ireland, 1922–1961* (Dublin, 2000) and *Social change and everyday life in Ireland 1850–1922* (Manchester, 2007).

DAVID FITZPATRICK is Professor of Modern History at Trinity College Dublin. His works include *Politics and Irish life, 1913–1921: provincial experience of war and revolution* (1977; new edn., Cork, 1998); *Oceans of consolation: personal accounts of Irish migration to Australia* (Cork, 1994); *The two Irelands, 1912–1939* (Oxford, 1998); and *Harry Boland's Irish revolution* (Cork, 2003). He also edited *Ireland and the First World War*, a pioneering collection of student essays published by the Trinity History Workshop in 1986. He is currently preparing a history of the Orange Order and a biography of John MacNeice, Louis MacNeice's father.

JOHN HORNE is Professor of Modern European History at Trinity College Dublin. He has published widely on the history of twentieth-century France and on the comparative history of the Great War, including editing *State, society and mobilization in Europe during the First World War* (Cambridge, 1997) and writing (with Alan Kramer) *German atrocities 1914. A history of denial* (Yale, 2001; translated into French and German). He is a member of the executive committee of the Research Centre of the Historial de la Grande Guerre at Péronne.

KEITH JEFFERY is Professor of British History at Queen's University Belfast. A leading specialist on the history of Ireland and the Great War, he delivered the Lees Knowles Lectures on military history at Cambridge University, published as *Ireland and the Great War* (Cambridge, 2000). His study of *Field Marshal Sir Henry Wilson: A political soldier* (Oxford, 2006) won the Templer Medal Book Prize.

JANE LEONARD has published widely on Ireland and the Great War since contributing to the Trinity History Workshop's seminal volume of that title (Dublin, 1986). As History Outreach Officer at the Ulster Museum (1997–2006), she curated displays on the Somme and other significant episodes in Irish history. She is currently a postgraduate student in politics at Queen's University Belfast.

PHILIP ORR is a researcher, freelance writer and historian from Carrickfergus. He has published *The road to the Somme. The men of the Ulster Division tell their story* (1987; new edn., Belfast, 2008), *Field of bones. An Irish division at Gallipoli* (Dublin, 2006) and *New loyalties—Christian faith and the Protestant working class* (Belfast, 2008).

CATRIONA PENNELL completed her PhD at Trinity College Dublin in 2008 on 'A kingdom united: British and Irish popular responses to the outbreak of war, July to December 1914'. She is currently a lecturer at the University of Cardiff. An aspect of her work on invasion fears has been published in Heather Jones, Jennifer O'Brien and Christoph Schmidt-Supprian (eds), *Untold war: new interpretations of the First World War* (Leiden, 2008).

NIAMH PUIRSÉIL lectures in the School of History and Archives at University College Dublin. A historian of Irish politics and labour, her publications include *The Irish Labour Party, 1922-1977* (Dublin, 2007) and (with Fintan Lane and Francis Devine) *Essays in Irish labour history: A festschrift for Elizabeth and John W. Boyle* (Dublin, 2008). She is joint editor of *Saothar*, the journal of the Irish Labour History Society.

'Halt! Who goes there?', detail from a 1915 recruitment poster. © Royal Irish Academy.

Selected reading

Arnold, Bruce 1981 *Orpen: Mirror to an age*. London. Cape.

Audoin-Rouzeau, Stéphane and Becker, Annette 2002 *14–18. Understanding the Great War* (translated by Catherine Temerson). New York. Hill and Wang. (First published 2000.)

Barr, Niall 2005 *The lion and the poppy: British veterans, politics and society, 1921–1939*. Westport, CT. Praeger.

Beaton, Fran 2000 *The Great War in Irish poetry: W.B. Yeats to Michael Longley*. Oxford. Oxford University Press.

Bew, Paul 1994 *Ideology and the Ulster question: Ulster unionism and Irish nationalism, 1912–1916*. Oxford. Clarendon Press.

Bew, Paul 1996 *John Redmond*. Dundalk. Dundalgan Press.

Bowman, Timothy 1999 The Irish recruiting campaign and anti-recruiting campaigns 1914–1918. In Bertrand Taithe and Tim Thornton (eds), *Propaganda, political rhetoric and identity, 1300–2000*, 223–38. Stroud. Sutton.

Bowman, Timothy 2003 *The Irish regiments in the Great War—discipline and morale*. Manchester. Manchester University Press.

Boyce, David George 1993 *'The sure confusing drum': Ireland and the First World War*. Swansea. University College of Swansea.

Braybon, Gail (ed.) 2004 *Evidence, history and the Great War. Historians and the impact of 1914–1918*. New York and Oxford. Berghahn.

Bull, Philip 2005 Sacrifice, liberalism and the Great War: the case of Ireland. *War and Society* **23**, 13–21.

Callan, Patrick 1987 Recruiting for the British Army in Ireland during the First World War. *The Irish Sword* **17**, 42–56.

Clear, Caitriona 2007 *Social change and everyday life in Ireland, 1850–1922*. Manchester. Manchester University Press.

Crean, Thomas N. 1994 Labour and politics in Kerry during the First World War. *Saothar* **19**, 27–39.

Cullen Owens, Rosemary 1984 *Smashing times: a history of the Irish women's suffrage movement, 1889–1922*. Dublin. Attic Press.

D'Arcy, Fergus 2007 *Remembering the war dead: British Commonwealth and international war graves in Ireland since 1914*. Dublin. The Stationery Office.

Dawe, Gerald (ed.) forthcoming *Earth voices whispering: Irish war poetry 1914–1945*. Belfast. Blackstaff Press.

Denman, Terence 1992 *Ireland's unknown soldiers: the 16th (Irish) Division in the Great War*. Dublin. Irish Academic Press.

Denman, Terence 1995 *A lonely grave: the life and death of William Redmond*. Dublin. Irish Academic Press.

Devine, Kathleen (ed.) 1999 *Modern Irish writers and the wars*. Gerrards Cross, Bucks. Colin Smythe.

De Wiel, Jérôme aan 2003 *The Catholic Church in Ireland 1914–1918: war and politics*. Dublin. Four Courts Press.

Dolan, Anne 2003 *Commemorating the Irish Civil War: history and memory, 1923–2000*. Cambridge. Cambridge University Press.

Dooley, Thomas P. 1995 *Irishmen or English soldiers? The times and world of a southern Catholic Irish man (1876–1916) enlisting in the British Army*. Liverpool. Liverpool University Press.

Dungan, Myles 1995 *Irish voices from the Great War*. Dublin. Irish Academic Press.

Dungan, Myles 1997 *They shall grow not old. Irish soldiers and the Great War*. Dublin. Four Courts Press.

Dudley Edwards, Ruth 2006 *Patrick Pearse: the triumph of failure* (new edn.). Dublin. Irish Academic Press. (First published 1977.)

Falls, Cyril 1998 *The history of the 36th (Ulster) Division* (new edn.). London. Constable. (First published 1922.)

Fitzpatrick, David 1995 The logic of collective sacrifice: Ireland and the British Army, 1914–1918. *Historical Journal* **38**, 1017–30.

Fitzpatrick, David 1996 Militarism in Ireland, 1900–1922. In Thomas Bartlett and Keith Jeffery (eds), *A military history of Ireland*, 379–406. Cambridge. Cambridge University Press.

Fitzpatrick, David 1998 *Politics and Irish life 1913–1921: provincial experience of war and revolution* (new edn.). Cork. Cork University Press. (First published 1977.)

Fitzpatrick, David 1980 Strikes in Ireland, 1914–1921. *Saothar* **6**, 26–39.

Fitzpatrick, David (ed.) 1986 *Ireland and the First World War*. Dublin. Lilliput Press and Trinity History Workshop.

Fitzpatrick David (ed.) 1990 *Revolution? Ireland 1917–1923*. Dublin. Trinity History Workshop.

Fussell, Paul 1975 *The Great War and modern memory*. Oxford. Oxford University Press.

Grayzel, Susan R. 1999 *Women's identities at war. Gender, motherhood and politics in Britain and France during the First World War*. Chapel Hill, NC. University of North Carolina Press.

Greaves, C. Desmond 1982 *The Irish Transport and General Workers' Union: the formative years, 1909–1923*. Dublin. Gill & Macmillan.

Gregory, Adrian 1994 *The silence of memory. Armistice Day 1919–1946*. Oxford. Berg.

Gregory, Adrian and Pašeta, Senia (eds) 2002 *Ireland and the Great War: 'A war to unite us all?'*. Manchester. Manchester University Press.

Harris, Henry 1968 *The Irish regiments in the First World War*. Cork. Mercier Press.

Hart, Peter 1998 *The I.R.A. and its enemies: violence and community in West Cork, 1916–1923*. Oxford. Clarendon Press.

Hart, Peter 2003 *The I.R.A. at war, 1916–1923*. Oxford. Oxford University Press.

Hennessy, Thomas 1998 *Dividing Ireland. World War I and partition*. London and New York. Routledge.

Horne, John 2006 James Connolly and the great divide: Ireland, Europe and the First World War. *Saothar* **31**, 75–83.

Horne, John (ed.) 1997 *State, society and mobilization in Europe during the First World War.* Cambridge. Cambridge University Press.

Horne, John and Kramer, Alan 2001 *German atrocities, 1914. A history of denial.* London and New Haven. Yale University Press.

Inglis, Ken S. 1998 *Sacred places. War memorials in the Australian landscape.* Melbourne. Melbourne University Press.

Jeffery, Keith 2000 *Ireland and the Great War.* Cambridge. Cambridge University Press.

Jeffery, Keith 2006 *Field Marshal Sir Henry Wilson: a political soldier.* Oxford. Oxford University Press.

Johnson, Nuala C. 2003 *Ireland, the Great War and the geography of remembrance.* Cambridge. Cambridge University Press.

Johnstone, Tom 1992 *Orange, green and khaki: the story of the Irish regiments in the Great War, 1914–18.* Dublin. Gill & Macmillan.

King, Alex 1998 *Memorials of the Great War in Britain: the symbolism and politics of remembrance.* Oxford. Oxford University Press.

Kipling, Rudyard 1997 *The Irish Guards in the Great War* (2 vols, new edn.). Staplehurst, Kent. Spellmount. (First published 1923.)

Laffan, Michael 1999 *The resurrection of Ireland. The Sinn Féin Party, 1916–1923.* Cambridge. Cambridge University Press.

Leonard, Jane 1997 'Facing the finger of scorn': veterans' memories of Ireland in the twentieth century. In Martin Edwards and Ken Lunn (eds), *War and memory in the twentieth century*, 59–72. Oxford. Berg.

Leonard, Jane 1990 Getting them at last: the IRA and ex-servicemen. In David Fitzpatrick (ed.), *Revolution? Ireland, 1917–1923*, 118–29. Dublin. Trinity History Workshop.

Leonard, Jane 1996 The twinge of memory: Armistice Day and Remembrance Sunday in Dublin since 1919. In Richard English and Graham Walker (eds), *Unionism in modern Ireland. New perspectives on politics and culture*, 99–114. Basingstoke. Macmillan.

Longley, Edna 1991 The Rising, the Somme and Irish memory. In Máirín Ní Dhonnchadha and Theo Dorgan (eds), *Revising the Rising*, 29–49. Derry. Field Day.

Macleod, Jenny 2005 *Reconsidering Gallipoli.* Manchester. Manchester University Press.

Martin, F.X. 1967 1916—myth, fact and mystery, *Studia Hibernica* 7, 7–125.

Maume, Patrick 1999 *The long gestation: Irish nationalist life 1891–1918.* Dublin. Gill & Macmillan.

McEwen, Yvonne 2006 *It's a long way to Tipperary: British and Irish nurses in the First World War.* Dunfermline. Cualann Press.

McMahon, Deirdre (ed.) 2004 *The Moynihan brothers in peace and war, 1909–1918.* Dublin. Irish Academic Press.

Mitchell, Arthur 1974 *Labour in Irish politics 1890–1930. The Irish labour movement in an age of revolution*. Dublin. Irish University Press.

Moran, Daniel and Waldron, Arthur (eds) 2003 *The people in arms. Military myth and national mobilization since the French Revolution*. Cambridge. Cambridge University Press.

Mosse, George 1990 *Fallen soldiers. Reshaping the memory of the world wars*. Ithaca, NY. Cornell University Press.

Murphy, Cliona 1989 *The women's suffrage movement and Irish society in the early twentieth century*. Hemel Hempstead. Harvester Wheatsheaf.

Murray, Peter 1990 The First World War and a Dublin distillery workforce: recruitment and redundancy at John Power and Sons, 1915–1917. *Saothar* **15**, 48–56.

Nevin, Donal 2005 *James Connolly. 'A full life'*. Dublin. Gill & Macmillan.

Ní Dhonnchadha, Máirín and Dorgan, Theo (eds) 1991 *Revising the Rising*. Derry. Field Day.

Novick, Ben 2001 *Conceiving revolution. Irish nationalist propaganda during the First World War*. Dublin. Four Courts Press.

O'Connor, Emmet 1988 *Syndicalism in Ireland, 1917–23*. Cork. Cork University Press.

O'Halpin, Eunan 1987 *The decline of the union: British Government in Ireland 1892–1920*. Dublin. Gill & Macmillan.

O'Rahilly, Alfred 1920 *Martyr priest: The life and death of Fr William Doyle S.J. who died in the 'Great War'*. London. Longmans Green.

Oram, Gerard 1998 *Worthless men: race, eugenics and the death penalty in the British Army during the First World War*. London. Francis Boutle.

Orr, Philip 2006 *Field of bones. An Irish division at Gallipoli*. Dublin. Lilliput Press.

Orr, Philip 2008 *The road to the Somme: men of the Ulster Division tell their story* (new edn.). Belfast. Blackstaff Press. (First published 1987.)

Prior, Robin and Wilson, Trevor 1996 *Passchendaele. The untold story*. London and New Haven. Yale University Press.

Prior, Robin and Wilson, Trevor 2005 *The Somme*. London and New Haven. Yale University Press.

Perry, Nicholas 2007 *Major General Nugent and the Ulster Division 1915–1918*. Stroud. Sutton.

Prost, Antoine and Winter, Jay 2005 *The Great War in history. Debates and controversies, 1914 to the present*. Cambridge. Cambridge University Press.

Staunton, Martin 1986 Kilrush, Co. Clare and the Royal Munster Fusiliers: the experience of an Irish town in the First World War. *The Irish Sword* **16**, 268–72.

Taylor, James 2002 *The 1ˢᵗ Royal Irish Rifles in the Great War*. Dublin. Four Courts Press.

Taylor, James 2005 *The 2ⁿᵈ Royal Irish Rifles in the First World War*. Dublin. Four Courts Press.

Thomson, Alistair 1994 *Anzac memories. Living with the legend*. Melbourne. Oxford University Press.

Todman, Dan 2005 *The Great War. Myth and memory*. London. Hambledon Continuum. [*on Britain*]

Upstone, Robert, Foster, R.F. and Fraser Jenkins, David 2005 *William Orpen. Politics, sex and death*. London. Philip Wilson & Imperial War Museum.

Urquhart, Diane 2000 *Women in Ulster politics 1890–1940*. Dublin. Irish Academic Press.

Vance, Jonathan 1997 *Death so noble. Memory, meaning and the First World War*. Vancouver. University of British Columbia Press. [*on Canada*]

Walsh, Oonagh (ed.) 2000 *An Englishwoman in Belfast: Rosamund Stephen's record of the Great War*. Cork. Cork University Press.

Wheatley, Michael 2005 *Nationalism and the Irish Party: provincial Ireland, 1910–1916*. Oxford. Oxford University Press.

Winter, Jay 1985 *The Great War and the British people*. London. Macmillan.

Winter, Jay 1995 *Sites of memory, sites of mourning. The Great War in European cultural history*. Cambridge. Cambridge University Press.

Winter, Jay and Sivan, Emmanuel (eds) 1999 *War and remembrance in the twentieth century*. Cambridge. Cambridge University Press.

NATIONAL PLEDGE

DENYING the right of the British Government to enforce Compulsory Service in this Country, we pledge ourselves solemnly one to another to resist Conscription by the most effective means at our disposal.

SIGNED

TCD, Samuels Collection: Sinn Féin national pledge, 1918. An electioneering ballad Sinn Féin Aboo! was printed on the reverse. Reproduced by permission of the Board, Trinity College Dublin.

Following page: Victory Parade in Dublin, 19 July 1919. © RTÉ Stills Library.

WHO CAN BEAT THIS PLUCKY FOUR?

'Who can beat this plucky four?'
Undated recruitment poster showing
soldiers from England, Ireland, Scotland
and Wales. Reproduced by permission of
the Board, Trinity College Dublin.

BUT ALL THE SAME
WE'RE WANTING MORE

Index

316

319

Following page: NLI, Ephemera Collection:
'Why not join the army for the period of the
war?', *c.* 1916. Issued by the DRI. Courtesy of
the National Library of Ireland.

WHY NOT JOIN

THE

ARMY

FOR THE

PERIOD OF THE WAR?

YOU WILL LIKE IT.

YOUR PALS WILL LIKE IT.

THE KAISER
WILL HATE IT.

Apply for particulars of Allowances, &c., or send a post card to Director of Recruiting in your District.

Issued by the Department for Recruiting in Ireland.   Wt. 6711.—1. 16.—DOLLARD, Dublin.